DUE DATE

APR 30			
NOV 2 8			
FEB 0 6 1994			
OCT 0 2 1994			
MAR 5 - 1995			
APR 21 1996			
			Printed in USA

WORKING PARENT

You Can Balance Job & Family

HAPPY CHILD

Caryl Waller Krueger

Abingdon Press

Nashville

Working Parent—Happy Child

Copyright © 1990 by Caryl Waller Krueger

This book is printed on acid-free paper.

Library of Congress Cataloging-in-Publication Data

Krueger, Caryl Waller, 1929–
    Working parent—happy child: you can balance job and family / Caryl Waller Krueger.
        p.   cm.
    ISBN 0-687-46191-X (pbk.: alk. paper)
    1. Parenting—United States. 2. Dual-career families—United States. 3. Children of working parents—United States. I. Title.
HQ755.8.K73   1990
306.874—dc20
                                                                    89-18266
                                                                        CIP

book designed and illustrated by J.S.Laughbaum

Some of the ideas in this book are from the author's books *1001 Things to Do with Your Kids,* copyright © 1988 by Caryl Waller Krueger, published by Abingdon Press, Nashville, Tennessee 37202; and *Six Weeks to Better Parenting,* copyright 1985 Pelican Publishing Company, Gretna, Louisiana 70053.

The author has made every effort to make the information and suggestions in this book practical and workable, but neither she nor the publisher assumes any responsibility for successes, failures, or other results of putting these ideas into practice.

MANUFACTURED IN THE UNITED STATES OF AMERICA

To
Sandra
for her determination
to be a loving mother
and a successful business woman

Acknowledgments

A book isn't written in a vacuum—especially a book about the wonderful people who make up a family. I am indebted to hundreds of working parents who took the time to fill out survey forms or to be interviewed. In many ways this is the story of their challenges and triumphs.

And special thanks go to Marie Newcom and Connie Constanz for helping tabulate the survey forms, Sheila Kinder and Cliff Krueger for reading the manuscript as it grew, Joan Franklin Smutny for sharing information about gifted children, Jean Mosteller for her help with the reading lists in chapter 17, and Cameron Krueger for providing computer technology support.

I'm also grateful for my wonderfully supportive husband and children, who encouraged this wife and mother to write and share a love for the important values learned only through family life.

Contents

Introduction: So You're a Working Parent 13

Chapter 1: Getting to Know You.................................... 15
Chapter 2: Touching Bases.......................................22
Chapter 3: You're Not Alone!.................................... 28
Chapter 4: The Alarm Goes Off....................................43
Chapter 5: Hey, Don't Skip Breakfast! Touch-Base Time #1..54
Chapter 6: Commuter's Express....................................62
Chapter 7: Keeping Alive from 9 to 5.............................69
Chapter 8: The Divided Heart: Touch-Base Time #2.............80
Chapter 9: Home at Last! Touch-Base Time #3....................93
Chapter 10: The Super Supper: Touch-Base Time #4........... 103
Chapter 11: One Special Hour: Touch-Base Time #5............ 117
Chapter 12: And so to Bed . . . : Touch-Base Time #6........ 129
Chapter 13: The Wow! Weekend....................................142
Chapter 14: T.V. and Your Bright Child...........................157
Chapter 15: Day-Care, School, and Your Smart Child.............169
Chapter 16: Extracurricular Stuff and Your Happy Child.......190
Chapter 17: Frosting on the Cake: Enriching Family Life........203
Chapter 18: S t r e t c h i n g Your Time...............................240
Chapter 19: Eight Great Traits of a Bright Child.................... 256
Chapter 20: Discipline and the Happy Child...........................281
Chapter 21: Cross-Country Forum.................................296
Chapter 22: Step by Step Together.. 305

Index...311

WORKING PARENT HAPPY CHILD

Introduction
So You're a Working Parent . . .

Let's face it: You have two jobs. *Why* you have two jobs, parenting and career, is your own business. *How to make the two jobs work* is my business.

Maybe you're a working parent because you don't want to starve, or because you want your child to go to college, or because you want some of life's extras for yourself, or because the satisfaction of the business world is essential to your own well-being. No matter what your reason, here you are, right in the middle of a balancing act.

I've known this balancing act well, so I also know some of the questions that wander through your thinking:

How can I find the time to do it all?
Is my child deprived of important things?
Should I feel guilty about our separation?
Will I be able to handle the challenges of parenting?
Who's really in charge of my life and my child's?
Is my spouse getting a fair share of me?
Is my job satisfaction sufficient to make the double effort
   worthwhile?
How can I have a bright and happy child?

With the help of my survey of hundreds of parents, I've found some good answers. This book will help you find those answers, too. It *is* possible to have a career and be an effective parent at the same time, but it requires dedication and organization—a plan that accomplishes what is necessary and leaves time for creative living.

Let me give you this motto:

Step by step I can do it!

13

Write this motto on several 3 × 5 cards. Put one on the refrigerator, one on your night table, one on the bathroom mirror, one on your desk at the office, one on the dashboard of the car, and one wherever else you'll see it often.

Why can you say "I can do it"? Because I'm going to share with you techniques and tested ideas that have worked for me and many, many other working parents.

When our first daughter was feeling hesitant about starting school, I often said, "You'll like it. You'll go in the car pool and you'll come home so smart!" On the morning of the first school day, her younger brother appeared at breakfast in his swimming trunks. I was baffled until he said, "I want to go in the pool too, so I can be smart." I wish it were that easy! But, believe me, it isn't so difficult once you have a plan.

Smart children are a joy to their parents, peers, teachers, and the community. But more important, a bright child is making the most of his own God-given talents. When young, this child can share his self-esteem and growing knowledge with his siblings and friends. And later, he can share it with the world.

You're going to learn my step-by-step method that makes the most of moments, builds success on success, brings the family together for a common goal—and results in a working parent with a happy child.

So, step by step, let's do it!

Caryl Waller Krueger

One

Getting to Know You

Connie and Kirk have a great marriage, two career tracks running successfully, a mortgaged house they plan to fix up someday, one old and one new car, friends from church and from a volleyball team, two charming little girls—and not enough time to enjoy all this. Kirk put his finger on the problem when he said, "Sometimes I don't think I know the kids. Our life moves so fast we just can't spare the time to sit down together and look at what we're doing and where we're going."

The time to stand back and assess past successes and failures, decide on short-range and long-range goals, and establish mutual interests is a must for Connie and Kirk—and for you, too.

This weekend when you have time, sit down with your family and answer this quick quiz. It will help pinpoint some of the areas that may be challenging for you. And it will focus on areas where this book can help you make some changes. Skip the questions that don't apply to your family.

Parent's Quiz
(Each parent should answer separately)

1. Does my day start on a high note and go up from there?
2. Am I satisfied with my child-care arrangements?
3. Is there at least an hour each day when I am wholly with my child?
4. Do I set social and learning goals for my child?
5. Do I set business, social, and learning goals for myself?
6. Am I spending time regularly to make our home a family center?
7. Am I finding the time to keep my marriage vital?
8. Do I arrange after-supper activities so that T.V. is not the sole highlight of the evening for the family?
9. Is there an enjoyable family event each weekend?
10. Do I understand the importance of thinking through my own unpleasant childhood experiences as well as my present-day angers and frustrations?
11. Am I usually able to work at my job without concern for my child's well-being?
12. Do I look forward to weekend time with my child, rather than feeling that this time is solely for my own rest and amusement?
13. Do I take my child to a museum, play, or concert as often as to the park or a movie?
14. Do I—or does someone else—read to my child at least 30 minutes a day, or do I encourage a reading child to read at least 30 minutes a day?
15. As work is done around the home, do I include my child, explain what I'm doing, and let her help?
16. Do I tell my child each day that I have confidence in him and in his ability to learn, that he is very special, and that I love him no matter what?
17. Do I know the name of my child's best friend?
18. Can I name something that really upsets my child and also something that really pleases her?
19. Do I know what my child really likes about me and what he most dislikes about me?
20. Do I know what my child likes to do with her free time and what she would like to do more often with me?

21. Do I know my child's favorite teacher and favorite subject, and his least favorite teacher and least favorite subject?
22. If I could buy my child the gift she most desires, do I know what it would be?
23. Am I aware of which of my child's accomplishments gives him the most pleasure?
24. Do I treat my job as parent with the same integrity and organization that I bring to my career?
25. Am I finding time to grow myself, through reading, classes, activities, or hobbies?
26. Do I have daily time to talk alone with my spouse about ourselves, our family, and current events?
27. Do I usually go to sleep feeling contented with my day?

The only score that matters on this quiz is the one you give yourself. Did you find that you are living in a house without knowing one another very well? Did you find that you are not encouraging your child to grow? And did you find that family activities are missing? A working parent who wants a bright child must see that family life is more than eating, sleeping, and looking at T.V. under the same roof!

Next, corral your child for a moment and try this quick quiz. If your child is under age three, some questions may require your thinking ahead about how he might answer them. Or you may want to rephrase the question. Skip questions that aren't pertinent to your child's age.

Kid's Quiz

1. Is it fun to live in this home?
2. Do you help with chores around the house?
3. Do you have a place for projects that you don't have to clean up very often?
4. Do you read—or are you read to—each day?
5. Do you know your family rules and what happens if you break them?
6. Do you have a relative (grandparent, uncle, cousin) with whom you feel very close?
7. If the television set disappeared for a week, could you name ten other things you'd like to do?
8. Are you happy about learning new skills and subjects?
9. Do you like family meal times?

10. Do you know your parents' favorite sport, music, food, book?
11. Do you know your parent's favorite school subject and least favorite subject?
12. Can you name something you do that upsets your parent?
13. Can you name something your parent thinks is special about you?
14. Do you know what your parents like to do for fun?
15. Do you remember what is your parent's most favorite family occasion and why?
16. Do you know something that your parent would like to do more often with you?
17. Do you know why your parents work?
18. Do you show your parents that you love them by your words and your acts?

You may want to talk in greater depth about some of the questions in the quiz. Each question is important for both parent and child, but especially important for a working parent who has less time to get involved in the small but meaningful elements of a child's life.

Getting to really know and appreciate your family is harder when you work, because you have fewer hours together. In addition, childhood is so brief. (You may not feel that way now, but when your child is eighteen you'll say, "Where did the years go?") During these learning years, you need a close relationship with your child as he develops. The child you know today will be a different child tomorrow. Children's needs, dreams, and challenges change frequently. So, you must keep in touch regularly each day.

Quantity Versus Quality Time

One parent said that her best "quality time" with her two children was on the freeway, during their drive to day-care and work. Although this parent and her children might have time for good talks during their daily commute, drive-thru parenting just isn't enough!

"Quality time" has been a popular concept to comfort parents into thinking that they can make up for hours of separation by a few intense hours together. But sometimes when the working parent is ready for togetherness with the child, the child is sleepy, wants to be alone, or is involved in some other project.

A working parent can't expect to be on hand for all the highlights of childhood. A parent may miss the first smile, the first word, the first step, the funny saying, the sad story told, the triumph of learning something new. These may not come during a brief "quality time" session. So, along with the quality times, we need the quantity times, too.

A working parent must make the most of those moments of togetherness with spouse and child. This does not mean that a working parent should smother the child with constant attention. Children still need time to be alone, to play on their own, to figure things out for themselves. It does mean that aside from important quality times, the family needs to grab quantities of other time (for going shopping, preparing supper, cleaning the house, washing the car) to enjoy one another.

Roots and Wings

We have two gifts to give our children: One is roots, the other is wings. We must see that our sons and daughters are rooted in knowledge, integrity, and love. And we also want them to take wings and fly on their own because they have learned self-government and self-esteem.

We give these gifts to our children through the expenditure of our abilities and our time. We need the ability to show a child how to live adventurously; we need the ability to help, to listen, to laugh, to change, to teach, to entertain, to love, to encourage. And, where our own abilities fall short, we must either acquire the ability ourselves or call on others to help.

Our time to accomplish all this must be both quality and quantity time. So, in our busy week, we have to balance career time with family time. We have to make time to come together for learning and loving.

And parents should remember that it is impossible to meet a child's ultimate need for self-knowledge and self-sufficiency without occasionally making the child unhappy. A child can't always know what is right for him to have and good for him to do. Your child's confidence in you must be continually growing so that he can accept your correction and guidance.

Some researchers are coming out with sad statistics on children of working parents. They say that these children are less confident, get poorer grades, get into more trouble, and so forth. But let's not be intimidated by such research. It makes good news to come up with a scary report, but *your* child doesn't have to be a part of it. The fact that you are reading this book indicates your interest in giving your youngster "wonder years." This requires planning and also the ability to know when to throw the plans away and do something adventuresome.

Where's the Fun Gone?

Today, almost 65 percent of mothers with school-age children work outside the home, and researchers say the number will increase to 80 percent in just a few years. With the entrance of many women into the work force, some of the good things of family life disappeared. What happened to those small things that make life more enjoyable and worthwhile—talking around the supper table, baking cookies and eating them immediately, long summer evenings in the yard, camping trips, the preparation for and anticipation of a holiday, walking in the rain, time to just do nothing?

Instead, many parents survive on fast food and jogging in the dark, working twelve-hour work days and paying for day-care that is just basic maintenance. The child knows only the rush to and from the day-care center or school and home, a hurried meal and television. There's no sense of a close community because nobody's home in Mister Roger's neighborhood.

This doesn't have to be. You can establish a strong sense of home and family, you can build memories, you can feel good about yourself and your child. To do this you need to develop your personal qualities of self-discipline, caring, orderliness, and creativity.

Being a parent doesn't automatically endow you with all these essential qualities. As your child learns and develops, so do you. Teaching a child to be orderly makes you more aware of your own disorder. Taking time to work together baking cookies for a playmate who is ill makes you aware of the needs of your own friends. Helping a child develop interest in a craft makes you realize that there can be more to your evenings than after-supper T.V.

So expect to grow—parenting is not something to "get through." A child's journey from babyhood to age eighteen should be one that both parent and child look back on with affection. If you aren't building good memories along the way, you need to look at how you spend your time as a family. If all your moments together are spent reminding, scolding, and instructing, you probably need some basic organizational changes that let you get through the routine and on to the fun. Yes, parenting *is* fun!

―――――――― *Parenting Point* ――――――――

Remember, all things are possible! Getting to know yourself and your youngster is not an impossible dream! It's a step-by-step process, one that begins with touching bases with your child during each weekday and continues through the weekend. Tell yourself often: "Step by step I can do it."

Chalkboard for Chapter One

Look closely at yourself, your family, and your job. Be realistic but also be challenging. Then fill in these lists:

Things I'd like to change in my relationship with my child:
1.
2.
3.

What I'd like to change in my relationship with my spouse:
1.
2.
3.

Personal changes I'd like to make in myself:
1.
2.
3.

Changes I'd like to make at my work place:
1.
2.
3.

Return to this page as you read and see how you are achieving your aims.

Two

Touching Bases

Ben is a list-maker. At one time both he and Robin worked late and they found the after-work needs of their two grade-schoolers almost overwhelming. Sometimes the kids asked so many questions and brought up so many new topics that Ben's head swirled. So, he started a list of things the kids wanted to talk about in depth and also those things that he or Robin wanted to settle when there was more time. After breakfast each Saturday there were groans as the dreaded list was brought out and discussed. Somehow, many of the items no longer seemed pertinent. Besides, Saturday was a day for action, not talk. There had to be a better way!

Far too many working parents find the weekdays so busy that they put off everything to the weekends. It's almost as if they only truly live on the weekends. They struggle through Monday to Friday figuring that Saturday and Sunday can make it all come out right.

This is like having a seedling of a precious and beautiful plant and ignoring it five days of the week. Then, when it looks sad and wilted, you drown it with water and fertilizer. When a few weeds come up in the pot the seedling is almost lost from sight. So you yank out the healthy weed and the sickly seedling gets uprooted, too. Parenting can be similar: days of ignoring family matters followed by overly intense attention and some bad decisions, and soon the main objective is lost from sight and family life becomes sickly and rootless.

Like young plants, our children thrive on *regular* cultivation. A working parent can't afford to be just a weekend parent. I know, you are tired from your day at the office and you think you need "me-time." But you can feel refreshed as well by "us-time," good weekday moments with your child.

Touch-Base Times

The weekend connection with your family will be much more productive if you nurture your togetherness during each weekday. I call these essential weekday times touch-base times. There are six of them:

1. At breakfast
2. From the office by telephone
3. Reunion at home
4. At supper
5. The special evening hour
6. Bedtime

Chapters 4 through 12 will take you through a typical work day and show you how to put these touch-base times to use. The touch-base times are your winning weekday tool.

Keeping in touch puts you close to your child—and your spouse—regularly and gives you a feeling of self-esteem even though you're very busy. And if you are in touch with your child's needs and interests, your child will be wiser and more confident.

Touch-Base Time Purposes

The touch-base times have four important purposes:

1. For communication during the weekday
2. As framework for allaying the fear of separation
3. As an automatic tool for time management
4. For reducing parental guilt feelings

Communication

Once you (as well as your spouse) commit yourself to including these touch-base times in your schedule, you'll find there are fewer misunderstandings ("I thought *you* were picking her up!"), less frustration ("What do you mean, you have to make a diorama of the Alps tonight?"), and a lot less guilt ("If only I were an at-home parent, I could . . . .")

In turn, you'll find opportunities to know your child better on a regular basis. "Tell me about your museum excursion as I peel this cucumber." "While I fold laundry, let's see if you can count as high as all the socks." "I'd love to hear you read to me as I get dressed for the meeting." "Let's look at the calendar and see what's fun this week." "We can talk about your school report on our grocery trip."

The six touch-base times become a framework for a child's contact with his parent during the day. Even the youngest toddler soon learns she can count on there being another touch-base time. This reduces a child's loneliness, longing for parental contact, and fear of separation.

The Fear of Separation

This fear of being separated from a parent is one of the strongest of all childhood fears. Research shows that it looms bigger than fear of monsters, fire, precipices, and punishment. Only the darkness is more feared—and we'll talk about that fear later.

A child sometimes can't see ahead to the end of the separation. Although *you* may know when you and your child will be in contact again, your young child may not, unless you tell her when you will talk with her or see her again.

A parent's last words when parting from a child should include these important elements:

- Love for the child
- Confidence that the child will have a successful time (at play, with the sitter, in school, etc.)
- That you look forward to hearing about the child's day when you are together again at the end of the day

This simple farewell routine is one of the best ways to get rid of the fear of separation. Some children may require more support. You may want to talk about what each of you will be doing while apart. You may let the child take along something from home as a reminder of family (a photo, a toy, a simple piece of jewelry to wear). And you may have to give the child something special to look forward to—a fun activity that will take place when you are together again. Lots of love and a little added attention are the best antidote for the fear of separation.

Automatic Time Management

The third purpose—an automatic tool for time management—is as important as the others. If you would give your child the gifts of roots and wings via your ability and your time, you have to use that time well.

Because you will make contact these six times each day, you will find that many little questions and problems can be handled then and there. There's no need to try to remember them or to put them on a list so you can bring them up later. Taking action at the time actually saves time, but it is also immensely satisfying to a child to have a simple solution immediately.

Certainly, answers to major problems can be postponed, but remember to say, "That's so important that I want to think about it and we'll talk about it after supper (or before bed, or next weekend)." Be sure to give a specific time to get together and solve the problem. And then, be sure you do!

But immediate solutions are usually the best. Allowing a problem to wait sometimes throws it out of proportion. And when answers to questions are put off, a young child may lose interest in the subject—or may not even remember why he wanted to know about it. The six touch-base times make you available as a parent, almost as available as the at-home parent. Kids can count on your support and interest during at least these six times of the day.

Feeling Guilty?

The touch-base times bring benefits to you, too, in the guilt department. In the survey I conducted before writing this book, 61 percent of working parents admitted to some guilt regarding being away from their children. The touch-base times don't put off parenting to a hazy future. Using them requires parenting at intervals during the work day. Thus, a parent has a feeling of success because he knows that, although he is not in touch at the moment, he will soon have that opportunity.

You experience less guilt when you evaluate your reasons for working. If you are part of a two-parent family, weigh the additional salary against the child-care costs, the pressures of work against the benefits. Write down your reasons for working and talk about them with your family. If you are working now because you have decided that this is the best plan for the present, don't chide yourself for having chosen the best plan! Look at the plan regularly to be sure that it remains your best parenting option. You may decide to modify it from time to time. But tell yourself that you have thought it through and this is the best option for now.

Working parents know that an at-home parent has more time with a child. But they can also realize that sometimes the at-home parent is lulled into squandering that time. There are many alluring ways to do so: taking on a volunteer activity that requires a major time commitment, enjoying a sport on a near full-time basis, pursuing inefficient home-making methods, engaging in worthless pursuits and vicarious living (some television and reading fall into this category). Thus, some at-home parents end up with no more time for their children than their working counterparts have. Their children may still come home to an empty house, no one to talk with, no parental direction.

In general though, the at-home parent has additional time to better manage the home. And of course there are additional opportunities, usually in the afternoon, to take part in child-related activities. These additional moments with children vary with the child's age, but the total time actually spent doing things *with* a child is between one and three hours. This then is the precious time the working parent is missing out on.

So be it. You will just work harder and better to include the same good things in your youngster's life. And that is my purpose, to show you how to be a working parent with a happy and intelligent child.

—————— *Parenting Point* ——————

Looking forward to being together again mitigates a child's fear of separation and a parent's feeling of guilt. Establish the six communication times as important weekday connections to your child. Then you can say: "Step by step, I can feel closer to my youngster because of our touch-base times!"

Chalkboard for Chapter Two

These are the good reasons I am working:
1.
2.
3.

These are the most difficult times of the day for me:
1.
2.

These times are hard because:
1.
2.

These are the times of day I feel closest to my child:
1.
2.

As you continue to read, you will find ways to organize the difficult times of the day and enjoy more times of closeness with your child.

Three

You're Not Alone!

Steve and Betsy love being parents of twins. After maternity leave, Betsy returned to her marketing job, yet she and Steve spent all their at-home hours nurturing the girls. There simply wasn't a moment left for other people or activities in their lives. Then Steve was offered a new position with better pay, but one that would consume many extra hours the first year. Although Betsy was thrilled about his advancement, she often felt abandoned and lonely in the evening and on weekends at home. The twins weren't great conversationalists yet, and Steve usually came home so late he just gulped dinner and fell in bed. Betsy suddenly realized that she needed adult companionship, occasional advice, and someone with whom she could talk and share her parenting challenges. But where could she find such help?

Tough times are easier to endure when we feel the support of another person. In two-parent families, one spouse counts heavily on the other. Sometimes that works, sometimes it doesn't. In single-parent families, there may be a good friend or relative—or no one—to count on.

This chapter is about supportive people: care-givers and teachers, good friends and relatives, coaches and counselors, and some who may be new to you. (Choosing and getting the most from a day-care facility, nursery school, and regular school are discussed in chapter 15, "Day-Care, School, and Your Smart Child.")

Beyond day-care and school, working parents need a team behind them. This is good for the parent and enriching for the child. They need to start their parental support group even before the baby arrives, and then enlarge it in all the years that follow.

Why this need? Can't you go it alone?

- Parents can't know everything. So they need other responsible people to rely on for answers to puzzling questions.
- Parents may know little or nothing about raising a child. Although the law requires a license to own a dog or be a manicurist, you needn't have any formal training to become a parent.
- Unexpected things happen. You want calm, caring back-up people during hectic times.
- A child needs to know not only parents and care-givers but also other people. He needs to be comfortable with people of varied personalities and know how to get along with them.
- A child learns more and learns about varied nonacademic subjects if exposed to others. A parent may not be able to sing lullabies or teach soccer or build toy rockets.

So, let's see the kinds of people you might choose, depending on the age of your child and your home situation. But first let's look at a very important person in your life.

The P.E.P.

Every parent needs a P.E.P.—a parental enrichment partner. In parenting, we know we can't do it all ourselves, we know we don't want to do it all alone, and we know certain aspects of life are more fun when we have a partner.

So, you need a PEP. The PEP should not be your spouse. You're both too close to those situations where you'll call on your PEP. You'll gain more if your PEP isn't under the same roof, and you certainly don't want your PEP looking over your shoulder. A little distance adds perspective. As soon as you know you're going to be a parent, be on the look-out for a family PEP.

What qualities should you look for in your PEP?

1. Parenting experience. Someone who has been a parent for a few years or many years will understand many of your challenges and can give you helpful perspectives. What may be a mountainous problem for you is often a surmountable hill for your PEP.

2. Nearness. You want to be able to reach your PEP when you need him or her. You don't want to have to call long distance or write a letter. The PEP has to be available right now or certainly within the day. This means that your PEP will live or work nearby. It means that your PEP will usually have the time to talk with you without disturbing the PEP's work or family. Sometimes you will be in contact by phone, sometimes in person. The PEP has to be handy.

3. Confidentiality. Don't choose a PEP who gossips or you'll find your problems blown out of proportion and part of neighborhood or party conversations. You want to be able to "dump" on your PEP without concern. This dumping is important since your PEP may recognize that what you describe as a current parenting problem may be two problems, or not a parenting problem at all, but rather something related to personal or business relationships.

4. Wisdom. Your PEP should not be a flighty or impractical person. The PEP should be intelligent but not erudite in a way that is humorless. A PEP with a sense of humor can often help you step back from a situation and see it for what it really may be: a funny, short-lived event without any deep psychological meaning. But your PEP also needs the wisdom to recognize when you need more help than he or she can offer.

5. Mutual respect. Your PEP should be someone who likes you and respects your abilities as a parent. The PEP shouldn't be a bossy, I-told-you-so person. The PEP should respect your position as parent and not try to take over your job. And the PEP should understand that you may not always accept the advice given. So, the PEP shouldn't be overly sensitive.

Now, when you *have* a PEP, that person is to be loved and cultivated. You might think that you would become greatly indebted to that person. How can you ever repay a PEP? You don't need to if you remember to "pass it along." That's a great way to reciprocate.

Let me tell you a story that illustrates this point of "passing it along." Early in my marriage, an older couple who were moving to smaller quarters gave my husband and me a large quantity of fine furniture and art objects. They were beautiful things that we would not have been able to buy while beginning our family, starting a new business, and paying the mortgage on a first house. When we tried to express our appreciation, the wife said that when she was new in business, an older associate had given her much time and many ideas that resulted in her getting a very satisfying and lucrative job, which turned into a fabulous life-long career. When she had asked the older associate how she could repay his kindness, he had said she should "pass it along." We were among her many "pass it along" recipients, and she asked that we remember to look for an opportunity to "pass it along."

Some years later, we were able to "pass it along" to a young couple who needed help at a crucial turning point in their lives. In turn, they told us later that they "passed it along" to a young woman who needed help in paying her college tuition. This young woman went into private nursing, and though she had few worldly goods, she "passed it along" by giving extra loving care beyond what was required professionally. At one home where she was very instrumental in nursing a woman back into good health, the husband of the woman was very impressed with her outstanding loving and caring nature. Of course he paid her well, but he also "passed it along" by giving in her honor an endowment to the nursing school so that more nurses could be trained. I don't know what has since happened in this chain, but it is a warm feeling to see the path of one kindness through many lives.

So don't feel guilty for leaning on your PEP. Just remember that there will be a time in your life when you can make a major gift of your time or talents to another. Accept the good that comes from your PEP and remember later to "pass it along."

PEP's come in all sizes, ages, sexes. Don't limit yourself by having a mental picture of a gray-haired grandma in a rocking chair dispensing sound advice. Your PEP could have a moustache and wear shorts and jogging shoes. Keep an open mind. Your PEP can be among the support people that we'll now discuss.

Your Support Team for When Your Child Is Young

You love your baby so much it's hard to part with her. Parents of a
new baby, particularly when the mother or father is on maternal-
paternal leave from work, want to stick close to their baby. This is
generally right to do, but there is another consideration.

The addition of a baby to a marriage changes the husband-wife
relationship because it adds a beloved little person who takes a share
of the time formerly allocated to the spouse. Sometimes that share of
the time can mean almost all their spare moments. Although the
twosome is now a threesome, there should still be twosome opportunities, and some of that time should be spent away from the cares of
the baby. Of course, if the baby has health problems, a parent may not
want to take this time away. But a normal baby—one who cries, sleeps,
burps, eats, occasionally upchucks, wants attention, drools, fusses—
may be left in competent care.

No matter how cooperative a baby you have or how good baby is at
napping or traveling with you, you need a little time away from him.
Three to four times a month is beneficial. These times away from
baby—whether it's dinner and a movie or a walk on the beach—keep
parents in tune with each other and keep the romance going. A strong
marriage is good for your child and averts the apathy that can lead to
divorce.

So you will need a care-giver available about once a week. And that
person must be one in whom you have confidence. It's hard to enjoy a
pleasantly planned evening out when harboring worried second
thoughts.

In the month before baby's arrival, determine who will be your first
sitter. If you have a willing parent, you have it made! In these
emancipated times, however, grandma may be having her own career
and needing her own free time, or grandpa may have talked her into
retiring to a sunny condo far away.

Interview baby-sitters! Look for adults and older teens of both
sexes. Invite them to your home to see how you function, or visit their
homes to see if you like where your baby will be cared for. Talk to
other parents to get an idea of costs, then candidly discuss rates of
payment with each sitter. Write down their fees so you understand
the basic charge and any extras.

Don't try to steal a sitter away from a friend or neighbor, but ask
those friends and their sitters for referrals. Usually sitters know other

sitters. And it isn't inappropriate to ask for references on anyone you don't personally know.

Be specific in asking the reference about the sitter: Did he feed the baby? Does he have experience with young babies? Was he neat in the kitchen and the changing area? Was the line always busy when you tried to call home, indicating that he was talking most of the time? Was he capable when the baby fussed? You'll be able to make a further assessment yourself when you've used a sitter one time. Did she follow instructions? Was she able to get the baby to drink the required amount of formula?

Don't stop when you've found just one sitter. Go for a short list (four to six) so that you have spares if one is busy or doesn't work out. Find a short-notice and nearby sitter also, one on whom you can count when some situation takes you away from home unexpectedly. This sitter may be more costly, but when you are in need, that may not be important.

Your Support Team for When Your Kids Are Toddler-Age

Once your child is old enough to be awake more of the time when a sitter is present, you may rely more heavily on competent teens. Again, include both boys and girls; both have talents to share with your child.

Before using a new teenage sitter, make an appointment for the day *before* he'll be needed. Use the extra time to familiarize him with your home. You'll want to talk about:

- Security of the home: locking doors, answering the door, security systems, answering the phone and what to say concerning your not being there.
- Child safety, emergencies, and important phone numbers
- Food available to eat and where it may be eaten
- Bedtimes and the pre-bedtime routine
- Activities and games, indoor and outdoor play
- Television—what shows are O.K. for a young child
- Telephone messages, telephone use

Show the sitter that you have the local emergency number on each phone and that other important numbers are in a prominent place (bulletin board, refrigerator door, desk). This list should include telephone numbers for:

- Emergencies (911 in many areas)
- Your PEP
- Doctor, including after-hours number
- Neighbor
- Nearest relative
- Close friend or friends

And, of course, leave a note with the number where you may be reached, whether you are at a friend's home, a movie, or a restaurant. *Write down* the time you plan to return as well.

Your Professional Problem-solving Support Team

Involved in the well-being of your child are many specialists who contribute ideas on health and education. These professionals can cost you money, so you should be well prepared when you go to them for help. This means that you should write down your questions in advance, and it certainly means that you should make notes on the wisdom they share. So often we think we will remember it all, but we can often forget an important part of the advice.

1. Pediatricians and other practitioners. These are often the most helpful in the child health-care area. When going to visit a pediatrician with a child who is ill, be sure to share all the symptoms, frequency of symptoms, and prior occurrences. Then keep the specialist informed with the response to treatment and other details. Guesswork has no place in parenting. Decide how you plan to care for your child's health and then see that you do it.

Choosing a doctor is more than reading the telephone listings. The recommendation of another parent is often the best lead. A family doctor, relative, or friend can often give suggestions, but if you are in a new area, you can always find a physician referral service through your municipal medical association. And remember, you're in charge of the choice and should feel free to change if you don't like the treatment, service, or charges. Parents need to be assertive in the care of their children.

When a young child is to visit a health care specialist, talk about what will happen at the office. Answer questions in a calm and reassuring manner. Encourage older children to participate in describing the problem and making notes on the suggested solution.

As a working parent, do your utmost in taking off the necessary time from work to take your child to the doctor. The presence of a parent is comforting, and hearing the suggested treatment firsthand is the best way to deal with the problem.

A child's sickness can bewilder a parent. That feeling of helplessness is allayed for the parent who takes an active part in the child's treatment, instead of just blindly following instructions without knowing why, and without assessing the success or failure of the treatment.

If an ill child is attended by a relative or other care-giver, be sure that you phone several times a day during the illness. Get a report on the child from the adult in charge and also talk with the child or send hugs and kisses. It is difficult to devote 100 percent attention to work when a child isn't well, but your immediate involvement and helpful attitude can speed the recovery.

2. Public and private social service agencies. These are authoritative sources of child-care information. They can also provide care when a family doesn't have the necessary funds for treatment of a special health-care problem. Again, you get more out of this service and feel more supported by the suggestions offered if you participate fully in describing the challenge and following the advice. Look in the business pages of your telephone directory for a listing of such businesses and agencies.

3. Parent support groups. These loosely organized groups are helpful, provided you remember that although the ideas presented have worked for one parent, they may not work for you. A few groups have professional leadership, who can provide valid suggestions.

Some groups are organized for new parents, some for parents of children with specific major health problems, others for support in the fight against drug use. Although such groups do much to put parents in touch with other families with similar problems, the camaraderie is sometimes more helpful than the suggestions shared.

4. Parent-teacher associations at schools. Although such groups can be routine and dull, many are now educating their members to more practical approaches to youth problems. Nursery schools may have programs on discipline, building self-esteem, and time management. Programs at grade and high schools present answers to the challenges of drug abuse, peer pressure, sex and AIDS, driver training, and safe and enjoyable parties and graduation celebrations.

5. *The religious worker.* A professional often overlooked is the religion-related worker. Churches and synagogues have ministers, rabbis, priests, and social workers with strong credentials who are eager to support the family in difficult times. Having made a church connection early in marriage is preferable to waiting until a problem arises and then seeking counsel.

Ideally, parents should feel good about relying on the ethics and comfort of their religion to sustain them and their children. When a parent finds a practical religion that helps in dealing with small problems, he is more likely to turn to it in a crisis.

6. *Professional writers and lecturers.* Parents shouldn't rule out self-education as part of professional support. Libraries and bookstores are filled with parenting books by well-respected writers. And local high schools and colleges often have parenting courses on specific parenting subjects such as toddlers, teen pregnancy, drugs, and sports pressures. Occasionally there are helpful television specials and videocassettes available that share professional parenting ideas.

Teachers—the Highlight of Your Support Team

Next to parents, there is no greater influence on a child than a teacher. The influence and encouragement from a good teacher will be remembered by your child long after the class subject is forgotten. The benefits that come from a good teacher can't be measured, and they often make the difference between an ordinary child and a smart child.

Teachers of very young children provide some of the warmth of parental love and caring. In this early-learning atmosphere, many of the first important lessons are taught. In fact, the majority of skills and attitudes we learn are taught in the first five years of life. Establishing a healthy attitude toward learning is one of the prime skills of a primary teacher. *What* a child learns is not so important as *how* he learns it and *how he feels* about learning it.

Teaching a child to grow in knowledge and be inquisitive, to accept failures but continue to strive for success, are great gifts from a teacher.

As a wise parent, you will want to establish your own family values and attitudes concerning sex, equality, controlled substances like drugs, democracy, business, welfare, religion, and so forth. Along the way, your child will meet teachers with different values (which could be equally good), and you will want your child to be ready to evaluate these and openly discuss the subjects with you. A time for discussion—ideally at supper on school nights—will keep you in touch with what your child is learning in these areas. And scanning the required text and reading-material for a course is your right, too.

Teachers have the opportunity to mold an impressionable child. Teaching about ethics, creation, sex, and morals has been so ignored by some families that schools are taking over these subjects. Parents may need in some cases to be aware of the aspects of just how these family-oriented subjects are being taught.

But above all, the warm relationship between teacher and student needs nurturing. How to do this is discussed in chapter 15: "Day-Care, School, and Your Smart Child."

The Enrichment Support Team

Beyond the PEP and professionals, there is a wealth of other adults, and some children too, who can be part of your supportive team. They can provide your child with loving care, develop talents and athletic abilities, and widen your child's horizons to include new and wonderful activities.

1. Leaders of after-school activities. These are an essential part of your support team because they provide a change of pace from the earlier part of the day. Library clubs, science clubs, boys' and girls' clubs, Camp Fire and Scout groups, and art, music, and dance lesson groups are just some of the possibilities.

The people involved in these activities contribute to a child's education in both obvious and subtle ways. Thus the qualifications of these leaders should be impeccable. Sometimes you will be given their credentials, sometimes not. A wise parent shouldn't just trust that the standards of those in leadership roles will be the standards he wants taught to his child. As time is available, parents should sit in on these sessions to learn just how they operate and what they teach beyond skills. Certainly, parents should engage in conversation with their children to determine exactly what is being taught and how it is being taught.

Most of these workers are caring people, and lifelong friendships between them and a child sometimes develop. This is both helpful and significant since these leaders usually work in areas where the working parent lacks time or talent.

Help a young child to know the leader sufficiently well to be able to speak comfortably with him. A child shouldn't be intimidated by the leader or coach. And support your child's choice of activities—as much as your job will permit. Sometimes the most you will be able to do is talk together about the activity. If you find that your child is bored with the activity after giving it a fair try, let her choose another activity.

2. *Good friends.* Whether they have children or not, your friends can become confidantes of your child. Sometimes asking your best friends to serve as godparents is an honor for them and a blessing for all of you.

Friends who have been in your home and have seen the way you care for your child may be willing to take over for a weekend or short vacation. Children who grow up around adults they see often, have more poise in the presence of all adults.

3. *Relatives.* Other family members shouldn't be overlooked, whether they live near or far. A letter of support and confidence from your mother who lives far from you, a telephone call from an uncle, or a quick visit by a nearby cousin can do much to lift your spirits.

Sometimes it takes a phone call from *you* to bring this kind of aid, but it is well worth it, especially when you need loving support. Close bonds with relatives are important as support for you, and also as a stabilizing factor in your child's life.

Parents who took part in our survey were *emphatic* about the need for supportive relatives. Those with relatives living nearby listed them as one of the top two most positive influences on their children.

Who says a person has to be a blood relative to care about kids? You may find aunties and uncles among your neighbors, on your sports team, at the office. Invite these folks over and see if the chemistry is right. Of course, you can't use these people solely as proxy relatives for your child; a good relationship means you'll have other social occasions just with them and without the kids. If you keep these relationships going through the years, children of these friends often become nearest and dearest to your children, providing them with wonderful proxy cousins.

What if grandparents are not close by? When we lived in Hawaii, the grandparents were far, far away. At church, however, we met a couple who were missing their grandchildren who lived in the Midwest. We enjoyed one another's company immediately, and these P.G.P.'s (proxy grandparents) became part of our extended family. Now, many moves and many years later, these loving and lovable PGP's are still a part of our lives.

Your PGP's are out there too. Look for them at church, at a retirement home, through friends or neighbors. This cost-free love connection can bring so much joy to your children.

4. Acquaintances. Sometimes you may have a friend from business, a professional club, or a sports team who just seems to be on the same wavelength with you. Don't overlook this person as part of your support team. Although she may not play a major role, sometimes her experiences can give you just the right view of a parenting problem. And when your children become teenagers and look ahead to their own careers, a talk with one of your business friends is often taken more seriously by your child than the same information coming from you. There are valuable and supportive ideas you can get from the dad up the block, the guy in your car pool, the woman you eat lunch with, the person next to you on the exercise bike at the club.

5. Neighborhood teens and preteens. Don't rule these out as too young to be a part of your support team! You'll gain a new appreciation for youth when you see what some teens can accomplish for you.

A single mom had a standing date with a responsible twelve-year-old, who would come by two evenings a week to look after the three children. This gave the mom time for a special long bath with a good book and time to manicure her nails or have an uninterrupted telephone visit with a friend.

A couple with two children hired a teenager who liked to cook to come in each Wednesday afternoon to make and serve supper. It cost a lot less than going out and the couple felt refreshed after this oasis in their busy week.

Many preteens enjoy occasional play with younger children. It increases the older child's self-esteem when he can share ideas with young playmates who are admiring listeners.

When going to the park, some parents take along a preteen to help keep tabs on the younger children and also to demonstrate new skills. Young children learn quickly from older children and enjoy being copy cats.

A Single Parent's Support Team

Some parents don't have any built-in support team. Either they are single parents, or their spouse is so indifferent that they essentially function as a single parent. Single parenting while working requires much determination, but the effort can pay off in a satisfying family life.

In addition to the professionals, volunteers, friends, and relatives already discussed, a single mom will want to be sure that her child has a close relationship with a caring male person. This can be an uncle or grandfather, neighbor or friend. Research has shown that children do not function as well when brought up in an all-female world, so start when a child is a baby to include men in family events.

Of course, the same is true for single dads. Because single dads are less common, however, society has been more supportive. A single father will want to encourage some of his women friends to help nurture his child. This doesn't mean that these women are trying out for the mother-wife job! Some women are far better at being a proxy mom than working at it on a 24-hour basis.

A wide circle of supportive friends and relatives is essential for the single working parent. Organized groups for single parents can do much to give support and provide a strong feeling of family. Many of the meetings are for single parents only, but there are also family activities, which bring all parents and children together. These can provide the warm feeling that the extended family brings.

Your Trading Partner

Among your acquaintances, look for a parent with a child of similar age to yours. Find opportunities to have both children together at one another's home. This trading-off of child supervision is usually thought of as an advantage for the parent who gets some free time in return for supervising two children at another time. But much more important, your child learns the way another family lives, how to understand and respect another parent, and the special feeling of having a close friend.

With neighborhood play much less common nowadays, your trading partner gives you a good substitute activity. You'll be pleased—and sometimes amazed—at the things your child will tell you about playtime at another house. You can adopt the good ideas your child shares, but when it is something you aren't keen on, use the line, "That's the way the Thompsons do it, but we do it this way." Make no judgmental comment that might get repeated!

Having a trading partner also provides a little socializing and time to compare ideas on the challenge of child rearing. Sometimes a trading partner turns into a lifelong friend, too.

If possible, let your trading partner be a different person from your PEP. This expands your circle of support. Some working parents form a playtime co-op in their neighborhood. No money is exchanged, but a log is kept of how many hours each family has used (when the child has been supervised by another parent) and how many hours the parent has given (time spent supervising other children). Such a child-sitting system can be a real money-saver.

Parenting Point

There can't be too much love and caring in a child's life. All parents, and especially working parents, need the assistance of others. Let your support team share the joy of watching your child grow in both wisdom and love. Together you can do it!

Chalkboard for Chapter Three

Start looking for the important people who will contribute to the all-around education and social experiences that smart children need. Try to find a supportive person in each of the following categories. It's up to you to make the connection and start what may be a lifelong relationship for your child. Complete this list and see how many you have:

SUPPORT PERSON AND PHONE NUMBER	DATE OF LAST CONTACT
__ Your PEP _____	_____
__ School teacher _____	_____
__ Relative _____	_____
__ Proxy relative _____	_____
__ Good friend _____	_____
__ Neighbor _____	_____
__ Religious counselor _____	_____
__ Health professional _____	_____
__ Competent sitter _____	_____
__ Social worker _____	_____
__ Parent support group _____	_____
__ Sport coach or teacher _____	_____
__ After-school activity volunteer _____	_____
__ Teacher (music, dance, etc.) _____	_____
__ Older children _____	_____
__ Trading partner _____	_____

You'll be more likely to call on members of your support team if you maintain communication with them, instead of just calling on them when in need. Keep working on this list until your contacts with your support team are natural, and frequent.

Four

The Alarm Goes Off

Diane is tired when she gets up and exhausted ninety minutes later when she leaves for work. First she gets husband Craig up and off to his early job, then awakens kindergartner Emily. Emily watches cartoons in her pajamas, then fusses over what to wear. When her car pool comes, she hasn't finished the now soggy cereal and storms out the door, forgetting the book she was supposed to take. Left alone with a large and as-yet-unfed Labrador retriever, Diane would really like to ignore the world and crawl back into bed. But her sales job calls, so she silently dresses and leaving the house a mess, runs to catch her bus. Another day has started the same dreary way.

As the saying goes, life is what is happening while you're busy doing the wrong things! Life goes by and sometimes we find we've talked about doing great things, but we've filled all our time with the dull things.

The working parent who wants to have a satisfying job and a happy and smart child needs to acquire a time-perspective that helps him through the routine and on to the wonderful!

Our survey of working parents shows that 48 percent say that mornings are the absolute *worst* time of the day for them (and for most others, mornings are the second worst time). Everything seems to go wrong, time flies, tempers flare, and suddenly another day is off to a rotten start.

Psychologists say that the mood of our day is usually set in the first thirty minutes we're awake. What is the first thirty minutes like at your house? Chaos? Threats? Nagging? Tears? Well, no more! Morning isn't the time to dish out the discipline. It's a time for self-discipline. So let's see how to bring calm order and even smiles to the morning drill.

The One and Only Purpose

The morning activities have a single purpose: to prepare you and your family for a productive day. Keep this constantly in mind and see that each thing you do contributes to this one and only purpose.

You want to send off a child ready to learn and enjoy his day-care or schooling. You want him to leave home with a feeling of confidence. You want him to feel he is capable. You want him to feel your love and interest. All of this contributes to his self-esteem, a most necessary quality for his day. You don't accomplish this by shouting "You're stupid" or pressuring him with "Hurry up!"

You also want to prepare yourself for the day. You need to be alert but calm in dealing with the family, yet ready and eager to do your job. This good attitude can turn a routine job into a vital one and a challenging job into a successful one. Each day you want to feel you've made some progress in your work.

So, to give you and your child the best chance for a successful day, you must resolve to organize the family in the morning. This is the most important time of day to have a routine and to stick to it.

The Typical Beginning

The day begins when the alarm goes off. This is usually the mom's alarm and she wakes spouse and then children. Right? Wrong! It is natural for the person being awakened to be antagonistic toward the person doing the awakening. Don't you get enough antagonism in your day without looking for it before your eyes are fully open? Besides, this procedure is a waste of your precious time. It makes others unnecessarily dependent on you. Far better is teaching family members to be self-governing. That's one of the prime goals of parenting. Your smart child is going to have to rise and shine every day of her life. It's time she learns how it's done.

It's accomplished by giving each person a simple alarm clock. Nothing fancy, nothing that resets and gives second chances, just the plain kind of clock that rings until the little button is pushed. Spouses shouldn't have too much trouble mastering this device! (Save your pampering wake-ups with breakfast in bed for the weekends.) On busy work days, adults should be independent and rise to the tune of their own alarm.

But what about kids? Any child more than three or four years of age can work an alarm. After all, toddlers understand the on-off button on the television set, and many understand far more complicated push-button learning games and simple computers. So give the child his own alarm. Many parents make a simple alarm clock one of the gifts for a child's fourth birthday with the encouraging statement that he is now old enough to be trusted to get up in the morning.

Place the alarm across the room from the child's bed and show her it works. Testing the sound of the buzzer is fun! And I guarantee you that, for the first few days, your child will answer the alarm and get up wholly on her own.

Then, about the fourth day, she'll turn it off and go back to sleep. Say nothing, get her up, keep quiet until nearly bedtime that evening. Then calmly say, "I see you turned off your alarm this morning and went back to bed for more sleep. Well, since you seem to need more sleep, your bedtime tonight is thirty minutes earlier. When you can get up when your alarm buzzes, I'll put your bedtime ahead to the usual hour."

It's that simple. And it's a lesson in consequences. Do the right thing (get up when the alarm rings) and things go right. Do the wrong thing (go back to bed) and things aren't so pleasant.

All Important "Me-Time"

The next step in your new morning program is to set your own alarm ten to fifteen minutes earlier than the children's, so you have some time before the action starts. Now this isn't the time to make pancakes or get your clothes in order. This is "me-time," an essential part of the day for moms and dads.

Don't trust yourself to have "me-time" in bed; you just might fall asleep and blow the whole plan. Find a special place to sit—on the patio, in the living room, even in your car. In this quiet away-from-it-all spot, let your mind be a blank piece of paper. Don't plan the day, just sit quietly and reflect on the possibilities a really good day holds. Think about the good things you already have in your life, not on what you think you're missing. Read something inspirational or religious, look out a window at the lacy design of a tree, close your eyes and listen to the morning doves, or just sit and see what pops into your mind. Remind yourself that in the next hour you are going to keep your temper, overlook arguments and whining meanness, and be grateful you're alive and have a healthy family.

At first, you may have to force yourself to sit down and do nothing for ten minutes. But after a few days of "me-time," you'll find all sorts of new and good ideas coming into your head, ideas that can make family life better.

Time Yourself

Do you know how many minutes you need to accomplish the necessary tasks of your morning before leaving for work? Amazingly, few people do. They have only a hazy idea of the needed time, and that's why they are often rushed and late. Parents and children should know the time it takes them to get ready each morning. How else will they know how to set the alarm?

One morning, write down the times needed for the following activities and tally them. Then check the times another morning to be sure you have them right. Parents should use this chart; a slightly different one for children follows. Time is needed to do this tabulation, but you will save time in the long run. Each of the activities on the chart is described below.

1. Me-time. Don't skimp on this important quiet moment before the day. Ten minutes is the minimum.

2. First bathroom time. This refers to the initial trip where shaving, showering, or bathing is included. Unless you have a multi-bathroom

	Your Time	Suggested Time *(in minutes)*
1. "Me-time"	————————	10
2. First bathroom time	————————	15
3. Bed making	————————	2
4. Dressing, make-up	————————	15
5. Infant-toddler help**	————————	10+
6. Tidying room	————————	3
7. Breakfast preparation*	————————	10*
or		
8. Morning tasks*	————————	10*
or		
9. Lunch making*	————————	10*
10. Breakfast eating	————————	10
11. Second bathroom time	————————	10
12. Desk check	————————	5
13. Farewell time	————————	5
14. Cushion	————————	10
YOUR TOTAL:	————————	105

** Omit if children don't need any special help.
 * A single parent with an infant may have to do all these himself,
   thus requiring additional time.

home, not everyone can be doing these at the same time, but each can
be doing something else on the list.

3. Bed making. Each family member makes his own bed. When
parents share a bed, it is perfectly acceptable for the dad to be the
bed-maker. There is nothing masculine or feminine about making a
bed. If you sleep in it, make it.

The same goes for children. A few patient lessons to show them
how to make a bed and how much nicer their rooms look afterward,
will save you reminders or the mistake of doing it yourself. Make it
easy for little hands by having a patterned spread that doesn't show a
few lumps underneath, or use a quilt that doubles as both blanket and
spread. Unless royalty is going to visit your house, perfectly made
beds are not a high priority. But do make them every day.

4. Dressing, make-up. There are too many morning decisions, so
select your clothes the night before. That way you know your outfit is
clean and ready to wear. And before kids go to bed, let them decide

the next day's outfit too. Hang suitable tops and bottoms together in the closet, clothing that you feel is appropriate and that a child is willing to wear. Each week there should be five or more outfits available. Let an elementary school-age child choose from these. Give younger children a choice of just two.

To keep up on local and world affairs, plug in a radio to a bedroom or bathroom outlet so that when you turn on the light, the radio automatically comes on tuned to a news station. You'll get more news this way and less distraction than from turning on a T.V. set. And you'll feel efficient for doing two things at once: dressing and being informed.

5. Infant-toddler help. With a baby in the house, determine the time needed to change his diaper, bathe, and dress him. Include nursing time, but do not include feeding time, which will be covered under #10. This basic care can be the work of one parent while the other is doing something else.

6. Tidying room. As you walk through your home, give each room a glance and pick up something "on-the-way." You'll be pleased with what just one sweep can do for your home's appearance. A child can be in charge of his own room or the family room. This is just a quick pick-up and shouldn't take much time.

A good rule for kids is: Toys on the floor are O.K., clothing and books are not O.K. Books go on tables, desks, or shelves. Clothing and towels get hung up or put in the dirty clothes hamper. Try not to place the hamper in the bathroom, because this congests an already crowded area. If the laundry area isn't convenient, put the hamper in the hall, or better yet, provide a plastic container for each bedroom closet.

7. Breakfast preparation. This often falls into the "mom's work" category, but there is no reason that dads can't do it or that two family members can't work together on it. An older child can often assume leadership. Make menus for the week and know in advance what you plan to serve. Prepare juice the night before. Have cereal and fruit available for extra-busy mornings.

Consider these more interesting breakfasts: peanut butter on toast with a fruit milkshake, a cereal sundae made of granola sprinkled on yogurt or ice cream, a grilled cheese sandwich and eggnog, pre-made and frozen waffles (thawed and served with pureed fruit toppings), crockpot oatmeal cooked overnight, made-ahead raisin oatmeal cookies with cheesy eggs. Who says breakfast has to be dull?

8. Morning tasks. While one parent is making breakfast, the other family members including toddlers should be contributing their fair share. These tasks might be: bringing in the newspaper, feeding pets, setting the table, emptying the dishwasher, entertaining the baby, making lunches, and taking out rubbish. A full discussion of useful chores for smart children is found in chapter 18: "S t r e t c h i n g Your Time."

9. Lunch making. This is an ideal task for a school-age child to do while a parent is making breakfast. This provides an occasion for conversation and also lets the parent supervise if needed. Advance preparation will speed this along. The weekly shopping list should include paper lunch bags and sandwich bags, plastic spoons and forks, big napkins, a variety of fruit, healthful breads and sandwich fillings, and tasty treats.

Some varieties of sandwiches can be made in advance and frozen (add the lettuce later), but lunch needn't always be a sandwich. Insulated lunch boxes mean that food will stay fresh and safe. For variety, try stoneground crackers and cheese, a tomato stuffed with tuna salad, hard-boiled eggs with dip, melon with cottage cheese as a topping, yogurt with fruit, frozen cooked meatballs that will thaw and can be eaten with a toothpick, or a thermos smoothie (frozen fruit, sparkling water, and tofu mixed in a blender). A granola bar or healthful cookies are a sweet treat with which to finish lunch.

Have a crayon handy so that an identifying name can be put on the lunch bag before packing.

10. Breakfast eating. This most important morning event is discussed in the next chapter. Allow ten to fifteen minutes for this essential get-together whether you're a family of two or ten.

11. Second bathroom time. Before leaving for the day, everyone gets a second visit. Oversee young children so that they brush their teeth thoroughly. Tell older children to brush as long as it takes to recite the alphabet, mentally naming something for each letter. Give family members ample time and privacy for bowel movements, since lack of time for this function can make a child uneasy or crabby during the day.

12. Desk check. Look at your date book or calendar so you are aware of every other person's activities that day and how they fit into your schedule. This way there are no surprises about who is where or what the pick-up time will be.

13. Farewell time. Family members may not all depart at the same moment. Take time to provide a good-bye of love and confidence for each. Remind little children of the next time you'll be together.

Near the exit door, have a "going shelf." This is where you put things going out the door: lunches and lunch money, school books and projects, library books, gym clothes, items going to Scout meetings, ballet shoes, outgoing mail, clothes for the cleaner, attaché cases, and any other item you promised to take or return to someone. Get the family in the habit of checking the "going shelf" at farewell time.

14. Cushion. When we fall, it's nice to land on a cushion. During the early morning, many things fall apart and don't turn out as planned. The phone rings, a child needs special comfort, a book is lost, a button falls off. Give yourself ten minutes for such occasions and when this cushion isn't needed, you can use that time for yourself.

Now, add up your times on the chart above, and you'll know just when to set your alarm for getting up on weekdays so you won't be frazzled, disorganized, or late. Encourage your spouse to do this also and read the accompanying text. In a two-parent family, the tabulation will be slightly different depending on the division of duties.

Time Your Child

Next, help your child make a similar tabulation. You will have to do this for younger children, but older ones will like doing it themselves. When a child knows how long it takes her to do the needed things each morning, she knows exactly the time to set her alarm.

	Child's Time	Suggested Time *(in minutes)*
1. First bathroom time*	_____	15*
2. Bed making	_____	3
3. Dressing*	_____	7*
4. Tidying room	_____	5
5. Morning tasks*	_____	10*
6. Breakfast eating	_____	10
7. Second bathroom time	_____	5
8. Farewell time	_____	5
9. Cushion	_____	5
TOTAL:	_____	65

*Times will vary with the age of the child (babies get off easy, teens will often take more time to dress), whether bath or shower time is at night or in the morning, and how many morning tasks you assign. Ten to fifteen minutes of chores is normal.

Your child's total will probably be a little more than an hour. Make the point that nothing on this list is optional and that you expect each item to be accomplished in order to start the day right for everyone. If one person fails to do a chore or is purposefully slow in front of the mirror, the entire family is affected.

See that the child's alarm is set in keeping with the time required. Give each child a list of what he is expected to do each morning. Make it a picture-list for nonreaders. Ask the child to post it in his room where he can see it. Make this rule: no playtime until the list is finished.

Our survey showed that one reason morning was such a bad time of day was that children *lacked direction* in getting themselves ready to go out the door. Insist that children take responsibility for accomplishing these necessary morning jobs. Praise for a good morning will help.

If a child continues to resist this basic organization you may need to offer incentives such as small rewards or extra privileges. And if that doesn't work, you can resort to a simple punishment such as the taking away of a favorite toy or activity. Remember that a smart child is self-disciplined and that young children are capable of this morning routine.

Although it may require a week or so to establish this routine, you'll find it makes for a happier and more confident family. A first-grader was once entrusted to our care for about two weeks because of a devastating storm in his home area. At first he resisted getting the necessary things accomplished in the morning, but by the time he returned home, our children had convinced him of the merits of a morning routine. He introduced this organization to his parents and his mother later reported that it gave their days a new, brighter beginning.

Sleepy Children

Educators say they have a difficult time the first hour of the school day because many children are still half asleep and many have not had an adequate breakfast. This makes concentration difficult. The same might be said of some adult employees!

Being awake at least an hour before coming to school is essential for children. A child's attitude toward learning is much better if she has been actively moving about, making decisions, talking, eating a nutritious breakfast, and so forth, before school. Remember, how the day goes often depends on how it starts!

Helpful Spouses

With two parents working, there is no such thing as "women's work." Parents should divide the morning tasks listed above so that one parent is not making breakfast *and* lunches *and* caring for the baby. Mom should not be the Little Red Hen and do it all alone. This show-off or martyr attitude is actually harmful since it denies the father the satisfaction of doing his share at home.

Our survey shows that most working mothers, unfortunately and very unfairly, are doing the same list of morning tasks as if they were at-home moms. This doesn't make for an honest and loving relationship. If parents work outside the home the same number of hours, the work inside the home *must* be equally divided.

If necessary, parents should sit down together and go over the list above. Each one can assume certain tasks with the understanding that they'll trade now and then. Both spouses are capable of the tasks that must be done.

—————— Parenting Point ——————

The day goes better when it starts with self-discipline. A smart child is even smarter when self-governed. Teaching a child—and yourself—to do the right things at the right time each morning is a lesson that goes on to bless the entire day. And remember, family equality begins in the morning! Step by step, together, you can do it!

Chalkboard for Chapter Four

Keep a little private calendar this month of your three important morning goals:

A. Your quiet, thoughtful "me-time."
B. Independence of family members (their ability to get up with their own alarm and then do things on their own).
C. An improved upbeat mood that comes from better morning organization and "me-time" thinking.

Put an A, B, or C after each date if you achieve that goal:

Day	
1	16
2	17
3	18
4	19
5	20
6	21
7	22
8	23
9	24
10	25
11	26
12	27
13	28
14	29
15	30
	31

Don't expect wonders the first few days. But you *will* see a gradual improvement.

Five

Hey, Don't Skip Breakfast! Touch-Base Time #1

Like a good dad, Bart waited in front of the library for Matt, his book-loving second-grader. After ten minutes he went inside but Matt was nowhere to be found. Feeling upset, he started for home, remembered something about chicken, and picked up a box at the Colonel's. He raced home, now worried about Matt, and when he burst into the kitchen there were Sheila and Matt calmly eating chicken! Sheila, rolling her eyeballs heavenward, said, "But I told you as you left this morning that I would get Matt and the chicken!" So the result for Bart was needless worry but lots of chicken to eat.

Mix-ups do occur when the family is rushing about in the morning. Sometimes not all family members get the messages right, and some get only half a message. Bart remembered something about chicken, but that was all. And he often picked up Matt on Wednesdays at the library. How could he be expected to keep it all straight? The routine was different every day. It wasn't at all like the office where employees understood their responsibilities. There were regular meetings, each person kept a detailed calendar, and you could always rely on your secretary to remind you.

What was needed was a morning board meeting at home! And that's just what can be done when the family has breakfast together. No one needs to take notes unless he wants too, yet each one is reminded of his appointments and responsibilities. But wouldn't that take a lot of time? Not at all, and the time investment is worth it!

In our survey, 52 percent of parents said they do *not* eat breakfast together. (Although 39 percent did eat together, 9 percent skipped the meal entirely or ate en route to work or school.) Not eating together means that there isn't one time when the entire family rallies before going off for the day. At the same time, half the parents surveyed said that morning was absolutely the *worst* time of the day, and these were usually the families who skipped this morning meal together.

When a family doesn't have breakfast together, there isn't a morning time with all present to take up important matters. This results in confusion, like Bart's, but it also has more serious consequences.

A working parent who wants a happy child must provide a morning send-off that prepares a child for the learning experiences ahead. Breakfast is the time.

How Long Does Breakfast Take?

Unless you have truly slow eaters, breakfast is a ten to fifteen minute event. But a most important event! A parent feeding an infant may require another five minutes in order to feed both himself and the baby. A slow eater should be encouraged to start promptly, even a few minutes ahead of the others.

Slow eaters are often not really slow at eating. Usually they are doodling and dawdling with their food, talking constantly, or dreaming and not paying attention to what's going on. If you have a child like this, remove distractions, encourage a normal eating pace, and give an incentive to finish about the same time as everyone else.

Sometimes a child eats slowly because she is not quite awake. If possible, children should be up and moving before breakfast and not come directly from their beds to the table.

But We Can't Eat Together!

That's the cry of many families where one parent leaves early, the other late, and the kids in the middle. However, there is still a way if you are really serious about being together in the morning. It is to schedule breakfast as the last event for the parent leaving early and the first or second event for the rest of the family. This may mean that kids eat in pj's, but it's better to spill on the pj's than on the outfit of the day.

If such a schedule is completely impossible, which it rarely is, then breakfast should still be an important time with one parent and the children.

Excuses are easily made that it can't be done, or that one doesn't need breakfast, or that one will grab breakfast "on the way." But for family solidarity, there is nothing like breakfast together.

Why Breakfast Is So Important

In the morning the family is preparing for hours of separation. They will probably not see one another for eight to ten hours, and already they have been separated through the many hours of the night.

Parents need to reestablish the warm and caring bonds of family that existed the evening before. The home is not a hotel where strangers just pass in the hallway. It is a haven that one returns to time and time again for nurturing and educating, as well as for sharing both sadness and happiness.

Unfortunately, today only T.V. sitcoms show the family gathered around cereal bowls laughing and eating together in the morning. Many real families eat "on the run," grabbing some sugar-coated sustenance and gulping down juice while racing for the door.

For the well-being of a working parent and a smart child, however, breakfast together is essential. This is touch-base time #1.

What Does Not *Go On at Breakfast*

To start with, breakfast is not a T.V.-watching time, nor is it the time to read the newspaper. It is not play time for kids, and it isn't homework time. All these things should be done before or after breakfast or during the evening before.

Most important, no one will want to come to the breakfast table if the get-together is just an occasion to be bawled out! So forget the mistakes of the morning, what happened with the sitter the night before, and petty suggestions or corrections. While there is a time and place for child discipline and discussions of marital shortcomings, the breakfast table is not it. Verbal upbraiding, whether mild or magnified, doesn't let the oatmeal go down easily. Avoid those upsetting comments and topics. Looking back has no place at breakfast. This is the time to look forward to a grand new day.

What Does *Go On at Breakfast*

Eating of course. But beyond good nutrition, which enables family members to function all morning, breakfast should include:

1. The plan for the day
2. When we meet again
3. Inspiration and education
4. News of the day
5. Confidence building
6. Love

Of course, it is understood that one person talks while the others eat. If everyone is conversing at once, breakfast will last until lunch! Although parents will do the majority of the talking, it's important to hear from the younger generation too. Sometimes a child will tell you about something that's been bugging him. If possible, settle it right then or before he leaves for the day.

Now, let's look at these six elements and see how they can easily fit into a short breakfast.

1. The plan for the day. Talk about this first. How does each family member get to work, day-care, and school? How do kids get home? What places will kids go after school and how will they get home from those places? Is there an errand to run on the way home? Who's preparing dinner? Be specific about times and meeting places. (It's a good idea to provide children with the telephone number of an at-home neighbor should the meeting plans not work out.)

You may also need to mention what needs to be taken along today: a toy, school project, lunch, money, books, Scout cookies, homework, a report, clothes to be dry cleaned. Are these things on the "going shelf"?

2. When we meet again. The family will usually be together at supper and for a period of time before supper. Sometimes though, a parent may be going on a business trip that will take her away from home for a few days. Whether the separation is to be days or just hours, the reunion needs to be described. These are good lines:

"When I get home from work, I'm looking forward to hearing what happened at day-care."

"My big meeting is today so I'll tell you about it at supper tonight."

"I'll be back Thursday but I'll phone tomorrow night at eight to see how your report went."

"We can use the time before supper to find your lost teddy bear. I know he's somewhere in the house."

"It's home-made pizza tonight so be ready to tell me your favorite topping."

"On his way home tonight, Grandpa is stopping by just to see you."

"I'm looking forward to being with you after work."

Such lines make a link across the hours of separation, hours that seem very long to young children. *You* know you'll be together again, but your child needs to be reassured. The fear of separation is reduced when a child understands when you will be with her once more. The child's fear of being unnecessary to the family (or even abandoned by the family) disappears when the parent shows interest in what the child will be doing during the separation.

We all like something to look forward to. For the family with working parents, the weekend often seems distant, especially on Monday morning! So talk about something nice that will happen on Wednesday and what will be very special about the weekend that is five days away. This means you have to have in mind a mid-week treat and a weekend special event, but that is part of parenting. You don't just let things happen, you need to *make* them happen.

3. Inspiration and education. Yes, a little "meat" can be included at breakfast. This usually comes from parents, but older children can also contribute. It's just a quick moment of learning for a working parent and a happy child. Here are some suggestions to get you started:

Keep a Bible at the table and read one Bible verse or one chapter of Psalms each morning. Bookstores and churches often have books of short inspirational quotations for reading in the morning.

Have a dictionary handy and let a child open it at random and point to a word. Read the word and give a simple definition. See who can use the word during breakfast. Then see who can use it at supper. Word-a-day calendars can also be purchased and kept at the table.

Try a little poetry. Two good books are *Read-Aloud Rhymes for the Very Young* (Jack Prelutsky, Knopf, 1986) and *The Oxford Book of American Light Verse* (William Harmon, Oxford University Press, 1979). Although three minutes is about all you'll probably spend on inspiration and education, this can become the highlight of breakfast. One survey family reported that the morning poem lifted the morning gloom at their house.

4. News of the day. Although your T.V. set is definitely off during breakfast (when it's on, it cuts down on communication within the family), you can still include the top news of the day. You can do this because you've had your news radio on while dressing (see chapter 4) or you've had a few moments to scan the newspaper. Make it quick and simple: "The World Series starts today." "Levant McDooley has reached the top of Mt. Everest." "It rained two inches in Dallas." "The city council approved the money for the new school." Choose your news headline in keeping with your child's age and also in keeping with special interests of those present.

Kids listen to and learn from parent-to-parent conversation. They not only learn the news, but they also observe the body language and hear the tone of voice (excited, depressed, pleased). Be alert to the subtle messages you're sending.

5. Confidence building. The hours ahead may be challenging for parents, but they can be downright intimidating for kids. Breakfast should build confidence, enabling a child to go forth ready to succeed. Consider your child's activities for the day and tie in to them like this:

"Your friends will like the dinosaur you're taking for show-and-tell."
"Your book report sounded good last night, so I know you'll give it easily."
"I like what you're wearing today."

"We worked hard making those cookies for Camp Fire and your friends will really enjoy them."
"It must feel good to have your homework finished."
"Take a deep breath and then work slowly through the math test. I know you'll do well."

Giving your child a feeling of self-esteem as he goes out into the world comes in part from your morning conversation concerning schoolwork, sports, play, and other activities.

6. Love. It's last on this list, but it should be foremost in your mind during the morning hours. Of course you love your child. Still she needs to be told often. You can't tell her too often! These expressions of love should come frequently from both mother and father.

After a weekend at home, some young children find Monday morning parting especially difficult. To remedy this in my family, busy though I was getting ready to leave for work, I always took time to hug each child and talk about the weekend just past and the good things ahead. One morning our younger daughter said to me in comforting tones, "Don't be sad Mommy. I love you and I'll do something fun with you tonight."

Some families end breakfast this way: Each takes the hand of the next person at the table. One starts by giving three squeezes to the next. This stands for "I love you." Next, four squeezes are sent around the circle, meaning "Have a great day." Finally, just two squeezes are sent for "Let's go!" Your family can make up its own messages and meanings.

Hugs, kisses, and love pats are also very important. And so are words of love:

"I love you so much."
"You're very special to me."
"I'm proud you're my kid."
"What would I do without you!"
"I love being your daddy."
"I love you no matter what."
"Always remember that I love you."

What a send-off! What a great ending for breakfast and your first touch-base time of the day. Try this system for a few weeks. You'll be amazed how much better you feel about the send-off you give family members, and yourself.

———— *Parenting Point* ————

A smart child and a working parent both have more satisfying days when the day starts with good nutrition. But don't forget the emotional nutrition that comes from giving your interest and love. Step by step, you can do it when you establish the tradition of breakfast together.

Chalkboard for Chapter Five

Here are a typical family's morning departure times:

7:05 A.M—Working father must leave home with one child, who is going to day-care.
7:35 A.M—Working mother must leave home, taking one child who is going to school.
8:00 A.M.—Older child must be ready to be picked up by the car pool.

Thus:

6:50 A.M.—The latest time that the family can have breakfast together. (The child departing at 8:00 A.M. will probably just be getting up. The working father and youngest child must be all set to leave shortly thereafter. Each morning schedule must be worked out to take all this into account.)

Now make a list of your family departure times:

_____ A.M.—Working father must leave home (taking a child
        en route to work?)
_____ A.M.—Working mother must leave home (taking a child
        en route to work?)
_____ A.M.—Child must be ready for car pool departure.
_____ A.M.—The latest time that family can have breakfast
        together.

Now that you know *when* breakfast must be, announce it to the entire family and make each family member a simple schedule that gets that person to the table for this all-important time!

Six

Commuter's Express

The worst thing about Marianne's job was getting there and back. She didn't mind the actual work, but the morning commute drained her energy before work, and the evening commute frazzled her otherwise good nature and spoiled the time she was soon to have with her son, Joshua. On top of all that, Marianne was acquiring a reputation for being late—late to work, late with her reports, even late in leaving the office. With forty-five minutes of commuting time each way, she realized that this hour and one-half was mostly nonproductive time for herself and her family. To top that, when she did get home, she was overwhelmed with odds and ends of other nonproductive things that needed her attention. And somehow, after spending time with Josh, she had no time left for herself.

Wouldn't it be grand if we could all live but five minutes from our jobs? What positive things we could do with all that wasted commuting time! However, commuting is a fact of life for most working parents, a time that many find boring and frustrating.

But this time *can* be well spent whether you take public transportation to work, commute by car pool, deliver a child to school or day-care en route, or drive alone. These minutes or hours of travel can be a gold mine of accomplishment, letting you arrive at work invigorated and return home at the end of the day eager to be with your family. And best of all, there are ways to use this time to make you a wiser parent and your child a more educated person.

First though, let's consider one of Marianne's problems: getting to work late. You can't arrive on time if you don't leave on time! People who are late for work are also most likely to be the ones late for the theater or the ball game, late to pick up a child, and late for meals. Being late is just a bad habit we acquire, and it doesn't have to plague our mornings or any other part of the day.

Car Pooling with Kids

If you drive your child—and other kids—to their morning destination, you probably have about ten minutes of talking time.

A pleasant conversation on some upcoming event, a fun car game, a question on a project, or asking how he feels about something, are good ways to use this one-on-one time. Don't fail to occasionally ask "What would *you* like to talk about?" You may be surprised at some of the responses!

This isn't the time to discipline a child. Remember that your aim is to help him start the day ready to learn. In-the-car confrontations can leave you both upset and cause you to drive less safely.

If there are several children in the car, you must keep them from wrestling or arguing by steering the conversation to happy topics. Try these easy car pool activities:

With younger children, let them name things they see along the road. When they know some numbers and letters, let them look for certain ones. Have them find something of a color you name. Sing little songs together. Teach rhymes. Try to tell a familiar story from memory and let the children do the sound effects.

With older children, play "I'm Going to Outer Space." It starts, "I'm going to outer space, and I'm taking an ape." The next child repeats that line and adds something to take beginning with the letter *b*. And on through the alphabet. Or have kids add up the numbers on license plates. Or play the connecting-words game: one person starts with a word such as *zoo*. The next person must name a word that begins with the last letter of *zoo*, such as *ostrich*. The next child must choose a word that begins with *h*, the last letter in *ostrich*, and so on. Or guess how many miles it will be to the destination, the winner getting first choice in car seating for the next day.

Whatever the activities, ensure that this special time together remains cheerful. Your last message should be "I love you." Because some of our kids didn't like to shout about love within earshot of their peers, we used the acronym RILY. It was our secret word. (Some thought it was the name of one of the children or our dog.) Only our family knew that it stood for "Remember, I love you."

Commuting with Other Adults

Whether you ride a train or bus, or car pool with others, the commuting time can be frittered away if you aren't careful. Daydreaming, watching the familiar landscape go by, idle conversation about last night's T.V. sitcom are worth five minutes or less. After that, it's time for better things. Of course, there is the exception of being part of an especially stimulating group of people whose conversation makes the trip amusing and educational. But such a gathering on wheels is definitely exceptional.

When a car pool has been running awhile in the same boring and unproductive vein, it is difficult to change it or to do things on your own. It's much easier when you're alone on public transportation to use the commute time to good advantage. Either way, be bold and take the initiative to use the time productively. Consider these activities:

Read the newspaper. This saves your having to read it in the evening when you have family things to do. The news doesn't change much during the day, and what *is* new you can catch on radio or television. In the car pool, certain shared news items can be springboards for conversation. Remind yourself to look for news you can use—as a business person and as a parent.

Read a book. Take along a paperback just for commuting time. This should be a book that you can read in short snatches, not one with hard-to-grasp concepts. This book can be a novel, a how-to book, or a book of inspiration. Some commuters like to use the time for business reading, selecting books that tie in with career aims.

Write notes. Social letters, thank-you notes, and other correspondence are items often put off. Writing them while traveling can make you feel good. A tablet with a sturdy backing makes writing easier while bumping along.

Plan your menus and grocery lists. You can do this and be part of the conversation at the same time. Then at home, it doesn't take long to add the items you find missing from your shelves. You'll save time when shopping from a list. And you'll save money by basing your shopping list on your menus, not on impulse.

Make other lists. Start your lists for Christmas, birthdays, and anniversaries—purchases, events to plan, foods to make ahead, decorations, gifts. Make a list of tasks that need doing around the house that weekend. List things you want to discuss with a spouse: travel, entertaining, parenting. List things you want to discuss with your child: allowances, sports, grades, overnights, telephoning relatives.

Consider parenting problems. Consider your biggest current problem: discipline, honesty, toilet training, dating, bad driving habits, and so on. Think about the problem and try to come up with some creative solutions. In the car pool, you may find some help from wise co-travelers.

Check your schedule. Carry your appointment book with you. Check to see what is forthcoming. List calls to be made, errands to be run, things to be accomplished at home and work. The mere fact that you write these things down in available time slots will make them easier to accomplish.

Of course, don't try to do all these things on one commuting trip. For example, you might write notes on Monday, make your shopping list each Thursday, and so forth.

Driving Alone

Don't feel sorry for yourself if you commute alone. This can be a real blessing and a calming way to start the day. There are no shouting children, no "helpful" backseat drivers, no diverting conversations, no boring questions to answer.

Although you don't have the opportunity to make lists, write notes, or read a book, this doesn't mean your time is to be wasted hearing the same news over and over again or muttering to yourself while caught in creeping traffic.

Here are three mind-freeing ideas:

1. Put a small tape recorder on your car seat and the microphone on your dashboard, kept in place with a piece of masking tape. Make a recorded letter to your mom or brother or good friend. Admit that you are driving alone and talking at the same time. Tell what's going on around you as you drive, as well as what's going on in your life. This will save your writing a letter later, and the recipient will love the alive feeling of your cassette letter.

2. Listen to a classical music station. The music is soothing and the announcer will teach you about less familiar classical pieces. Let commuting time be music appreciation time.

3. Read a book! Well, listen to a book. It matters not if your car hasn't a built-in tape player; take one along. With so many freeway commuters today, several companies provide thousands of wonderful books on tape for commuters to rent and enjoy. These companies will send you a catalog so you can choose from current novels, nonfiction, and self-help books. You can even have the entire Bible read to you.

One of the biggest companies is Books on Tape, Box 7900, Newport Beach, CA 92658 (telephone: 1-800-626-3333). No, I don't have stock in the company, but it's so great I wish I did!

Because many working parents don't have the time to read, this is an easy way to "read" at least a book each month while driving. (Some people also listen while shaving, bathing, cooking, cleaning, repairing, walking, and so on.) You can rent an entire unabridged first-rate novel on cassettes for about the same price as buying the book. And better still, many libraries now have collections of cassette books that you can borrow free of charge.

You can listen for pleasure or knowledge. Maybe you feel there is a hole in your education. Books on tape can fill in that hole and expand your knowledge. You may prefer to stay abreast of best sellers, or go back and cover the classics. They're all available on cassette.

It's hard to think of many better ways to spend the commuting time than listening to a really good book. The great authors of the past and the hot new writers are your companions, and "reading" in this way gives you a feeling of great accomplishment. It can be a window to the world for a busy working parent.

There is no longer an excuse to be a literary illiterate. And you will find many fine books on tape that will appeal to your children too. They can be listened to while doing tasks, dressing, or enjoying crafts.

Deep-breathing Time

No matter how you've spent your travel time, you have one more activity before starting work. It's called deep-breathing time. This is both a physical and a mental exercise.

No doubt you've been sitting for some minutes during your commute. As you arrive at your job, stand up extra straight, throw your shoulders back, and take three deep breaths. As you do, say to yourself:

It's good to be alive!
It's great to have a job!
It's grand to be a parent!

Now is the time for your mind to shift gears. Think of your child and know that he is having a happy and adventuresome time in the good care of those who will love him and teach him. Then, confident that your child is well cared for, shift mental gears to your job.

This is the start of a new day on the job. Whatever went wrong, whatever hurtful thing was said, whatever you found dissatisfying is now past. That was yesterday. This is today.

Think of what you hope to accomplish today. It may be a mountain of a project, it may be something as small as working on a clear desk-top. Set one or two goals for this day alone. These goals might be to give 100 percent attention to each task, to smile at a coworker, to find something complimentary to say to a subordinate, to speak frankly and with dignity to a boss, to eat a sensible lunch, to finish something that is already started, to write with newly sharpened pencils, to make fewer mistakes, to be receptive to new ideas, to be a willing worker.

As you leave the bus or cross the parking lot, determine that you will not let pettiness spoil the good day you have begun for yourself.

You've done all the right things in starting this day and now you deserve the best.

Parenting Point

Working parents need to attend to many details and they can do some of these projects in spare moments while commuting. This fitting a project into otherwise wasted time is sometimes called "working in the cracks" and frees up home time for family togetherness. Use the time getting to work to enrich the day ahead. Step by step, you can learn to do this.

Chalkboard for Chapter Six

Here are some goals to check off as you achieve them:

For before leaving home:

1. Determine not to be a tardy person. Put together a morning schedule that gets you out the door on time.
2. Use a counter or shelf near the exit door for the family "going shelf." Explain how it is to be used and see that it is.

For commuting time:

1. Select different activities for the car, bus, or train depending on whether you are with children or other business people, or are alone. Make a list of at least five things you are willing to try:

1.

2.

3.

4.

5.

2. Start giving yourself deep-breathing time just before your work day begins.

Seven

Keeping Alive from 9 to 5

Susan had started work again after five years at home with Leslie and Johnny. Now that they were in school, she was eager to resume her career. Husband Bruce agreed that the extra salary would go into a savings account, first for a house with a back yard and then for college educations. But back at her job, Susan felt that her boss was watching her—and watching her disapprovingly. Had the work place changed in five years? She worried about her appearance, her skill in speaking with her associates, her time off when Leslie was sick, her performance at meetings. Even though she had toiled very hard at home while the children were toddlers, this was different and she found it difficult to get back into the 9 to 5 working mode.

There is a lot more gossip about working moms than working dads. Some say mothers are just in it for the money, others say they can't shift gears and become professionals; now that they have two jobs, the work place is a second job and gets second-rate attention.

Certainly it is correct to feel that family comes first, but this doesn't have to mean that you treat the work place in an off-hand manner. We can cultivate the ability to do two—or more—things well. The problem arises when we have to concentrate on something entirely different—our job—after we've been thinking and acting so much in the parenting realm.

Shifting Gears

Ideally, the mental shift from parenting to career comes in the time that elapses between leaving home and arriving at the job. By the time you reach your work place, you should be thinking about the responsibilities, challenges, and opportunities of your job. This is now your priority.

How do you do this? With discipline! It is easier when you are confident that your child is happy in her activities while separated from you. It is easier when you can actually see the things that your salary provides. It is easier when you know that your job makes a difference for the better and benefits you as a whole person.

But you also need to remind yourself that you are being paid to work at the job. You aren't being paid to be a parent. So it becomes a matter of your integrity not to confuse working time with parenting time.

This doesn't mean that an occasional thought, conversational comment, or phone call cannot concern your important job of parenting. But you will be happier and more successful in your work if you treat your 9 to 5 hours in a businesslike way.

One mom in my survey said, "My child is in my thoughts every moment of the working day." It's quite difficult to do a good job at the office when the mind is somewhere else. This same mother expressed guilt over being separated from her child during the day—a concern she hadn't thought through to a conclusion.

Eventually, most parents *will* be separated from their children for longer periods, until the day arrives when they live in separate places and communication becomes the weekly phone call or visit. So this weaning process needs to start early in the parent-child relationship. It must come gradually by moments and hours so that it isn't a blow when it becomes days and weeks.

This acceptance of being separated from your child doesn't mean you love your child any less than an at-home parent. And it doesn't mean you should heap guilt on yourself. About 61 percent of the mothers in our survey expressed guilt about working. This was more common among mothers who held jobs for their own personal satisfaction or to provide extras, rather than among those working to make ends meet. But once you decide that it is best to work, you have to compartmentalize your thinking.

When you divorce the work place job from the parenting job, it means that you value your work and the tangible and intangible benefits it brings you. You have decided to be both parent and business person. You have good reasons for making that decision. Now you have to carry it out to the very best of your ability.

Although this tug-of-war to give 100 percent dedication to the job may seem to apply more to working mothers than to working dads, we are seeing more and more fathers whose work is also affected by events at home: a child's health and academic progress, the pressure on the marital relationship when both spouses work, the lack of time for family togetherness and personal private time.

So we all need to shift gears, to trust that our child is well and happy, to put our minds to work giving a top performance every day from 9 to 5.

What Bosses Say

When increasingly greater numbers of women began to enter the workforce in the early 1980s, I conducted an opinion survey of bosses—men and women—who had mothers of young children in their departments. These managers were asked if they found any differences in attitude between working fathers and working mothers. The answer was a vehement and decided "Yes!"

With few exceptions, the fathers were categorized as more businesslike and dedicated to their jobs. This was often because the fathers had worked continuously whereas mothers were likely to have had time off during a child's infancy. And now the mothers were learning how to handle both parenting and working. No doubt as more women are in the work force for a longer period of time, and more men take on a share of home tasks and child-care, these statistics will change and there will be little or no gender difference in professional competency.

There is another factor. Mothers in general are more closely tied emotionally to their children than are fathers. This too may change as dads perform more parenting duties, as increasing numbers are doing. These emotional ties between parent and child often make separation difficult. This is especially evident at the start of the work day. A mother may already have been up for hours, giving home and children her 100 percent effort, before having to deal with the challenges of business.

The bosses interviewed said that women have problems in these areas: absenteeism, gossip, time abuse, attitude, and lack of professionalism. Let's consider these five areas of comment by bosses who are both male and female, old and young, blue collar and white collar.

Absenteeism

When one large Midwestern company established its own day-care center, female absenteeism dropped by two-thirds. Male absenteeism was unchanged.

In about 90 percent of two-parent working families, the mother delivers children to day-care or school, attends the parent-teacher conferences, is the parent called when a child isn't well, and remains at home with a sick child.

Sometimes the nature of a father's job keeps him from doing his share in this area. But in many cases, the mother performs these duties merely because society has made her accustomed to doing things a certain way. Dad teaches whittling; mom bandages the cut fingers. Dad dresses himself for the office and eats breakfast, mom dresses herself and the children and then feeds everyone breakfast. Dad doesn't know how to care for and amuse a sick child; mom is so good at making chicken soup and playing bedside games.

New parents should start out trying to be equally competent in child-care. As children grow, parents can express their expanding individualities by learning more about certain aspects of their children's lives. There is no reason that mothers can't be sport coaches and dads design costumes for the class play. It's just that we're so used to it the other way around.

Today, a mother's need to care for a child is the main cause of absenteeism. When carried to extremes, absenteeism can be the cause of poor work performance, lack of promotion, and sometimes the loss of the job.

But absenteeism is not always caused by the needs of the children. The personal health of the worker is often involved. Here again statistics show that women "lose" by requiring more days off from work for health reasons. However, this is changing, and in the last decade it has moved toward equivalency.

Women, who usually carry a larger at-home workload than their spouses or carry the whole burden as a single parent, are frequently fatigued and more susceptible to illness. On the other hand, women are better at staying on the job when their health is marginal; they seem better able to cope with headaches, minor illness, and of course monthly discomfort. Bosses did admit that women seemed to try harder to keep working when not feeling well.

Because chronic absenteeism can affect job performance, a parent should endeavor to avoid the reputation of being a "sometimes worker." Certainly, when a parent or a child is ill, time off from work is a necessity. Sometimes one member of a parent's support team (see chapter 3) can take over and care for a sick child. Knowing that a child isn't well and still having to be at work, is one of the most difficult aspects of holding a job while parenting.

In two-parent families, consideration should be given to sharing the days taken off work in order to care for a child. With fathers doing more, this could change the reputation for excessive absenteeism that working mothers now have.

Office Talk

The cliché of gossiping women gathered around the coffee pot or in the rest room isn't disappearing much. The employers questioned felt that women wasted company time with unnecessary chitchat. Such talk is usually about family concerns.

Women, still being the prime-movers in child-care, are more interested in sharing the child's progress, solving problems, learning new ideas, getting advice from others, and telling charming kid-stories. Certainly, men gab but usually not about the family. Until recently, parenting conversation wasn't considered as manly as talk about politics or sports. Men are more apt to gossip on nonfamily matters, whereas women function more on the two-track system: worker and parent. Often this doesn't leave time to contemplate the Middle East turmoil or the latest baseball player trade. Mothers in our survey reported that they had very little time to read or learn new things while both working and parenting. The challenges to their dual lives are sometimes overwhelming.

The problem with all informal office conversation about the family—by dads or mothers—is that it tends to bring the worker's thoughts back to the child and the matter of separation. And this often interrupts the flow of office thinking and makes it more difficult to return to business matters after a break.

Sometimes excessive office talk stems from the desire to know more about the outside world. It is understandable that when one is mostly at home or at the office, the important—or trivial—news of what is going on elsewhere makes one feel more alive and part of the action. But often these conversations become gossip sessions about coworkers, the evils of management, and poor company policies.

All workers, not just parents, could benefit from engaging in less gossip. Office gossip is rarely helpful and is frequently hurtful. It adds to stress and creates factions. And often, it isn't even true!

Test yourself for a week. En route home, think about the social conversations you had at the office. How did you feel after these conversations? Enlightened or invigorated? Resentful or suspicious? Note how many different topics were covered. Consider any idea that would be useful at work or at home. Pull from these conversations—if possible—interesting, factual items you can share at supper. If there is nothing worth sharing, you may want to improve the time spent in office chatter.

We all need the change of pace that these casual conversations can bring, but we don't need the reputation for wasting time on useless talk. And that is just what bosses feel that many women do.

Time Abuse

One of the biggest complaints employers in our survey had against all workers is that they didn't work the prescribed number of hours. It is interesting that men have the reputation for taking overly long lunches and leaving too early at the end of the day. Women have the reputation for arriving late and then taking long breaks (of course these are generalities). Too, according to the complaints, the body might be present for eight hours, but the mind was out to lunch a lot of the time.

All told, most bosses questioned were more critical of women than of men in the area of time abuse. When questioned, they said that men often did business at lunch or on the way home. This probably isn't true, but it's the unfavorable picture women must deal with at present.

To be sure you aren't abusing your company's policies, keep track of your time for a week or so. Be very specific, down to the minute. Note when you arrive and leave, when you start a break and when you return, when you leave your desk for lunch and when you are back at work. You may find that such a record is a useful tool during salary negotiations. It could back up your claim of being a dedicated worker.

Attitude

Who wants an employee who acts as if he is doing his boss a big favor just by turning up?

How we view the relationship between work and the consequences of our work is vital. At the beginning of this chapter, we saw Susan, motivated to work so that she and Bruce could afford better housing now and college tuitions later for their two children.

Motive plays a big part in attitude. We do a better job and our attitude is more upbeat when we are working for a good purpose. The expectation of a good reward for our work speeds our progress!

In my survey, 42 percent of mothers worked to make ends meet, and another 31 percent worked to provide family extras. But a great number, 28 percent, were working for personal satisfaction.

The mothers working to make ends meet felt the least guilt and commonly said their children understood their reasons for working. The mothers working to provide extras had a slightly greater measure of guilt, yet felt that their children also understood why they worked. However, mothers holding a job for personal satisfaction had the greatest amount of guilt and the least success in explaining to children why they worked. Some of these mothers, employed for their own well-being, had serious regrets about not being an at-home mom. Although their attitude toward their job was more *selfish* than *selfless*, they could not escape the subtle worry about not actually *having* to be in the work place. Guilt—or the lack of it—affects attitude. Workers who value their jobs are more effective.

Mothers who hold down a job for personal satisfaction need to accept the fact that outside work fulfills an inner need for them, a need they feel cannot be satisfied in any other way. Some of these mothers may want to examine their motives for working to be sure that they have considered all the options available for using their time during important child-rearing years. A part-time career or a home office may be an answer.

A poor work attitude is often manifested by those parents who escape to the office. Working to escape home life is not unusual for both mothers and fathers. When children are baffling, difficult, or in trouble, the work place can seem like a safe and sane haven. But unfortunately, these parents bring their frustrations with them.

Dedication to work and dedication to parenting can and should go hand in hand. A commitment to a company and to a task within that company means you will use all the business knowledge you can find to fulfill the commitment. The same goes for parenting. The business skills of organization, discipline, fact-finding, testing different solutions, listening to others, and making changes are just as useful at home. The answers are out there if you look for them.

Several bosses complained that women who talk so much about wanting equality with men sometimes separate themselves from male coworkers. They give the appearance of being disinterested in what male coworkers think or can offer. Occasionally women are justly right in being wary of male coworkers, but usually cooperation regardless of gender is more advantageous to work progress.

One woman employer pointed out that some women who work for her have a mental picture of themselves as second-class workers. Thus, their attitude is less upbeat, less solution-oriented than that of men in similar positions. They feel that their work is to carry out orders, not originate new, creative ideas.

The final comment from bosses regarding attitude was that mothers often seem unhappy about working. They don't smile or seem to enjoy a light moment. They seem tired and pressured, and are more apt than men to be grumpy. One woman manager said, "I know that many of my women employees are putting in time until they can retire to full-time home-making." Although this may be the desire of some mothers, it shouldn't be an attitude that is so evident.

Many women don't want to work, but have to. So if work is a task that absolutely must be done, it is much better to do it in a willing way. A mean disposition harms the offender more than the coworkers.

Professionalism

The employers in the survey really grew hurtful on this subject! Both male and female bosses found vast differences between working women and working men. In general, the men were seen to be far more professional. However, for women who were employed at the same company for more than two years, the differences almost disappeared, showing that experience brings a more professional attitude.

The bosses began their diatribe with appearance. Men dressed "more appropriately" for the work place. One female vice-president admitted that men's wardrobes were more routine so it was easier for the men to look professional. For men, she mentioned these no-nos: wrinkled or frayed shirts, suits in need of cleaning, unpolished shoes, white socks with dark shoes, patterned ties that fight with patterned shirts, and unkempt fingernails.

The same vice-president accused women employees of wearing overly flashy colors, huge dangling earrings and other party jewelry, unbecomingly tight clothes, and even clothing that inhibited the ability to bend over, climb stairs, or comfortably cross legs! In general, dresses, skirts and tops, or suits were considered far more professional than slacks. Slacks were only acceptable for workers not having to meet the public or in jobs that required pants. Variety was not nearly so important as appropriateness to the job situation.

Sensible shoes rather than spike heels or strappy sandals were preferred by all bosses, as were simple non-bouffant hairstyles. Most modern hairstyles were acceptable with the exception of unnaturally colored hair. Managers also objected to overpowering perfumes that scented entire work areas.

Make-up that approached the theatrical took a lot of flack. Since many work situations bring workers and customers as close as two feet, make-up should be applied with that proximity in mind. Few jobs require the exaggerated make-up that makes one look good from twenty-five feet away!

For many medical and food-processing jobs, women wear white uniforms or white smocks. These are supposed to provide a sanitary and professional look. However, managers said that they produced the opposite effect when they were ill-fitting, soiled, or in need of mending.

Certainly, when women return to the work place after a maternity leave, they may have a problem fitting back into work clothing. After all, you don't get something for nothing! But usually a mother can alter clothing until her weight returns to normal or wear fuller tops and jackets.

When a woman goes back to work after a long absence, she may not have a complete work wardrobe on hand. Borrowing some clothes from a friend who is the same size may be the answer until the paychecks provide money for more variety.

All employers found gum-chewing very unprofessional. And all but a few said that the use of profanity was a definite detriment to professionalism. Employers worried that those whose in-office language was spiced with four-letter words would become so comfortable with that vocabulary that they couldn't control it when dealing with customers.

But professionalism means even more. One employer said that he wished his women employees were more discreet in sharing their personal lives with him and one another. He felt that talking about last-night's argument, drug use by children, stopped-up plumbing, and what to serve at supper were matters best discussed elsewhere or during work-breaks. He added that many companies now provide a counseling service that can help with serious family problems.

When you as a working parent are wrapped up in child and family matters, you are wise to consider just how much to share at the office, how much to tell friends, and how much to keep to yourself. When working with good friends, you may find that the line sometimes becomes blurred. But no matter how much of your personal life comes into the office, it is best shared during breaks or lunch.

When a working parent leaves the job for home, it shouldn't be with a feeling of merely having scraped through the hours. These are hours you'll never have again, so make them worthwhile. If you take pride in your accomplishments on the job, you establish a good frame of mind for the family time ahead.

On the way home, shift gears again, this time from working parent to at-home parent. Leave the job behind as much as possible. After all, there is always tomorrow.

Parenting Point

Love your job! How can that help you have a happy child? Your attitude toward work rubs off on your youngster, affecting his attitude toward school work and eventual career. So your improved attitude can make both you and your child even smarter. Be grateful you have a job that provides necessities or extras for your family. Don't just fill your job, overflow it! Step by step, you can make your hours from 9 to 5 better!

Chalkboard for Chapter Seven

Although you may not be able to make overnight changes in your relationship to your job, expect steady improvement. Consider the five areas listed below and make an honest appraisal of how an employer would grade you in these areas. Grade yourself from A to F. Then regrade yourself in one month, and again in two months. If your grade hasn't improved, keep trying.

Topic	Grade Now	In 1 Month	In 2 Months
Absenteeism			
Gossip			
Time Abuse			
Attitude			
Professionalism			

For one improved grade, give yourself a big smile. For two improved grades, congratulate yourself. For three improved grades, tell a friend. For four improved grades, give yourself a treat. For five improved grades, have a celebration!

Eight

The Divided Heart Touch-Base Time #2

Mid-afternoons are the hardest time in Michelle's work day. Whether she is at her desk or out making a call, she wonders what Chad is doing. Has he remembered it is the day for his after-school reading enrichment class? Did he get home safely afterward? Will he choose a healthful snack or is he eating an entire bag of potato chips? Is he afraid of being in the apartment alone? Will he immediately turn on the T.V. and spend the afternoon in limbo until she arrives? And, to top all this, Michelle is feeling her mid-afternoon energy low that makes the minutes creep toward quitting time.

This longing feeling, this wondering about family while at work, has been called "the divided heart syndrome." It frequently happens to mothers and is happening to fathers more often. There is nothing wrong with feeling this need to know how a child is, but a parent must also know the right things to do about it. Just wondering doesn't accomplish anything, and it often wastes time.

One large-company switchboard operator says that she doesn't need to look at the clock to know it is 3:30 in the afternoon. The switchboard just lights up as parents call home to check on children. Employers recognize this and sometimes complain that work stops for about thirty minutes when it is after-school time.

It should be part of the "bill of rights" of every working parent that he is entitled to a parenting phone call once each day. Let's not even consider whether it is a toll call, or whether it takes five minutes; let's remember instead that contact with a child once during the work day brings peace of mind to the parent and a sense of being loved to the child. Now, what employer would not be in favor of such an important five minutes! Only a scrooge would deny a working parent this important touch-base time.

Your Second Touch-Base Time of the Day

The breakfast send-off was touch-base time #1. It brought a sense of love and organization to the start of the day. Touch-base time #1 is very important!

Touch-base time #2 reinforces that love and reminds a child of the parent's care and concern for her. Both touch-base times provide elements of organization, and organization is a top priority for folks doing the two jobs of working and parenting.

If touch-base time #2 is given a few moments of advance thought, it doesn't have to result in a lengthy conversation. In-depth news and comments from parent and child can be shared at supper. This call has but three purposes, which can be handled briefly:

- To reassure the parent that all is well
- To give the child some reminder of afternoon activities
- To tell the child how much you care for her and what time you'll be home

This touch-base time may not be a phone call if your child is in a day-care situation where phone calls upset the planned schedule of activities. But if your child is in a home-care situation you may be reassured by a very brief phone call, especially if you have a new baby or a child who has not been well.

There are alternatives to this five-minute telephone call, but let's consider the phone contact first.

Touching Bases with a Phone Call

What kinds of things do you say to a child when you reach him on the phone?

- Ask about school, being specific. Did the report go well? Was the test hard? (These questions can be answered with a yes-no.) To keep this brief, say you'll want to hear all the details at dinner.
- Check to see that he feels comfortable at home, has locked the door and taken other safety precautions.
- Give some direction: Eat an apple, teach the dog a trick, start homework, call a friend, set the supper table, work on a puzzle or craft.
- Ask him to be thinking of something the family can do together after supper.
- Tell him that you love him and what time you will see him.

Tailor your points to your own child. Be brief, but talk enough to feel satisfied.

When I worked in an advertising agency I called home at the time I knew the kids would have returned from nursery school and grade school. The oldest always answered the phone, and knowing that I first wanted an update, she would give a brief summary of activities : "The artist is out skateboarding, the actress is in the doll corner, the little guy is spilling his juice, and I have everything under control." Then we'd have time for a short, pleasant conversation. It was just what I needed.

When telephoning a care-giver, your conversation will vary with the age of your child. Ask the questions that are important to you. (Did the baby take all her formula? Is my toddler playing happily today? Is the bruised knee O.K.?) Then reaffirm the time you'll pick up your child—or the time you'll be home—and get off the phone.

The Late-Afternoon Phone Call

Sometimes a parent will be delayed getting home or to the care facility. It may not make a difference to the care facility, but if a child (or spouse) is at home and expecting you, the late-afternoon phone call is a courtesy.

Again, the call needn't be long. It can include as little as, "I'm delayed but will be home by 7. I love you." "I'm just leaving and will see you soon." "I'll be there for supper. Give Daddy a hug for me."

One mother who works part-time and is home by three o'clock says that the late-afternoon phone call from her spouse lets her use her afternoon time to best advantage. And it makes for a prepared-on-time supper, too! She knows how much time she has to play with her children before starting the meal. She likes not being left in limbo!

Alternatives to the Phone Call

If it is impossible for you to place a call, arrange with a member of your support team to make it for you. Let this person know what you want asked and how to respond if necessary. It's not the same as your own call, but it does give you peace of mind. And if your support-team member talks directly with your child, it can give the child reassurance and a feeling of being cared about.

Sometimes a phone call isn't at all possible. Your child may be going from school to a club or other activity where you can't reach her by phone. These options allow you to keep in touch:

A short note. In the morning, write a short note and put it in the child's lunch box or pocket, reminding her to read it after school. The note can be brief: "I'm looking forward to supper with you and hearing about the Brownie meeting. I'll pick you up at 5:30 in front of the church. I'll be at 123-4567 if you need me. Love you! Dad"

A note at home. Like the phone call, the note left on the kitchen counter reassures a child of your interest, gives direction to her after-school time, and tells her how much you love her. You can't overdo this. Even if the note is similar each day, take a moment to write it. We all like to receive "mail."

A cassette tape. Kids love recorded messages, but this method requires a bit more organization of you. Some parents record a message the night before to be listened to in the afternoon when the child gets home. The child turns on the player and hears your voice; this alone can be very comforting. Then, you can enumerate things to do and end with love.

Touching Bases When You Can't Have Any Contact

There may be many reasons that you can't be in contact with your child in mid-afternoon. Perhaps your child is still an infant, or in a large day-care center, or can't read yet, or you are out of reach of a phone. You are still entitled to touch base with your child—mentally.

Take five minutes of your afternoon break to think about how wonderful it is to have a child. Go over in your mind the things your child is learning, all the good and correct things he does, how much you love him. Think of his progress, whether it is in giant leaps or faltering steps. Jot down something special you've thought of and share it when you next see your child—or spouse. Your child will like knowing that you thought of him during the day and that you wrote down something to tell him.

Some parents who work at a desk enjoy looking at a family photo. This is a reminder of the unique nature of the family as society's most important organizational unit and your very special family group.

One parent has kept a journal of thoughts, thoughts that came to him while sitting at his desk taking five minutes out for touch-base time. He used a simple cloth-covered lined-paper book, available in any stationery store. He didn't organize what he wanted to say, he let it come directly from his heart to the page. It was his special way of reaching out and touching his child in the midst of a busy day.

He kept this journal for many years, then gave it to his daughter when she went off to college. Here are some of the entries made through the years:

"You pouted a little as I put you into Mrs. Carlson's arms this morning, but I could tell she was going to love you as I do."

"I was surprised this morning when you walked right into your room at day-care and didn't look back or hang on my knee or cry anymore."

"There is still a trace of gum under one of my fingernails! That was such a mess yesterday, getting the gum out of your hair. But you do look cute with short hair!"

"What a day on the soccer field! You handled the team loss well and I'm proud of you."

"How could we have lived under the same roof and I never have known you were such an actress. Last night's play was great and you said your lines perfectly."

"I am totally amazed with what you know about engines! I think you're going to be teaching me a few things. I never even taught you how to add oil or change a filter."

"Your mom and I really miss you this week, but I'm thinking of all the great things you're learning at camp."

"This was a worrisome weekend for us, but now that it's over, I'm going to try to do a better job of communicating with you.

"Asking Dean over for supper was a good idea. I feel better about him now."

"I was wrong about the car and will tell you so tonight. Yes, parents make mistakes, too."

"The calendar says it's just a month before you start college. I hope we've told you all the things you'll need to know, most of all that we love you and have confidence in you."

Such random thoughts recorded almost every day are a beautiful and lasting way to keep in touch with your child as she grows and changes.

When You Are at Home in the Afternoon

It's a wonderful privilege for either parent to have a job that lets that parent be at home in mid-afternoon. Some teaching positions, part-time jobs, and flextime jobs bring a parent back home about the same time a child arrives home from school or let a parent pick up a child from day-care after naptime.

This extra time is really special and shouldn't be frittered away on reading the mail, making phone calls, or taking a nap. It can be refreshing to be with your child for a relaxing hour or more.

When touch-base time #2 means actual togetherness, it can change the remainder of the day very positively. The time can be allocated in many different ways, but here are some of the essential elements:

The drive home. If you pick up your child and drive your child home, *don't* start the conversation with either of these two questions: Were you good today? (Would a child volunteer that he was naughty? Even if he did, this conversation would end up being a downer.) What did you do today? (A child has done so much, she is apt to just generalize.) It's better to begin with very casual conversation: "It's been a hot day." "I'm glad you were ready to go." "We have to stop at the store a minute." This is a winding-down time for both of you. Save deep conversation for later.

If you must ask questions, try ones like these: "Have you decided what we should do after supper?" "Who did you play with today?" "What's that interesting rolled-up paper you're carrying?" This isn't the time to be combative or corrective.

Snack-and-tell time. Your child has had a wealth of experiences, some good, some bad, some new, some boring. You'll learn about these if you share an afternoon snack. Juice, fruit, crackers and cheese, yogurt, and carrots and other veggies make good snacks. Leave the cookies and cakes for dessert after supper. Now is the time to just listen. This is hard. After all, you want to know what's been going on. Let there be a little silence. Silence is fine sometimes. You may be surprised at the things your child will say if you just let her talk when she's ready.

After a while you can ask about the book report, the homework assignment, the piano lesson, how the shirt lost its button. Ask what happened that was funny or different or scary. You'll get an insight into your child's thoughts, priorities, reactions, likes and dislikes.

A group activity. If you are a working parent at home in the afternoon, consider the importance of participating in organized group activities such as Scouts or Camp Fire with your child. Shared activities can be good bonding experiences and build memories, too.

A change-of-pace activity. For school-age children, most of the day has been spent sitting down and working. The diligent student may want to do homework immediately upon arriving home. Instead, encourage a change-of-pace activity, such as going outside to play with a friend, bicycling to the library or park, making brownies, working on a craft or hobby, or possibly watching a *very good* T.V. show. At least thirty minutes should be spent in this way, to revitalize both body and mind.

If your child is old enough to do some of these things on his own, you may want to choose a change-of-pace activity for yourself. Depending on the amount of activity in your job, this could be very physical or mental, or just plain relaxing. Such an activity might be exercising, writing a letter, calling a friend, washing the car, making a cake, playing tennis, sewing, reading a book.

Quiet time for homework, a time for chores, and supper preparation time are not part of your afternoon touch-base time. They belong in touch-base time #3, which occurs just before supper.

Parents who have afternoon free-time with their children have the privilege of an extra time for closeness. These moments are precious; don't waste them, don't let them slip away.

For many parents, touch-base time #2, the mid-afternoon touch-base time, is the hardest to achieve. It takes dedication to the family to make contact with your child—verbally on the phone, via a note, in your thoughts, or in person. But the results—a happier and more secure child—are worth it, so see that you have this important touch-base time.

Latchkey Children

One product of our changing society is the latchkey child. The term was coined in the early nineteenth century to describe children who wore house keys on strings around their necks.

With the rising need for two incomes to make ends meet (and unfortunately for many this means an unnecessary, exorbitant standard of living), and the increasing number of single parents, the number of latchkey children increases each year. Often after-school programs are unavailable or unaffordable, so a child returns to an empty house or apartment.

Today there are more than two and a half million latchkey children, some as young as five. (High school children may also fit this category, but they are not part of the official count.) Although the latchkey system is not the most desirable, for some parents it is the only option.

Even if you do not have a latchkey child, you should be concerned about their welfare. There are latchkey children in almost every neighborhood, and your child probably has latchkey friends.

The emotional and intellectual progress of these young people is important to all society. A community of concerned citizens can have a tremendous impact through the development of programs that help all children. Some programs are: after-school television shows just for at-home children, a neighborhood plan where one parent makes contact with all latchkey children, and a telephone help-line to answer questions from latchkey children.

You are the best judge of your child's maturity level and ability to be home alone. Age is not always the deciding factor. There are very mature eight-year-olds, but there are also thirteen-year-olds who can't be trusted alone. In general, age ten should be the minimum.

Children vary in their feelings about being left on their own. Some feel proud and confident, but others feel sad and deserted.

Research on a generation of latchkey children is just beginning to come in. Some of it is very discouraging, revealing low academic scores and high drug use and run-ins with the police. But the latchkey system can also be very successful if a parent can instill a sense of responsibility and common sense in a child.

If you decide to permit your child to be at home alone, safety will be your main concern, but these additional risks should be considered before starting:

Emotional stumbling blocks. Some latchkey children are hurt because they cannot handle the feelings of loneliness, boredom, abandonment, rejection, insecurity, and fear. Instead of feeling independent, they feel deserted and the experience lowers their self-esteem.

Wasted time. Will the child accomplish something or just look at T.V.? Will he take time for play, do his chores and homework, take good phone messages, and if necessary look after younger siblings?

Lack of responsibility. Is the child competent to care for herself or for a younger child? Does she know what to do in case of an emergency? Will she remain calm or will she panic?

Poor influences. A child needs parental guidance and self-confidence to overcome the pressures from peers to engage in illegal or destructive activities. Can he learn to say "no" to those who try to persuade him to join in activities of which you disapprove: smoking, alcohol and other drug abuse, shoplifting and petty theft, and so on? It takes a strong-minded, well-trained child to combat these evils on his own.

Safety. Parents need to cover the "what ifs" with all children and particularly with those left alone for long periods of time. When a child is very young, make sure she knows her full name, address, and telephone number.

Safety must be taught in three areas: creating a safe home environment, rehearsing special situations, and teaching skills.

1. A safe home environment. Unfortunately, door and window locks seem to be a necessity. See that your house is completely lockable. Trim the bushes near your door or windows so no one can hide behind them.

In many communities, a member of the local police department will come into your home for a safety check of doors, windows, locks, and lighting. You may want to install new locks or a front door peephole.

Check for safety in these areas also: unloaded and locked-up guns; matches, medicines, and cleaning supplies out of reach of young children; appliances made inaccessible that are difficult or dangerous to use or are malfunctioning.

Check your home for fire hazards and make sure that smoke alarms, furnace, and water heater are in good repair. Have a fire extinguisher available and show your child how to use it.

See that a list of telephone numbers is posted prominently and point it out often. The list should contain numbers to call in case of emergencies, police and fire departments, doctor and ambulance, poison control center, relative or neighbor, and parents' work places.

2. Rehearsing special situations. Take time to simulate special situations with your child. Alleviate fear by reassuring a child that he may not need some of these skills, but you want him to know what to do just the same. A parent or friend can help you set up these situations:

- *What to do if the doorbell rings*
- *How to answer the telephone*
- *Action to take if a fire starts*
- *What to do if a stranger approaches*
- *What if he finds a window is broken or a door is open*
- *How to care for simple injuries*

3. Teaching skills. A child on her own needs certain skills for safety, good health, and effective time use. See that your child knows how to use the stove and other appliances, how to look up a word in the dictionary or a topic in the encyclopedia, how to select a nutritious snack, where to put a message if she is going out to play or to the store.

Children function better when they know the house rules. Give your children parameters about what they can and cannot do, and how you expect them to act in special situations.

Just what is a latchkey child to be doing during the two or three hours before a parent returns? You can post suggestions for activities on the refrigerator door or make a list for each day depending on the age of your child. Include some of these:

Exercise. Give a child permission to play at school or in the park as a change of pace from sedentary school work. Perhaps you or a neighbor has a yard for safe after-school play. And if a child must remain in the house, provide a simple exercise mat and a chinning bar.

Reading for fun. Go to the library often enough so that a child has on hand several good books to read. Start him reading the book at the library or when you are around. This gets the child "into" the book and he will be more likely to pick it up and continue reading it on his own.

Chores. Provide a weekly or monthly chart and refer a child to it each day. Add any special task. Be specific about what you expect: feeding the dog, taking the laundry from the dryer, then folding and delivering it to each bedroom, putting the potatoes in the oven at five o'clock, 400 degrees. When you come home, be very appreciative about what she has been doing, and gently encourage her to finish any undone task.

Creative activities. Don't let a child's life become regimented. Encourage a variety of crafts and hobbies. Don't always steer boys toward making airplane models and girls toward doing embroidery. A few ideas for both sexes to try are these: stamp collecting, scrapbook making, sewing, model building, rock collecting, bird-watching, writing a pen pal.

Making a cassette tape. Let your child make a tape for you, telling things he might otherwise forget. Listen to it as you change clothes after work.

Cooking for fun. By encouraging and not pressuring, you can have a pint-sized gourmet chef. Find recipes that require a minimum of ingredients and appliance use. Start with making strawberry gelatin and no-bake pies. Work up to cakes and cookies. Many parents allow latchkey children to prepare each day's dessert.

Homework. Show a child you appreciate knowledge and occasionally give him an example of how you are still learning yourself. Research shows that homework is best done before the evening hours. Although older children may have to work both before and after supper, encourage younger ones to start their assignments before you return home. Show interest in the homework as soon as you have time. (For homework ideas, see chapter 15: *Day-Care, School, and Your Smart Child.*)

As a parent of a latchkey child, you need to be very flexible and communicative. Be specific about what you expect, what is right and wrong, where you are, and when you'll be home. Be sure to inform a child of even minor changes. Many latchkey children worry when parents are even fifteen minutes late.

As a child grows, change the after-school activities. And be prepared to change rules and arrangements if they aren't working just right. Give more privileges or take away some, depending on the situation.

See if there is a suitable organized activity for your latchkey child to participate in after school. If there isn't, work with other parents and groups to start one. You'll find help from schools, churches, park systems, day-care facilities, even employers. Talk with schools and your public transportation company about "late buses" so that children can safely take advantage of special after-school activities without the lonely walk home.

You can get more latchkey ideas and information from these national groups:

The School-Age Child Care Project, Wellesley College Center for Research on Women, 828 Washington Street, Wellesley, MA 02181.

Child Care Action Campaign, 132 West 43rd Street, New York, NY 10036

Catalyst, Resources for Today's Parents, Department RTP, 250 Park Avenue South, New York, NY 10003-1459.

And when you are home in the afternoon, be a good friend and neighbor to nearby latchkey children. You don't need to take on the care of such a child unless you wish to, but sometimes it is a great comfort to him to know that another adult is nearby or just a phone call away in case of an emergency.

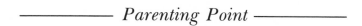

Parenting Point

Communication is a key to good parenting. Plan now to determine ways to include your child in your work day. It takes as little as five minutes, but this is an important five minutes. Use your own creativity to find communication opportunities. Step by step, you can do it, and when you do, you'll both feel great.

Chalkboard for Chapter Eight

Try different ways of being in touch with your child. Cross off those that are impossible for you. Try the others several times this month.

_____ 1. Mid-afternoon phone call.
_____ 2. Late-afternoon phone call.
_____ 3. Phone call to your child by someone else.
_____ 4. Note placed in school lunch box or pocket.
_____ 5. Note left at home for after school.
_____ 6. Cassette message left at home for after school.
_____ 7. A five-minute love-break for thinking about your child.
_____ 8. If you are at home in the afternoon, use this additional time for special togetherness with your child.
_____ 9. Whether or not you have a latchkey child, investigate what your community provides in the way of after-school alternatives for these children.

Nine

Home at Last!
Touch-Base Time #3

Most evenings Paul arrives home about an hour after his wife, Piper, does. He happily scoops up one of the kids and is surprised to find Piper looking beat. She says that this first hour at home after her work day is absolutely the worst sixty minutes of her day. Nothing seems to go right, the kids are vying for her attention, everyone is hungry, and supper isn't even started. Oh how Piper wants a few moments for herself! But she feels guilty about wanting time alone and so she quickly changes her clothes, starts the meal, tidies up the family room, feeds the cat, and tries to deal with the children. This often results in her shouting at them about something trivial. By the time hungry Paul appears, she sometimes feels like just throwing the supper at him. How she wishes it could be different!

Even more hectic than the hour before leaving for work in the morning, the first hour home in the evening gets the worst rating in my survey of working parents. They say, "The kids just shout and argue," "I'm *so* darned tired after work I can't even think about being a parent," "We eat stupid fast-food suppers because there's no time to cook," "Each child wants my attention and I can't concentrate on anything," "This could devastate my marriage."

Dealing with this hour before supper is a little like putting out a fire. Parents wonder, "Where should I begin? How can I manage these kids? How can I explain with everyone shouting? Who is hurting and needs immediate attention? Does anyone care or appreciate what I'm going through? Why is the excitement so high? What's in the mail? What can I do with the frozen meat?"

First, we must realize that both parent and child need to be calm. Relaxing from job tensions may have happened on the way home, but often it hasn't. The change of scene to home life comes when most family members are tired and hungry. Often, children also want a parent's 100 percent attention at a time when a parent wants only *quiet* and a moment alone.

Now that the hours of separation are over, a parent has to recognize a child's heartfelt desire to be once more cared for by the parent. No matter how good the day-care, school, or after-school activity, there is nothing like Mommy or Daddy. All the pent-up questions and comments and problems of the day come tumbling out. This can almost be too much for a parent who has been dealing with questions and comments and problems for the eight preceding hours.

Since nothing positive is accomplished by ignoring children at this critical moment, a working parent needs to know what to do and how to do it most efficiently. It is now that the child's needs take precedence. But this doesn't mean that all the time is child-related and the parent gets nothing.

This touch-base time #3 involves a certain number of activities, and, if they are performed in the right order, it can provide satisfaction for both child and parent.

It falls to the first parent home to perform some necessary tasks in preparation for the supper and evening times, times that should be the best of the day. While there is no escaping the kids, tell yourself that your time *will* come!

The Homecoming

The homecoming may start when you pick up a child for the ride home, or when you come in the door and are greeted eagerly (or apathetically) by the child waiting for you. Three things need to happen *immediately:* acknowledgment, interest, and relaxation. The first letters of those three words are *a, i, r.* AIR! And a little fresh air and breathing room is just what is needed in this all-important touch-base time.

If you take time to put these three elements into your homecoming, you'll find that the remainder of the time before supper can be productive, harmonious, and happy. AIR time is only a few minutes, so let's breathe in a little AIR and take each of the three words separately.

Acknowledgment—for the First Letter in AIR

At times, we all need to be noticed. In fact, we love attention! As a parent, you want your child to notice your arrival home, which signals the good things you will do together. And in turn, your child wants you to be aware of him and his activities.

The moment you see your child again—baby, toddler, grade-schooler, or teen—should be one of joyful acknowledgment. This comes in the form of a happy greeting, a kiss, a hug, lap-sitting, or an arm around the shoulder. Let this affectionate style of greeting start early in a child's life and continue all the years ahead.

It isn't necessary to exchange a torrent of words, but what *is* needed is a renewal of the parent-child love-relationship. It can be words, acts, or a combination. It needn't be eloquent or dramatic; simple and sincere is best.

This acknowledgment of each other takes only a minute of your time, and it is the necessary first step.

Interest—for the Middle Letter in AIR

Now comes a show of interest, which is another important sign of caring. Again, this needn't be a lengthy dialogue. In fact, it's best when the interest makes a link to a later event, giving continuity to the family evening together.

You might say, "Did you go on the field trip? I want you to tell me all about it when we have our juice." "Have you received the test results yet? Let's look at them before supper." "Did you get a new piece of music at your lesson? Let's play it together after supper."

Note that these are easy questions, ones that can be quickly answered at this very busy time. There is nothing argumentative or judgmental about them. But, and this is most important, getting more details is not put off to some hazy time called "later."

"Later" often never comes. Many parents use it as a method of getting rid of an uninteresting or uncomfortable topic. Kids—even little ones—are wise enough to recognize this crutch and they learn quickly that "later" usually means "never." They begin to realize that "later" carries that "Don't bother me, I'm not interested" implication.

So, you need to be specific. Rather than say "later," say: "At snack time," "Before supper," "After supper," "At bedtime," "As soon as Mom is home to hear it," "First thing Saturday." Then be a person of your word. If you think you aren't apt to remember, actually write down the subject in question and the time you have promised to talk about it. Put your note on the counter, table, T.V., in your pocket, or wherever you'll be most likely to see it.

One reason little kids hound and pester is because they don't have a conception of time. When a parent says "later" and doesn't mean it, the child soon learns that "later" has no meaning. He equates "later" with "never." So when the parent says "later" the child doesn't believe him and, wanting an answer, he just keeps pestering. Unfailing attention to what you've promised to do puts kids in the habit of believing you. If you form the good habit of remembering those "later" promises, the child will believe you and bother you less during your truly busy times. That way everyone wins.

With older children, you can also say, "I will try hard to remember," "You should remind me," "Don't forget to bring it up."

It improves a child's self-esteem to know that you really have an interest in her and her activities, even though there isn't enough time to go into details at the moment. Like *a* for acknowledgment, *i* for interest takes only a minute or two.

Relaxation—for the Last Letter in AIR

In order to breathe, we need the *r* in air. A few minutes of relaxation can serve three worthwhile purposes. It can let us unwind, it can soothe an overactive child, and it can also take the edge off suppertime hunger.

In our survey, 71 percent of parents said that their families were "starved," "famished," "desperately hungry," or "ready to eat the moment they get in the door." In order to satisfy the need to eat immediately, many parents bring home more costly fast foods or serve less nourishing supper foods just because these foods require no preparation time. Such a meal is often a meal on the run without much value—nutritionally, emotionally, or intellectually.

The better answer is to have a moment of sit-down relaxation and a small part of the meal. Make an appetizer course a tradition at your house. Doesn't that sound elegant! Tailor the appetizer to the age of your child and his ability and willingness to eat a full meal later. Often a very small appetizer will suffice.

Let children toddler age and older help prepare the snack. It should be very simple and take almost no time to prepare. It can be something you planned to serve at supper anyway. Some quick ideas are: a sliced banana in milk, crackers and cheese, cucumber sticks with yogurt, hot chocolate, fruit juice, apple sauce, a graham cracker. These items should be ready to go on cupboard or refrigerator shelves. Select this item the night before so that your homecoming can be really relaxed.

Don't eat standing up and certainly don't turn on the T.V.! Sit down together in a comfortable spot, one that won't be damaged by a spill or a few crumbs. Out on the porch, at the kitchen counter, in the family room, or just sitting on the floor makes this different from the meal ahead. Listen, munch, listen, talk, listen, smile, listen, appreciate, listen. You may have noted the frequency of the word *listen!* Children have so much to pour out to you: The small events from their day seem large to them. Give your child the opportunity to talk while you relax and just listen.

Now you've had a minute of acknowledgment and a minute of interest followed by a few minutes of relaxing refreshment. All together, this probably won't take more than ten minutes.

AIR Works!

What a difference this ten minutes can make. Get into the habit of having AIR time the first thing when you and your children are together again. This rids you of weary and hungry feelings, omits the need for kids to pester, and solidifies the loving parent-child relationship. It is definitely worth ten minutes of your time. It will make the remainder of the hour before supper go more smoothly.

Parents who have consistently tried AIR time find that they are ready to take on the other important aspects of touch-base time #3.

Onward with Touch-Base Time #3

Now that you've satisfied those immediate demands for attention, you are ready to continue with two other essential parts of this late-afternoon touch-base time. These two can usually fit into the time remaining before supper.

These are quiet time and "helps" time. Although both the working parent and the happy child should have quiet time and helps time, they may not always be doing these simultaneously with each other. Just the same, the two activities are important because they provide a regular framework for activity that cuts down on boredom, complaints, whining, arguments, and aimless television viewing.

This is a time for parent-child cooperation. Sometimes as children grow older, their activities bring them home later, just in time for supper. But since older children have more evening time than younger siblings, the quiet time and "helps" time activities still fit into their schedule, but later.

Start early with your child to teach her that, although other families may have other methods, your family has a regular routine to benefit everyone. (Of course, be ready to change your certain way to a better way too.) Two of the things that your family does a certain way at a certain time are just these: quiet time and "helps" time.

Quiet Time

All children can benefit from a quiet time after being very active. Most children have an afternoon activity that uses up energy, so they are ready for quiet time during the hour before supper. The active time might have been after-school play or a sport or Scouts. When that is over, it's time for something not as physically active.

During quiet time, younger children can read or be read to, draw, cut and paste, solve puzzles, write Grandpa, or enjoy other quiet activities. Establish this quiet time in babyhood and continue it. Learning to work or play quietly for a specified period of time produces better work habits and an increased attention span. School teachers will thank you for teaching these skills!

Don't always tell a younger child what to do during this quiet time. Be ready with suggestions if needed, but let the choice be made by the child. When you let young children choose the activity themselves, they will work at it alone (or with your occasional encouragement) for a longer period of time.

Older children should use this time for homework. Although homework is best done *before* supper, teens may have to work again after supper in order to complete assignments.

The place for quiet time is very important. A child should not be squeezed in the middle of a pile of toys, or stretched out on a bed, or sitting in front of the television set. A well-lighted table and comfortable chair are ideal, even for a toddler. After all, you are setting the standards for lifelong good study habits.

Younger children will need books, crayons, scissors, and paste. Older ones should have a good dictionary, sharp pencils, and erasers. A good-sized working surface that doesn't require clean-up before supper is best.

Younger and older children should learn to work together in the same area. (There are years of classrooms and dorm rooms ahead where learning to concentrate is an asset.) Teach respect for learning, the importance of not copying or even touching a sibling's work without asking, how to work quietly, and the merits of finishing a job. Such lessons make this time invaluable.

A parent is entitled to quiet time, too, and can have that quiet time near the children in order to encourage good work habits and maintain order if necessary. One day I felt so tired that I stretched out to read on the family room sofa near the playing children. Soon I was sound asleep. Since they had never seen me take a nap, they went and found the family Bible, sat down on the floor next to me, and pretended to be reading it, assuming I was dying! When I suddenly awoke they were so pleased! But there are better ways for a parent to be refreshed.

A parent should use this short quiet time for something very special. The mail, which consists of a few good items and a large quantity of bills and junk mail, can wait until evening! Choose a project that gives you pleasure: reading, phoning a friend, exercising, making a quick cake, writing, using the computer, sewing, and so forth.

A child's quiet time should last fifteen to forty-five minutes, depending on age and amount of homework, but fifteen minutes is the minimum. And during this pre-dinner quiet time, don't make the rule, "You can see T.V. when you finish your homework." This just means that homework will be hastily and carelessly whipped out. Tell a child to read or choose another quiet activity when homework is finished.

"Helps" Time

The final fifteen minutes or so of touch-base time #3 consists of doing helpful things—things that make our family special.

Children need to contribute to the well-being of the home each day of the week. This is discussed in detail in chapter 18, "S t r e t c h i n g Your Time." Any child more than age three should have several useful tasks that lighten a parent's workload. Even younger children can learn to be helpful, and every little bit helps.

Remember that it is important for a child to learn to do these tasks around the house as part of your plan to help him eventually function entirely on his own. This is vital preparation for the child's future! Such seemingly minor accomplishments also build self-esteem and encourage camaraderie in the family.

So, when about fifteen minutes remain until supper will be ready, end quiet time and encourage the doing of daily chores. No one but baby is exempt!

Supper Preparation

In the ideal working family, one parent takes the lead in supper preparation, with assistance from the children and spouse. Supper is worth fifteen to twenty-five minutes of preparation time, but some foods such as baked potatoes or a meat loaf may have to be started during quiet time. In families where a child is home in the afternoon, the child should have certain assignments concerning supper preparation.

A parent's duty is to know in advance what the meal is going to be. This is the result of weekly menu-planning and shopping from a grocery list. Although it takes time to make menus and shopping lists, doing so saves time and worry—particularly those what-is-there-to-eat-tonight delays that beset many working parents.

Sometimes, a little preparation the evening before can reduce the time for supper preparation the next day when everyone is busy.

Making a molded salad or cupcakes, cleaning the broccoli, or mixing the juice concentrate takes a few minutes the night before but makes a big difference the next day. One family has as a morning "help" for one child the clearing of the breakfast table and the setting of the supper table.

The entire evening goes better if supper is nearly ready when the last family member arrives home. Achieving this is not an impossible feat. It takes a little concern for others combined with good time management.

It's important for spouses to return home on time for supper and for kids to come back promptly from play or other activities. Supper together is a "must."

In addition to the elements of a meal that can be prepared in advance (table setting, salad making, dessert preparation), other parts of the meal can be partially prepared: vegetables cooked to near-tenderness, beverages in glasses in the refrigerator, the casserole ready and held on warm in the oven.

Don't raise kids who are illiterate in the kitchen! Remember that the kitchen is no longer a woman's department or a wife's domain. There are kitchen jobs for both parents, as well as for toddlers and all older children. Cooking together can be relaxing and fun, a time to talk, and a time for spelling word tests, races, and playing word games.

Make the Worst Hour into a Better Hour

The hour before supper may never be the highlight of your day, but it doesn't have to be a disaster, either. Touch-base time #3 can be a precious time of renewal for you and your child. It prepares for and precedes the best times of your day. Don't skimp on the time for your child's homework or "helps." These two activities make for a much wiser child. Remember that you'll feel far more able to achieve your before-supper goals if you start with AIR time.

Parenting Point

At last the separation is over! Soon the family reunion will begin. Take time to help your child and yourself get ready for the important hours ahead. Relaxing together and then working together, step by step, will make this difficult time a happier time for all.

Chalkboard for Chapter Nine

Make a list of a dozen pleasant activities that can be done in as little as fifteen minutes. These can be brief enjoyments like rolling on the bed with your toddler, taking a quick shower while an older child supervises a younger one, relaxing on the patio, or starting a project that you can put down and finish later.

You deserve this short afternoon respite after a busy work day. Add to your list as you think of other restful activities.

1.
2.
3.
4.
5.
6.
7.
8.
9.
10.
11.
12.

Ten

The Super Supper
Touch-Base Time #4

I t's a typical suppertime at the Baxter house. Bill is eating like a robot, watching the sports segment on the living room T.V. Marsha doesn't care about sports so she sits on a kitchen stool reading the newspaper and munching. Eddy and Freddy have left their unfinished plates and are busy on the family room floor with their road racer cars and tracks. For twenty minutes the parents haven't said a word. When the sports news ends, Bill pats his stomach and says, "Well, I guess supper is over."

Supper is over? To be honest, supper hasn't even begun! An indeterminate amount of eating has gone on, there's been play, entertainment, and reading, but none of this adds up to a real supper.

One definition of the word *supper* is: an informal dinner hour, eaten at a table with the participants engaging in light conversation. Few families today actually sit down at a table for supper, and even fewer engage in conversation, light or heavy! The consumer information department of the Pillsbury Company reports on a fifteen-year study of family eating habits: "Families are putting less emphasis on sharing a meal and if the trend continues, the family meal could be extinct by the year 2000."

Why no suppertime togetherness and conversation? The answer is simple. When the T.V. is talking, the family is *not* talking. This doesn't mean that the supper participants are necessarily giving their attention to the T.V. They may be engaged in other activities or just sitting in a stupor. Some may not even be sitting, but just walking past the food and snacking now and then. This habit of grazing is currently popular, but it's no substitute for the many nutritious and non-nutritious benefits of a real family supper.

Who Needs Suppertime, Anyway?

Parents do. Children do. This is the parent-child reunion time. A reunion is a joyous coming together. Little by little the family has returned home late in the afternoon and early evening. There may have been some activities that brought together parts of the family. Perhaps homework or cooking has been a joint activity of a parent and a child.

But now, there is to be the reunion of the entire family, in one place, at one time.

Like the pre-supper events, the after-supper activities and bedtime routine engage only parts of the family, so this meal may be the one after-work opportunity for everyone to be together. The family has been separated more than one-third of the day. Parents have been working, experiencing challenges, triumphs, and even some frustrations. Children have been learning and playing, testing relationships, trying new skills, and also experiencing challenges, triumphs, and even some frustrations. These activities now need a forum, a place where they can be discussed and put in perspective, where some conclusions can be reached, where love and care can be expressed.

The Need for Touch-Base Time #4

Supper is the fourth touch-base time in the day. It is one of the longer and more important times a working parent has with a child.

Breakfast, the first touch-base time, inspires the family for the day. Supper, the fourth touch-base time, educates the family for the day. This education is of the pleasantest kind; it isn't forced learning, but casual sharing.

In our survey of parents, 85 percent of the families *do* eat supper together. Good as this is, the percentage is steadily decreasing. Families who do have this reunion time speak glowingly of it:

"It is the best time of the day!"
"I'm tired, but my child refreshes me."
"We can just talk and talk."
"It's a time when we really get to know each other."
"I feel so close to my son as we talk about his day."
"At last a time to answer all those questions."
"Our kids ask us about our day, too."
"Supper is what holds our family together until we have more time on the weekend."
"We look back on our suppertimes as part of our family's great memories."

Certainly, the highlight of the meal is talk. And it should be, since good communication is the glue of family life. It holds the family together in a close and caring way. Communication is an exchange of news, of problems, of ideas, and most of all it is a sign of interest and love.

Excuses, Excuses!

So why don't families eat together more? There are many excuses, but, with a few exceptions, the excuses are poor. Eating together does require some advance planning. Eating together can bring out a latent fear of what will happen if family members are forced to talk with each other. Eating together can result in parents hearing some things they don't want to hear. Eating together requires a certain organization and we tend to shy away from organization even though it may be the best thing for us.

Excuse #1: We don't all get home at the same time, so I just feed the kids.

Answer: Give the kids some fruit and crackers or a cup of soup and then eat supper together later when everyone is finally home.

Excuse #2: There is too much to do when we all get home. All of us want to do our own thing.

Answer: The evening, after supper, is the time for individual activities. This supper reunion takes priority. The home is not a hotel and restaurant, it is a place where the inhabitants interact with one another, and in order for interaction to take place, the inhabitants must come together. Suppertime is a logical time for this interaction.

Excuse #3: Our daughter is on the soccer team and doesn't get home until after supper.

Answer: Like Excuse #1, let other family members have an appetizer to stave off hunger, then eat when your daughter gets home.

Excuse #4: Our older children have places they want to go in the evening.

Answer: Fine; they can go to those places—after supper. (Weekday after-dinner excursions by older children should be held to a minimum and permitted only when homework is completely finished.) Teens have been with friends all day. Now the family comes first.

Excuse #5: We like to catch the T.V. news with supper.

Answer: If the family is so desperately in need of a news update, family members should turn on the radio while coming home or preparing supper. The news will still be available when supper is over.

Excuse #6: We've never eaten supper together.

Answer: There is no time like the present to start this wonderful tradition. It's easiest to establish the "supper together" habit when children are young and then keep it going until they're off to college or career. There are some things in family life that are "givens" and supper together should be one of them. We have found that our college and career kids still love to come home where there is a chatty and relaxed supper—something definitely missing in their busy fast-food lives.

Excuse #7: What could we possibly do at supper? It sounds boring!

Answer: Read on. That's what this chapter is about—having an enjoyable meal and conversation. Dinnertime can be great for its nutritional value, but it also has values that are informational, humorous, educational, exciting, and loving.

Excuse #8: I can remember that my dad used supper as the time to bawl out us kids or to pontificate on some pet subject. Mom sat meekly by. We kids found that if we started an argument, we'd get sent from the table—and we liked that!

Answer: Set a few guidelines: no monologues, no arguments, no putdowns, no ridicule, no leaving the table until the meal is over. Joking is fine if it isn't cruel. Body language is important: Avoid scowling and slouching. Parents need to set an example for interesting talk and good humor.

The Super Supper Setting

If supper *doesn't* consist of eating while watching T.V., reading the paper, or playing, just what does it include? First, let's consider the supper setting. Eat at a table. See that the chairs are comfortable and of the correct height. If you are eating on a carpeted floor, spread a piece of plastic under the baby's high chair.

Include in the table setting a napkin ring and a no-iron cloth napkin. A cloth napkin doesn't float away as paper ones do. Children raised in fast-food places may never have seen a cloth napkin. Knowing how to properly use a napkin is part of growing up.

Supper doesn't always have to be in the same place. The table may be on the patio in good weather. The table may be the living room coffee table with everyone sitting around it on the floor. Or, you can have a picnic on the back yard grass. Even supper in the room of one of the kids can be fun. These alternatives can add variety to the usual dining room or kitchen table setting.

Put something in the center of the table, other than salt, pepper, and catsup. Your centerpiece can be flowers, a green plant, an interesting toy, an art object, a picture from a magazine. Change your centerpiece regularly, and often let a child select the next piece. The centerpiece is often a conversation starter.

Candles add a special effect. Voices are softer, food looks better, the room takes on a glow. Even the simplest foods become special in candlelight. Let one responsible child be in charge of candle lighting and extinguishing. Kids love to light matches so this reminds younger children that matches are used only with adult supervision.

Teach little children to sit down and stay seated. A few tears at first will pay off in a longer attention span and a less fussy child. Don't raise a child who wants "down" before others finish eating. And be sure there are no adult eat-and-runs, either! If needed, give the baby a toy for amusement. (When a little child is excused early, that means an adult has to keep track of the child, spoiling the dinner for that adult.) It's educational for a child to sit and eat, or just sit and listen. A child who has been taught to remain seated is much more pleasant company at a restaurant, too.

How Long Does the Super Supper Take?

Actual eating and talking should last a minimum of twenty-five to thirty minutes. If less time is used, the family isn't eating enough or chewing enough or chatting enough. This togetherness time is important so don't rush through it.

Teach children that they do not leave the table until a parent says the meal is over. If a child needs to go to the bathroom, teach that child the correct way to ask to be excused. Bathrooming and hand-washing though, should come before dinner because such interruptions stop the flow of conversation.

Telephone calls can also interrupt supper conversation and shorten togetherness time. So discourage leaving the table for phone calls. Designate one older child (or a parent if children are too young) to answer all phone calls and take messages. The friends of older children will soon learn not to call during mealtime.

Balanced nutrition should be part of family education starting when kids are young. Don't force a child to overeat. Eating should be done slowly, with each mouthful chewed well, so that the food is truly savored. Practice setting down the fork between each mouthful instead of continually shoving in more food. These are the good habits of trim people.

Elements of a Super Supper

The family is seated, the food is on the table. What happens now? Here are six elements that will be the basic contents of your super supper.

1. Informal talking. One person talks while the others eat. Adults should try not to direct the conversation. Let topics come up naturally. You may be surprised, sometimes shocked, at the things a child wants to talk about.

The main conversational topic will be the events of the day. Sometimes there has been an exciting happening, sometimes there has been a hurtful occurrence. If you listen carefully, you can learn what is important to your child. Often you can defuse bad feelings or redirect a child's thinking into better channels through your own reaction and comments. But this is no time for discipline or discussion of what to do about a bad report from school.

A supper conversation brings continuity to family life when a parent or a child asks a question that is a link to the day before: "Did you settle the argument with Keith?" "Did the rehearsal go better today?" "How did the second meeting with the manager turn out?"

Don't hesitate to talk to children about your own work and some of your problems. Youthful ingenuity may give you some good ideas. Don't let your child be like this toddler, who was asked what his dad did all day. He said, "He sits in a traffic jam." Tell your child about more than the problems of getting to work; tell him what goes on in the work place.

A child may bring a personal problem to the family in hopes of finding a solution. This shows again a child's need for family, and such a discussion should be handled with care and love.

2. Current events. It's important for children from toddlers to teens to know about important happenings outside their own sphere of action. Older children may participate in the discussion with their parents, but younger children will mainly listen and eat. Play down disasters. Rather, talk about an election, a scientific discovery, a new building in town, a sporting event, and so forth.

The key words in such discussions are "What do you think?" Ask this question often. Surveys show that children who are frequently asked questions exhibit higher test scores than those who are never questioned. Remember that. And ask the child's opinion casually; don't phrase the question in an argumentative or baiting way. Then, use the answers to promote a deeper discussion of the topic. Questions make your child smarter.

Encourage children to bring to the table a clipping from the day's newspaper. Young children may bring a picture or cartoon. Don't judge what is brought. Just let the child talk about it. Let kids read from an article if they wish. These items can be springboards for discussion. And most important, this idea of bringing a clipping to supper encourages children of all ages to look through the daily paper. That alone makes a smarter child.

3. Upcoming events. At breakfast you went over the plans for the day. At supper, talk about what will happen after supper, but most important, what the family will be doing on the weekend ahead.

Some parents have no idea of plans for the weekend ahead, so having to share at supper forces them to actually plan something: a visit to a relative, a work project at home, attendance at a sporting event, a movie, a trip to the zoo. Remember to discuss with kids what they would *like* to do instead of unilaterally telling them what they must do on the coming weekend. Allow time for individual activities. These discussions of future events give continuity to family life. We all like to look forward to happy events!

4. Music. Before supper begins, turn on an all-music station, or better yet, play some recordings. It's fine if the record or tape repeats. Although the music is primarily for background, it can also be educational. Tell children the name of what is being played: a Beethoven concerto, dance music, a Sousa march. Set the volume so that it doesn't interfere with conversation. If you repeat the same music in a few days, you may find that a child recognizes it and can name it.

When children are young, music without lyrics is best since lyrics can distract little ones. As children grow older, let them take turns with you in selecting music for supper. Let children play their own favorite musical recordings—preschool rhyming songs, rock, or country and western. Being exposed to a variety of music is broadening, and it is often surprising for parents and kids to find that they appreciate and actually enjoy music they were unfamiliar with.

5. The continuing book. When my husband first brought a book to the supper table, there were groans! The kids thought this was going to be "educational," that is, pretty grim. However, he'd selected an exciting book that would appeal to the varied ages, and one we hadn't read either. The first day, he read for just five minutes as the kids finished eating. The second day, one said, "Let's get to the reading." The five minutes was increased to about ten minutes. As the book got more compelling, a child said, "Let's read more." But no, we didn't allow that! Ten minutes was the maximum. Oh, how the anticipation built. How would the story come out? We still remember that first book! In the years afterward, dozens of books were read, some serious, some funny, all memorable.

Children who read well can be permitted to read a page or so, but the reading should not be a test of ability. It's for fun, and the comprehension is best when the reading is accurate, smooth, and uninterrupted.

Even when friends shared supper, the kids would insist on the book reading, bringing visitors up-to-date on the story so far. Once, when our older son returned home from college, he placed a book on the dining table and said, "This is the book we're going to read together during my vacation."

If you need ideas on books to read, check out this handy book at your library: *The Read-Aloud Handbook* (James Trelease, Penguin, 1985). It will give you many great ideas for your supper reading-time, and bedtime reading too.

Book reading at supper may at first sound boring. But, once you try it, it will become one of the things that makes supper special. Remember to keep it brief, ten minutes at most.

All together, with eating, talking, sharing, and reading, supper will probably consume less than thirty minutes. This is a very relaxing thirty minutes and a tradition that should be established early in family life.

Now we've listed five of the six elements of supper. The last is the *least* important. It is table manners.

What About Table Manners?

6. Table manners. Certainly you want your children to know how to eat in a civilized manner at home, in restaurants, and eventually at parties, on dates, and at business events. Good manners become second nature when they are taught gradually and calmly. And suppertime is the forum for teaching table manners.

But mealtime shouldn't be one continuous lesson in good manners. This will take away from the joy of being together. You should establish good manners in a consistent, but low-key way.

Each week, choose, from the list below, one table manner to teach. Manners are not masculine or feminine, and good manners should be taught *by* both fathers and mothers and *to* both sons and daughters.

At the very beginning of the Monday meal, talk briefly about the manner you are emphasizing for the week. You might say, "Tonight we are going to remember to ask for the salt and pepper to be passed, instead of just reaching across the table for them. Remember, they go around the table to the person requesting them, and the salt and pepper travel together." That's all. The next night you can touch on the subject even more briefly.

At the end of a meal, you might comment on the manner in a positive, appreciative way. Perhaps you've been working on not talking with a mouth full of food. If the family has made progress here, be sure to mention it!

These are the basic manners you will teach your child so that she will not embarrass herself in public or be considered crude.

1. Eat with elbows off the table. This is one of the hardest rules for teens, who seem to have the knack of nearly lying down on the table!

2. Eat with the mouth closed. Gross eating habits can spoil a meal—and a reputation.

3. Pass serving dishes around the table. Discourage reaching across the table or past others. Teach the family to ask, "May I have some on the way?"

4. Know how much food to take. At a buffet for eight persons, a child who hasn't learned his math at home may see a plate of eight stuffed tomatoes and take two, leaving one diner with none! If there are four in your family, show children that each portion should be one-fourth or a bit less. Teach a child also to take a small amount first and ask for seconds later, instead of taking a large amount and possibly leaving some of it on his plate.

5. Try new foods. Explain to the family that the food you serve is safe to eat and that all foods should be tried since they are not poisonous. (Take into consideration allergies and preferences, though.) When a new food is first served, let a child have a "royalty serving." This is just one tablespoonful, but this amount must be eaten. You will often find that the next time the food is served, the child eats a normal-sized serving.

6. Ask to be excused. There are very few reasons to leave the table during a meal, but teach a child how to ask to be excused. And, at the end of the meal, let one child say, "May the family all be excused?"

7. Start to eat all together. (Saying a blessing helps to start the meal right.) Although you may occasionally make exceptions, teach the family to start eating when *everyone* is seated, served, and a parent picks up a fork.

8. Know how to use various eating utensils and a napkin. Teach children how to cut meat (and not to cut it all at once), the difference between salad and dinner forks, how to use a soup spoon and where it goes when finished, and how to break bread or rolls and use a butter

knife. Demonstrate also how eating utensils go at the four o'clock position when you're finished eating. Show how a napkin is placed in the lap, how it is used during the meal, and to place it to the left of the plate at the end of the meal. (It is not rumpled in a ball and tossed on the table!)

9. Know how to handle emergencies. Explain what should be done with a bone or piece of food that can't possibly be eaten, how to remove it from the mouth gracefully, where to put it on the plate. Parents should learn—and teach their children—the Heimlich maneuver method of dislodging food caught in the throat. This could be life-saving information.

10. Coughing and sneezing at the table require a hand over the mouth, as they do elsewhere. Eating is not a time for grossness in manners (or in conversation).

Once each year, have a bad manners supper. Let everyone try all the bad manners imaginable. See who has absolutely the worst manners. This will be fun and get a lot of laughs, but it will also make bad manners so memorable that good manners will become more important.

When the Meal Is Over

The book has been enjoyed, the eating is over, the napkin is on the left side of the plate, and the family is excused. Often at this point there is a mad dash for T.V., toys, telephone, or homework.

But there is one more activity that requires family cooperation: cleaning up after the supper. Particularly in a family with working parents, the clean-up after a meal should be accomplished together and as quickly as possible. Many hands do make light work, and everyone from the toddler on up should have an assignment.

All family members but the baby can carry their own dishes to the kitchen sink. Parents and teens are good at putting any leftovers in small dishes and into the refrigerator. The person with the best sense of organization can load the dishwasher. Without a dishwasher, a teen or parent can wash the dishes and a young child can dry them.

A toddler can stand on a stool and wipe the counters and table clean. And young children can be in charge of sweeping the floor if necessary. With this kind of joint activity, the clean-up shouldn't take more than five to ten minutes.

Eating Out

Increasingly, the busy family eats supper out. Our survey shows that the average family eats out at least twice a week. Good conversation and good manners are still a part of the meal.

Since eating out is a treat (no preparation, no clean-up, no "I-don't-like-spinach" comments), don't rush through it. Certainly, you don't hog a table for an hour while other diners wait, but you should use the occasion to eat slowly and enjoy the time together. Eating out is more expensive than eating at home, so get your money's worth by savoring the experience.

Eating out also provides different topics for discussion. "What do you think is the healthiest food to order here?" "What food on the menu probably has the most calories?" "Who can guess how much the total bill will be?" "What would it cost to make this meal at home?" "Who is the brightest dressed person in this restaurant?" "What do you think her profession is?" "What will that tall man order?"

Don't hesitate to teach children to read the right-hand column on the menu. The price of a meal is something that kids should be cognizant of as soon as they learn to read. Before ordering, they should be given a price limit. Let them weigh the value of a more expensive item against a less expensive one.

New words pop up at restaurants too. Expand a child's vocabulary by explaining the meaning of terms such as *braised, consommé, béarnaise sauce, prawns, torte.* And on that special occasion when a menu is in another language, you can teach a few new words such as *fromage, poisson, linguini, crème, crêpe, rigatoni, rouladen, knackwurst,* and *mit schlag.*

Unless you're in a very elegant restaurant, it's acceptable to let an older child check the addition on the bill. A child can also take the money to the cashier, after having figured just what change she should bring back.

It's a good math lesson in percentages to let kids figure the tip, whether it is to be 10 percent, 15 percent, or 20 percent depending on the service.

Don't let the eating-out experience become routine. Keep it special. Try different restaurants. When going to the same old place, try new items on the menu.

The Return of Supper

A generation ago, the family gathered after work around the oil-cloth covered table. The mother had been laboring at home, the children in the fields or at part-time jobs, the father working on the farm or in town. Usually, the father dominated the supper conversation. It was sometimes an opportunity for putdowns, recriminations, or stern warnings about the dangers facing youth.

Despite all this, the table was also the forum for a lot of education. It was there that children first heard words like *democracy, justice, rights, ownership*. Most of a young person's moral, ethical, and political knowledge came from these conversations at supper.

Today, with both parents out in the world, the conversation should be more lively and diverse. Dad no longer dominates. Mom voices opinions, as do the children. New ideas are discussed and new words introduced: *segregation, welfare, abortion, unions, evolution, capitalism, socialism,* and *acid rain* are all fair game at the table.

Some forecasters predict the resurgence of family dining—and that can't happen soon enough! The supper table provides a family with the most positive way of communicating on a regular basis. Here is a daily opportunity for intimacy that mustn't be passed up.

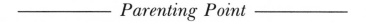

Parenting Point

A suppertime that builds poise, conversational ability, and knowledge makes a smarter child. And a big bonus is the building of memories, memories that come from being together. Certainly, eating together requires some planning, but when you see all the rewards of the supper reunion, you'll give it high priority. With family cooperation, step by step you can do it!

Chalkboard for Chapter Ten

Break new ground by establishing a super supper most nights at your house. For the first month, write down your plans. After a month or so, you won't need to be so organized because the supper reunion will naturally become a habit and eventually a happy tradition.

Week One
  Music to be selected by: _____
  News clipping to be brought by: _____
  Table manner to be practiced: _____
  Book being read: _____

Week Two
  Music to be selected by: _____
  News clipping to be brought by: _____
  Table manner to be practiced: _____
  Book being read: _____

Week Three
  Music to be selected by: _____
  News clipping to be brought by: _____
  Table manner to be practiced: _____
  Book being read: _____

Week Four
  Music to be selected by: _____
  News clipping to be brought by: _____
  Table manner to be practiced: _____
  Book being read: _____

Eleven

One Special Hour Touch-Base Time #5

David feels he deserves a special hour after supper. Nothing is going to stop him from stretching out with his shoes off, getting a little snooze, then tackling his stack of reading while keeping one eye on the T.V. Five-year-old Amanda has other ideas and soon creeps up on the edge of the sofa and plops herself down on her daddy. "Hey, give me some peace!" he says. Undaunted, Amanda asks, "What are you doing?" David mutters, "I'm busy, kiddo. Gimme a break, it was a hard day." "But I want to do something with you," she insists with a pout. "I'll do anything you want this weekend. Ask me then," he says with a sigh. Amanda wanders off, saying to herself, "But it was only a little tiny thing . . ."

No one will argue that a working parent should not guard and treasure the few free hours after supper. After all, it may be the only

117

really relaxing time of the day. But it is also a special time between parent and child. So there comes the interpersonal conflict, as David had with Amanda, and also the mental conflict, in the form of nagging thoughts about whether a parent is spending enough time with his child.

Certainly, a parent's needs are important: time for reading, attending to the mail and paying bills, watching a favorite television show, making a few phone calls, going for a walk with your mate. All of these are valid time consumers in the evening.

But you have chosen to be a parent, and a child's needs are important too. You've been away from each other all day, returned home, had supper, and now it is time for some casual time together. This time makes a significant improvement in a child's social and academic skills, so it's time you can't omit in your quest for a smart and happy child. The time is as important for new-borns as it is for those about to leave the nest!

But What About Me?

A parent may agree with the need to be a parent, but still feel "entitled" to "me-time." Yes, a parent will definitely have her own important time, but it may not come first. Let's put things in the correct order!

Say that supper is over by seven o'clock. Babies and toddlers are in bed within the hour, grade-schoolers certainly by eight-thirty, and older children somewhat later. And working parents may find that ten o'clock is their own best bedtime. So a parent has about three hours of after-supper time to schedule. Out of that should come the necessary time for building the parent-child relationship. Then, the remainder of the time is all yours.

So, the answer to the "What about me?" question is: kids first, parents second.

How Much Time?

A recent survey (reported by Richard Louv, *San Diego Union*, August 28, 1988) says that the typical working parent averages two minutes of one-on-one time with a child each work day. That's appalling! So, let's not be typical or average, let's be extraordinary!

Although it will vary from child to child, somewhere from twenty to sixty minutes is sufficient. Then, a parent can be off to his own pursuits until bedtime. Parents of a baby can enjoy about thirty minutes of reading, finger-play, and singing. Parents of young children may devote the maximum sixty-minute time (keeping in mind that some independent play is important here, too). And parents of teens may find that twenty minutes is all that can be sandwiched in.

Whether you have just twenty minutes or an hour, this evening time together is very precious. That's why it is called one special hour: Your time together happens within the hour after supper, a time when the family members feel warm and close to one another. You will probably not spend the entire hour *with* your child, but you will be on hand, available for conversation, ready to help when needed.

Top Priority: Touch-Base Time #5

There may have been some short moments you spent with a child in the late afternoon. And your supper together was a good *group* experience.

This after-supper time differs from the supper together because it is strictly a *one-on-one* time. Although it may seem hard to take the time for after-supper togetherness, it is necessary. A single parent who has all the home chores to do alone must be especially diligent in setting aside the time.

If you are part of a two-parent family, you have the luxury of taking turns being with a child. Both parents don't need to be parenting the same evening (unless there are a lot of kids!). But this important contact shouldn't be left to mothers only, nor should it evolve into moms being with daughters and dads being with sons.

Time together before supper is often hectic and fragmented. Perhaps you've had to put off a decision or conversation that a child wants. Now is the time for it. And if there is need for correction and a disciplinary discussion, this is the best time for it. When report cards and messages from teachers come home, consider them after supper when both parent and child are fed and calm.

But touch-base time #5 is mostly a very pleasant time. It should leave a parent relaxed and ready for her own free time just ahead. It is your best time during the week for enriching your child's life. You will be amazed at how much you can do together in less than sixty minutes.

So, let's pretend it's seven o'clock at your house. Are you stretched out like David, ignoring Amanda? Here are some refreshing alternatives.

One Special Hour with Babies and Toddlers

In preparation for bedtime, this special hour together should be an active time. The bedtime routine will follow and it will help a child wind down for sleep.

The hour after supper needs to be divided between togetherness activities and independent play. Children who have been in day-care most of the day may have had plenty of group play and supervised activities. Hence, part of this hour should be set aside for a young child to do things on his own. Yes, babies and toddlers need to be alone too.

Thus it is important for very young children to learn how to play by themselves. That's why a playpen is so important for babies and young toddlers. The playpen provides a safe place for this play. Considering the small size of a child, it is not a tiny cage! If a child is two feet tall and the playpen 4 × 4, this is the same as a five-foot-six person in an 11 × 11 area. You can do lots of things in 121 square feet!

Certainly, toddlers can learn to climb out of the playpen, but you can also tell them "no" and put them back in. There are many fascinating toys that can amuse a young child for long periods of time. And a child learns to play in one area, not fretfully all over the house. He knows that this is *his* play area where he can do as he wishes.

The playpen teaches a child two important lessons: (1) to be creative with what is at hand for play, and (2) to play with the same toys in a variety of different ways, thus utilizing ingenuity and expanding the attention span. Without parental interference, or with just a brief suggestion or demonstration to get things started, this will happen. That's why wise parents start the playpen routine when a child is a baby. It is a comfortable alternate location where a child feels at home and secure.

And if a child frets a bit, or throws all the toys over the railing, that's a worthy lesson too. We don't always get exactly what we want, and we need to take care of what we already have.

An older toddler can enjoy the same secure play in her room. A Dutch door, an expanding gate, or a screen door will let a parent keep track of a child playing in a child-safe room. Of course, making a child's room safe should be a priority. Cords, lamps, outlets, tall stacks of books, plastic bags, unsecured bookshelves—whatever could be dangerous—should be made safe, removed from a toddler's reach, or fastened down well.

The playpen and the child-safe room provide a parent with leisure time without concern for a child's well-being. But beyond this solo playtime, the special hour is one of parent-child togetherness. Sometimes the togetherness time should be first and the individual playtime second. Other days, turn it around the other way.

Baby-toddler activities for the special hour might include:

1. Playing finger-games. Start with "This Little Piggy" and add others like "This Old Man" and "Teenie Weenie Spider." Here is an opportunity to hold a child while you play together at the same time.

2. Exploring toys. You may be surprised to learn that many children don't know how to use the toys they own. Often children have so many toys that play means mainly moving them around. Take just one toy at a time and put the others out of the way. Together, look carefully at it; let the child show you what she knows about it. Then, introduce a new idea, a new way of playing. When the child seems to have tired of playing, introduce a second toy and see what interesting play can result.

3. Trying simple crafts. Don't buy big craft kits or sets of sixty-four crayons for very young children. Show a child how to use yarn, crepe paper, or string, lacing it through big holes in a piece of cardboard. Let a child practice holding a crayon and drawing on plain paper (don't bother with coloring books yet). Explore the good feeling of soft clay. Don't try to figure out what a child molds with it; any shape is fine.

4. Singing songs. Sing to babies, teach songs to toddlers little by little. Make rhythm instruments out of wooden spoons, kitchen whisks, and old metal pots. Put dried peas into a plastic container, tape it shut, and then shake it in time with music. Invest in some sing-along cassettes suitable for very young children.

5. Playing simple games. Put a string on the floor and see who can walk the length of it without falling off. Have a doorway chinning bar and practice hanging from it. Play with all the balls in the house by sitting on the floor with legs outstretched and rolling the balls back and forth.

Take turns playing "Where shall we go?" A parent may ask, "Where shall we go if we want to read? (A child leads to the bookshelf.) Where shall we go to find ice? (to the freezer). Where shall we go to find rain? (to the shower). You can keep this going for a long time. Vary it by hopping, skipping, or crawling to the destination, or carrying a child piggy-back.

6. *Making a playhouse.* Throw a sheet over a card table. Then gather dolls, animals, dishes, and toys and move in. You play the part of the baby in the family; let your toddler be the parent.

7. *Going places.* For variety try a quick after-dinner excursion. Yes, there are interesting places you can go in less than an hour. Destinations (depending on distance, weather, remaining sunlight) can be: the home of a neighbor or relative, the park, the ice cream store. Or, try a walk around the block with the baby in a stroller.

You'll notice that these activities did not include television or book reading. There is little of interest to babies and toddlers on T.V., so don't waste precious time on that. And book reading is part of the winding-down bedtime routine discussed in the next chapter.

Read the next section on after-supper activities for grade-schoolers. You may find some of them adaptable to your toddler.

One Special Hour for Grade-schoolers

So many new experiences are part of grade school. It's sometimes hard to keep up with all a child is learning—both academically and socially. This after-supper time is an opportunity to observe and listen and ask. A nonthreatening, comfortable, and supportive home atmosphere provides the setting for problem-solving and memory-building activities with your child.

Just having a parent readily available is a good beginning. But it is also important to have a planned activity together, something that brings you together physically and permits conversation.

A grade-schooler may also need time to complete homework, telephone a friend, prepare for a Scout meeting, and so on. But if homework is started before supper, there should be one-on-one time available after supper. Again, this requires only one parent, but remember, mothers and dads should spend time with both daughters and sons.

If you have a safe yard, grade-school children will also enjoy after-supper outside play. Even if it gets dark, this kind of play can be stimulating fun. Hide and seek, tag, King of the Mountain, and other games can be enjoyed by flashlight.

The activities most important, though, are those *you* share with a child. Consider these activities, all taking less than an hour, and some requiring as little as ten minutes.

1. Establish the after-supper game. A continuing game can become a great family tradition. A trivia game, a jigsaw puzzle, a few hands of pinochle or hearts—all these are relaxing. Consider having a place where a box game can be played without having to put it away. That way you can have fifteen minutes of Monopoly or Scrabble each night and continue the next evening.

2. Enjoy a brisk walk. You may have to sell the idea on the basis that you, the parent, need exercise. Walking in the semidarkness is conducive to intimate conversation and confidence-sharing. Sometimes make it an all-family walk or, when days are longer, a neighborhood bike ride. Cycling is great exercise, but you'll find that the conversation is not as good in a group.

3. Practice a sports skill. Throw balls in baskets, practice hitting baseballs and catching footballs, sink a can in the back lawn and practice golf putting, hit tennis balls against a wall, work out with an exercise video, go to the community pool and swim for thirty minutes, or play table tennis. These may sound like work to some adults, but they'll refresh you and please your child.

4. Work on a craft. One of the best pick-up activities is a craft or a hobby. Sometimes you may work together on the same project, sometimes you may work side-by-side on different projects. Consider woodworking, sketching, sewing, porcelain painting, pottery-making, ceramics, stamp or coin collecting, refinishing furniture, flower arranging, collage making, gourmet cooking, soap carving, model train building. Visit a craft store to see the variety of choices.

5. Bake something. In some families a parent and child prepare dessert *after* supper and serve it about an hour later. Whenever kids are to take a food snack to school or to an activity, prepare it together. It's less expensive and more fun than just buying it. Help a child start his own box of recipes, and, on a gift occasion, give a child his own cookbook.

Start simple and keep it simple. Baking projects should take thirty minutes or less. And the child should be enthusiastic about the product, so don't make butterscotch pudding if the child prefers vanilla. On the other hand, don't get in a rut; try new recipes. Our children took turns working with one parent to make a dessert. Usually, it was a pudding, or cup cakes, or a fruit cobbler. But when one child became interested in wok cooking, he insisted we make a dessert in the wok. At first I was doubtful, but we created a concoction of nuts, canned mandarin oranges, and vanilla cookie pieces tossed in a very small amount of butter and brown sugar. This hot dessert became a favorite on cold nights.

6. Go places. When a weekday night needs a lift, plan an after-supper excursion. Ensure that it fits within an hour's time. Let a grade-schooler choose what would be most enjoyable: a visit with a friend or relative, a quick trip to the library, a walk through a safe park, browsing time in one nearby store, a neighborhood bicycle ride, a drive to the boat harbor or to an airport to watch planes take off. The actual destination isn't so important as the change-of-pace togetherness.

During the grade-school years, a child starts the important steps toward complete independence. This daily time together helps to keep you current on what your young person likes to do, what concerns her, what skills she is learning, and what she is thinking.

One Special Hour for Teenagers

Let's be realistic! The chances are almost nil of your having an hour after supper with a teen. But, along with being realistic, remember that you are the parent in charge, and that in general your ideas are good, practical, and workable. So assert your parental privilege and see that you have at least some togetherness time with your teen.

If in the earlier years you've established the habit of being together after supper, it will be easier to still have twenty minutes together. If you don't have this tradition, appeal to a teen's fairness to try togetherness time for a month. He may find that it's a pleasant change of pace from an otherwise hectic schedule.

If a teen has homework, stop in her room with a snack and ask if you can be of any help (proofreading, testing, finding supplies). This shows your interest in what she's learning and keeps you in touch with your youngster.

Within reason, discourage a teen from going out on the weekday evenings. Because of after-school activities, homework may be the evening priority. If you don't let a teen get in the habit of "going places," you won't have to argue about it. Kids who are home on school nights make better grades and get into less trouble. School nights should not be social nights. Of course, a phone call or two of moderate length, a change-of-pace activity in the middle of homework, and some relaxing reading or a small amount of good television-viewing after the homework is finished, can fill out the evening.

So, if you are going to have togetherness with a teen, you have to grab it when you can and gently insist on it when it looks impossible. Beyond helping with homework, the best activities with teens include the following:

1. Sharing a physical activity. Try fifteen minutes of jogging or cycling, a quick basketball game, a thirty-minute swim session, a video home workout on the living room floor. The after-supper walk is a good option, too.

2. Playing a game. As with younger children, build the tradition of an after-supper game such as backgammon or checkers. Chess is a good game that can be played over several nights' duration. Just put a poker chip or coin under the last piece moved. Find other sophisticated card games and box games that can take as little as fifteen minutes.

3. Working together on a project. Build a bookshelf, clean a cupboard, paint a table, design and sew a jacket, change the oil in the car. Such activities often go better with two working together. Be sure to say that you'd like help for a specific length of time (ten minutes is good) and then stick to your estimate. Being needed by you adds to a teen's self-esteem as well as his knowledge and ability to accomplish tasks and projects.

4. Enjoying a little music and literature. Sit together quietly on a sofa and look through a book or magazine together. You'll learn about your teen's likes and dislikes by commenting on or discussing items in the magazine. Or, if you or he plays the piano or guitar, sing a few songs together. If you don't play well, you can play one hand and your teen the other.

5. Making special plans. It can be his party, your party, or a family event. Have paper ready to make notes and write down good ideas. Together plan foods, games, the guest list, music, costumes if any, and important do's and don'ts. Work out a time schedule that gives you both the time to enjoy the preparations and the event. Being "in" on plans makes a teen feel respected and confided in—needed and essential to the family!

The parents in my survey said that the time immediately after supper was the best weekday time. They felt closest to their child at this time and again at bedtime. Parents were almost unanimous in feeling that after-supper activities were essential to keeping the family together between weekends.

Most said that, after spending time with their child, they weren't as tired as before. They were more able to perform some necessary tasks and still have some time for relaxation before bed. And this gave them a feeling of success.

However, the survey participants said that T.V. viewing was the most common after-supper activity. About 75 percent of families permitted kids to watch *two* hours of television on weekdays! But remember, when the T.V. is on, conversation is off. And time to talk is meaningful for all age groups. Many working parents complain that there isn't enough time to *connect* with their kids, yet what is needed is to *disconnect* the T.V. Conversation can combine with other activities, but not with T.V.

The survey showed that the other evening activities in order of preference were: reading, shopping, games, outside play, sports, and hobbies, and these are activities that can make for a smarter child. Most of them can bring parents and children closer together than T.V. viewing.

If this after-supper hour is the best parent-child time of the day, a parent needs to consider carefully just how the precious time should be spent. The excuse that kids are "too busy" is just that—an excuse. Kids are able to find time for the two *t*'s: *t*elevision and *t*elephoning. So make time for the third and most important *t*: *t*ogetherness.

The Togetherness Rating

Failing to plan, coax, insist, design, and create activities for after supper means that your family can be an interactive family only on the weekends. Your weekday time together will be at the barest minimum. This is no way to run a family! And as children grow older, you will find that you lose touch with them.

Both closeness and memories are built on day-to-day events, no matter how small. This precious after-supper time is the focal point of your weekday parenting activity. Don't skimp on it.

When you have spent some time with your child in the after-supper hour, take time to consider how well you connected with her. Was the conversation easy and tension-free? Was your child open and honest rather than guarded and defensive? Was the time useful in solving a problem, having fun together, achieving something, or just getting to know each other better? If so, your togetherness time was constructive and you have a high togetherness rating.

At first, your togetherness time may only achieve one or two of these goals, but when you establish time with your child regularly, you will find that your "score" goes up. You and your child will actually look forward to this one-on-one time.

If you find that you're not enjoying this time, you're probably pressing too hard. Change the activity to something nonstressful and less verbal. (A walk or a board game may be the answer.) Then, slowly build on this simple project and add more-involved activities and more-controversial topics.

When you enjoy regular weekday time with your child, you feel confident about going on with your own evening activities, knowing you have fulfilled an important parenting responsibility.

The time spent means that your child will be smarter, too. Just think of all the knowledge you can share in this one precious hour—from yourself, from books and games, about sports and hobbies.

Parenting Point

After supper is your most essential weekday parenting time. Even if you share only twenty minutes with your child, make this valuable connection. Research by the Educational Testing Service of Princeton, New Jersey, shows that kids who are talked with are brighter and more creative than those who are left alone or permitted to watch T.V. You can have a smarter child and be a more effective working parent when you share "one precious hour." Step by step you can do it, and when you have, you'll want to do it every evening.

Chalkboard for Chapter Eleven

Chart how you feel about your evening parenting activities. For the next two weeks, try to have togetherness time after supper. Keep track of the time spent and what activity you did together. Then give yourself a togetherness rating:

3 if you felt that the time was valuably spent.
2 if you felt that it was moderately useful.
1 if you felt that the time was useless.

	MINUTES SPENT AND ACTIVITY	ACTIVITY RATING
WEEK ONE:		
Monday	_____	_____
Tuesday	_____	_____
Wednesday	_____	_____
Thursday	_____	_____
Friday	_____	_____
WEEK TWO:		
Monday	_____	_____
Tuesday	_____	_____
Wednesday	_____	_____
Thursday	_____	_____
Friday	_____	_____

If your togetherness rating is most often a *1*, keep a chart like this for several more weeks. Eventually, you'll find your rating going up even with the most difficult kids!

Twelve

And so to Bed . . .
Touch-Base Time #6

Margaret loves the bedtime routine, but husband Jerry does his best to stay out of it. Second-grader Chris and toddler Todd have a playful time in the bathtub, and then they run about the house playing hide-and-seek before Margaret tucks them both in. Chris goes right to sleep, but Todd is out of bed almost immediately. His reasons are always inventive: He is both hungry and thirsty, he isn't sleepy and would like to watch T.V. "just a minute," he sees a scary shadow in his room. Margaret tries to satisfy his whims and get him back in bed but he always comes up with a new excuse. So she agrees to lie down with him until he falls asleep. Soon both Todd and Margaret are sound asleep. After nearly an hour, Jerry realizes she isn't around so he finds her and awakens her. She says she has a busy day tomorrow and might as well go off to bed right away. Jerry says nothing but feels left out and lonely.

Going to bed should be a pleasant experience for both children and parents. It should signify the end of one successful day and the hope for another good day to come. It should not be a boring routine, a marathon of games, a rehearsal of fears, or a contest of wits that leaves a parent frustrated and exhausted.

Bedtime requires a routine, a routine that permits some variables, but one that both parent and child can count on. This is not the hour for action and adventure. That was enjoyed in the period after supper. The bedtime routine should be a time to wind down, one that prepares a child for quietness and sleep.

You will remember that reading was *not* suggested as part of the after-supper touch-base time, an active time. That is because reading is the keystone of the bedtime routine. And daily opportunities for reading good books are one of the best avenues a parent has to increase a child's knowledge.

The Last Touch-Base Time: #6

Now begins a working parent's last moments of daily contact. You have had some brief touch-base times: breakfast, after school, before supper. And you have had some longer touch-base times: supper and the hour following.

Now comes touch-base time #6, one that varies in length depending on the age of your child, yet is as important for a six-month-old baby as for a sixteen-year-old high-schooler.

There are many elements in this interlude. Some of these you will do *for* very young children, some you will do *with* toddlers and grade-school children, and some of them will be done *alone* by preteens and teens.

Like many systems you teach at home, the before-bed routine gives a child the opportunity to accomplish some essentials, to enjoy moments of relaxation and education, and to exercise self-government, which prepares him for life on his own.

The Bedtime Routine

You can tailor the activities to suit your own family situation, but the following activities are the recommended end-of-day essentials.

In two-parent families, one parent may supervise one night while the other has "the night off." Or the work can be divided between both parents. But don't get into the sexist habit of moms always giving the baths and helping make lunches while dads read the bedtime adventure stories.

It's important to start the bedtime routine when a baby is born and keep it going until a child is grown and leaves home. Don't skip this section because your teen goes to bed on her own. Although many of the activities no longer require your supervision, many still apply. So read it all and pick and choose what your child needs.

1. The Bath

For babies and preschoolers, the bath provides a warm and calming experience, necessary as a prelude for good sleep. Some parents like to bathe children before supper, but this can make for sleepy children at the table and during the active time following. Being in clean pajamas can also limit the important after-supper activities.

Save bath time for about thirty minutes before bedtime. For young children, this is a good time for conversation, story-telling, and fun with bath toys. Two young children will enjoy bathing together.

When babies become toddlers, start showing them how to bathe themselves properly. You didn't think lessons were needed? Yes, kids need to know where to start washing their bodies and where to finish. They need to know how to safely wash ears, how to give themselves a good shampoo, how to brush fingernails and toenails, how to carefully wash the tummy button and private parts.

Unless you actually demonstrate all this and establish good washing practices, bathing will be merely soaking, and showering will be just getting wet. Neither of these really cleans the body. So, yes, you do have to give lessons!

Never leave young bathers alone. Not for a moment. Not to answer the phone. Not to get a towel. It's not worth the danger or the anxiety. Small children can get into all sorts of trouble in just a few seconds. Get everything ready beforehand and stay in the bathroom until they are safely out of the tub.

By the time a child is in grade school, she should be bathing herself, and bathing alone, not with siblings or parents. A radio or cassette player—placed a safe distance from the tub or shower—makes this time more enjoyable, particularly for those kids who just "hate to bathe."

Some older children prefer to shower in the morning, which is fine if it doesn't take away from others' bathroom time during the often-rushed morning. Parents of teens may still have to influence the cleanliness routine by buying and encouraging the use of good shampoos, conditioners, creams, powders, and deodorants. If you don't encourage bodily cleanliness and the value of certain personal-care products, your kids will be learning from peers (which may or may not be helpful) or they will be fair game for faddish advertising (and you'll find that they are spending money on every new product invented).

Today we live and work in more confined spaces than in the old days and the weekly bath has been replaced by the daily bath or shower. So teach your child how to bathe and see that he has the time for cleanliness each day.

2. Next-Day Clothing Preparation

Before bed is the time to make decisions on what to wear next day—and to be sure that the desired outfit is clean and all the buttons present.

Clothes selection is an opportunity for a child to make a choice, an important step in self-government. A parent can suggest several acceptable outfits or combinations from which a child may choose.

Teach toddlers the names of colors and show which combinations of colors look best together. But don't be too exacting—a child should *like* what he wears, and style isn't particularly important. (Quite often with young children, it is the parent who is overly conscious of style, whereas the kids couldn't care less.)

For young children, put the chosen outfit on one hanger—shirt, pants, underwear, even the socks. Put the shoes right underneath so there can be no doubt about what to put on in the morning. Toddlers should be encouraged to help dress themselves and learn to do it completely alone by age four.

Older children should have a section of their closet where all the clothes are acceptable for wearing to school. They can just choose whatever they want from that section. These clothes should be separated from weekend clothes, dress-up or party clothes, and work clothes. Teach children early that clean, mended clothes are always acceptable, that dirty ragged clothes are not.

Help a teen assemble a wardrobe in which she feels comfortable. Trendy and expensive clothes need not be part of the wardrobe. Talk with other parents about controlling teen clothing purchases so that expensive name-brand clothes aren't essential to a teen's acceptance by her peers.

Setting a clothing budget is one way to show a teen the importance of wise clothing selections and good maintenance. He will soon see that he can have one name-brand shirt or two just-as-good house-brand shirts. And he will think twice about the purple patent leather low-slung belt that costs thirty dollars and is out of fashion four months later. This is excellent preparation for the future when a young adult has his own money to spend and is on a tight budget.

Although toys on the bedroom floor are acceptable, clothing is not. Before bed is the time to pick clothing up and put dirty laundry items in the hamper. (Once a week is often enough for the toys to be picked up unless you expect a visit from royalty.)

3. Next-Day Take-alongs

Now is the time to gather books, homework, show-and-tell items, lunch money, and items for after-school activities. All these should be put on the "going shelf."

Lunches can be started and sandwiches put in the refrigerator along with other foods awaiting the morning assembly. The empty lunch box or bag should be put on the "going shelf" as a reminder in the morning to pack and take the lunch.

4. Snack Time

Perhaps the family has not had dessert after supper. A dessert or snack at this time is fine, but it should be minimal. A child should have this snack with you in the kitchen or dining area. Try not to serve it in front of the T.V., because the child will watch whatever is already on, and you may have trouble getting her to go to bed until that show is completely over.

For variety, put the snack on a tray and bring it to the bedroom as she is preparing for bed. She'll love being "served" in this way. Surprise teens with a small snack to eat as they are finishing their homework. Studying goes better if there is a break in the middle for dessert or a little family conversation.

5. Reading

Bedtime is the time for a good book or two. Encourage kids who can read to enjoy leisure reading for at least fifteen minutes before bed.

For nonreaders or new readers, this is your opportunity to share books and story telling. It's a good lap-time activity that is pleasant and educational. Read his familiar favorite stories along with some new ones you choose. Reading together is an intimate activity and one that prepares a young child for sleep.

Don't read any set number of books. One toddler got cranky when a grandparent tucked him in after three books. He insisted, "My dad always reads *seven* books." Be flexible, read at least one complete story, more if you have more time.

6. *Final Things*

The last things before tucking a child in are a trip to the bathroom, teeth brushing, and a little drink of water. For a responsible child, a small glass of water on the night table can save her a trip out of bed.

7. *Love Time*

The parents in my survey listed bedtime as one of the two most favorite weekday times, saying they felt closest to their child at this time. In the survey, 79 percent said that they used bedtime as one more occasion to express love to a child. Unfortunately, the other 21 percent of parents said that they didn't tell their children daily of their love for them.

I hope you've told your child you love her: when she went off to school, when you made contact in the afternoon, or when you returned home. Whether or not you've already verbalized your love, you have one more opportunity. It is now, before a child goes to sleep.

It doesn't matter how old your child is, whether you've had an argument, or whether you're the one going to bed and your teen is staying up later. If you go to bed before your teenager, be sure to kiss him goodnight before you tuck yourself in. Before sleep, love time is a must.

Some younger children like being carried off to bed "fireman style." Others like to cuddle with a parent. Some like lap-sitting—just being held quietly.

Older children like bear hugs. Just because your child becomes thirteen is no reason to stop hugs and kisses. Keep it going daily to keep it natural.

Beyond physical expressions of love are the all-important verbal expressions. Lines like these should be among your last words to your child before she falls asleep:

"Remember, I love you."
"I'll always love you, no matter what."
"You're very special to me."
"I'm glad you're my kid."
"You were great today."
"Today was a better day than yesterday."
"I'm proud of you."
"I'll check on you in a little while."

This last sentence is important for younger children who have some fear of the dark or going to bed alone.

Last come bedtime prayers. Start with babies to sing or say a short prayer. Teach older children bedtime prayers that are meaningful. (You'll find some new ones in my book *1001 Things to Do with Your Kids,* Abingdon Press, 1988.) Prayers can do much to reassure a child and to calm nighttime fears.

Bedtime Fears

About 60 percent of children under ten are afraid of darkness and almost as many are afraid of being alone (*Children* magazine survey, 1988). Specific fears of monsters and ghosts, storms and natural disasters, and of animals and insects, affect more than 40 percent of children.

Such fears keep some children from falling asleep and also cause some to get out of bed several times in the night. Bedtime fears are usually gone by the time a child is a teen, but what can you do to help a younger child?

Depending on the magnitude of the fear, you may do some or all of these things:

• Talk openly about the fear. Explain that darkness is not a "thing" but just the absence of light. Show the nothingness of the dark by asking a child where it goes when you turn the light on. Tell a child that you will be near in case there is a storm. And tell a child that monsters and ghosts are definitely not real.

• Have only calm before-bed activities, not games that excite a child. Be sure you aren't reading creepy bedtime stories. Don't permit scary or violent T.V. or movie viewing.

● Install a nightlight in the child's bedroom. This can be an inexpensive solution. The first time it is used, show a child the various shadows that the light makes on the wall, and demonstrate how much of his bedroom the nightlight permits him to see.

Our older son really liked the comfort of a nightlight. When he started grade school, I wondered if he would ever give it up but decided not to make an issue of it since we were working on other aspects of maturity at the time. One night after he'd been put to bed, he came out of his room and brought the nightlight to us. He said, "This thing is keeping me awake. I don't know why you make me have it. Let's give it to my little brother. I bet he'll be able to sleep with it on."

So don't worry about the nightlight's becoming a habit. Few kids go off to college with one!

● Place a bell on the night table. Let your child practice ringing the bell to summon help. Then go out of the room, shut the door, and let the child ring the bell. See how fast you can return to her. Enforce your rule that if the bell is used for trivial needs it will be removed. (You might tell the story of the boy who cried "wolf" too many times.)

● Tell your child that you will be close by and that you will look in on him regularly. Do so within a few minutes, while he is still awake, and continue until the child falls asleep. But make these brief, nonconversational checks or they could turn into a play for attention. Your nearness can be very reassuring.

● Read poetry to the child. The soothing rhythms of poetry can bring calmness and sleep. Sit in a chair near the child's bed. Do *not* lie down with her. Lying down with her would start something that you cannot continue, and you would be denying your child the opportunity to triumph over the fear and grow in independence.

Should the problem of bedtime fears continue over a long period of time, you may want to seek professional help. You will probably find, however, that this bedtime routine erases most fears.

The Pest

Some children want a few extras before bed. It doesn't matter to them that they have already been to the bathroom, had a snack and drink, heard a story, been hugged and kissed, and said their prayers. They would like more to eat, one more story, or the chance to watch a little more television. Once a parent gives in to frivolous demands, the child keeps it up and becomes a bedtime pest.

This constant interruption of what is now the parents' precious time can make bedtime unpleasant for everyone. It is no longer a peaceful happy time, but a constant hassle. So get control of the situation.

First, if your child is well and you have been through the bedtime routine, there is no need to give in. This requires courage when the little person in his jammies appears at your elbow and speaks so appealingly. But don't weaken. Once you do, you have started a bedtime tradition that you don't want and won't like. You know what is best for your child and that includes the right amount of sleep.

It is far better to plan ahead and let a child stay up later than to let him wheedle you into it. Say occasionally to a child, "I want you to stay up a little later tonight to see the full moon," or, "The documentary on whales is so special that you can go to bed later tonight."

By the time a child is able to climb out of his crib or bed, and able to open his room door and find you, he is old enough to understand that certain acts are right and others are wrong. Constantly getting out of bed is wrong. Quickly and gently lead him back to his room. (Do not pick him up.) Firmly put him to bed. Do not make a lot of conversation. Simply say, "This is your bedtime. Goodnight. I love you." You may have to do this several times before the pest understands that you will not change your mind.

If this fails, go one step farther. Tell the child that he is permitted to get out of bed for three reasons only. These reasons are: (1) He is ill. (2) The house is on fire. (3) He wants to be punished.

A child who claims to be ill should not be treated to food or television. Attend to her needs, then tell her you'll check on her and care for her as required right in her bed. The child usually gets the message that you are serious, and so she'll not get out of bed unless she wants punishment. Let the punishment be known in advance. One of the best punishments for a bedtime pest is to set her bedtime fifteen minutes earlier the next night. Whatever punishment you choose, you must follow through on it.

A child can also be told that it isn't mandatory that he sleep. He is welcome to play with his teddy bear or sing to himself. Older kids might like to listen to a radio tuned to an all-music station. If children share a room, however, singing and radio playing are not appropriate.

Be sure that you have set a child's bedtime in keeping with his age, physical activity, and sleep needs. Crankiness is often a sign that a child needs more sleep. Children who need less sleep should be given a longer playtime before the bedtime routine. They may also be given an extended reading time.

The Family Bed

In recent years there has been publicity about the family bed—a bed where parents and child or children all sleep together.

Proponents speak of the closeness that this brings. Some even say that this doesn't impede the parents' sexual relationship!

The family bed usually starts when a nursing mother finds that having the baby at hand is a great convenience. Once the habit is established though and the baby becomes a toddler, he insists on staying in the parents' bed. And soon it is very hard to stop the practice without a big fuss, so parents just give in.

As new babies join the family, they also join the bed group. One father happily reported that at his house seven sleep in one king-sized bed! One wonders how efficient working dads and moms are the next day.

More and more child development specialists are beginning to speak out against the idea of the family bed. I am emphatically opposed to the family bed concept for these well-researched and fact-based reasons:

1. Each year numerous babies are suffocated by parents who accidentally roll over a baby during sleep. More often it is a father who does this, but some mothers have done it also. Why risk killing a baby for the convenience of being able to nurse it quickly?

2. Closeness is important; in fact, it is so important that it should be a part of family life long *before* bedtime. If sleeping in the same bed is the main time for closeness, parents should examine how they use the time before and after supper, and provide time for closeness then. Closeness and tenderness are too important to be put off until one is sleepy.

3. Although children should not feel ashamed about their

sexuality, being present when parents are having intercourse can be very upsetting to most children. It results in a child's feeling alienated and left out, and it can also cause harmful attachments to or fantasies about a parent. Sex in marriage should not be a taboo topic, but it doesn't need to be taught by demonstration.

4. Parents have a right and privilege to have private times without children present. The high incidence of divorce is partly the result of lack of time for parents to relate to each other. The time after children are asleep in their own beds, the time preparing for the next day and preparing for bed, and the time together in bed before sleep are one-on-one times for parents. These times are necessary for the strength of the marriage, especially because parents have been separated much of the day.

5. Laziness is one reason for the family bed. It means that parents don't have to go through the bedtime routine and then leave the child alone. It is easier—*but not better*—to sleep together. That way a parent doesn't have to deal with a child's calling out, getting up, or having other special needs. Proponents of the family bed also point out the advantage of there being only one bed to make each day.

6. Family members go to bed at different times and fall asleep at different rates. When everyone is in the same bed, one can disturb another, and someone is inevitably deprived of sleep.

7. The sleeping surface is important. A child in her own bed sleeps in a fairly level and healthful position. She can move around, stretch out, or curl up. In a family bed, the parents, being heavier, depress areas of the bed, and thus children often sleep on a slope. This isn't as good for the back and it forces children to sleep in a crowded or closed position since there isn't room to spread out. This makes sleep less restful.

8. Most important, the family bed is undesirable because it deprives a child of his independence. Learning to be self-governing is one of the key lessons of childhood. A child needs his own space. He needs to achieve the confidence that enables him to be alone. He needs to overcome his fear of darkness. Going to bed in his own bed adds to his self-esteem. He takes pride in his room, his own special private place. And he learns the importance of being on his own.

Setting Bedtimes

If you find your child frequently awake more than thirty minutes after bedtime, consider setting her bedtime later. Conversely, if a child is sleepy and apathetic during the evening, consider setting bedtime a little earlier.

A child's bedtime should be flexible, not rigid. For example, a third-grader's bedtime might be anywhere from 8:30 to 8:45: She has the choice of being tucked in at 8:30 or at any time up to 8:45—but no later. Make it clear that the fifteen-minute grace period is just that; it is not sixteen or twenty minutes extra.

Each year after summer vacation, in which there have probably been later bedtimes, change a child's bedtime in preparation for the new school year. You should also do this with teens, since lack of sleep is a significant problem for that age group. Teachers report incidences of high school students too tired to work efficiently and actually sleeping in classes.

Make "Bedtime Setting Day" a big deal for younger children. Mark it on the calendar in advance. Talk with each child separately and discuss how well—or how poorly—that child went to bed during the last school year. Reward goodness with a bedtime that is five to fifteen minutes later. Let a child offer her own suggestions and be sure you listen. Don't let the time that a television show ends influence your decision. Weeknight T.V. has little place in the busy family's life.

Weekends and vacations call for more relaxed bedtime hours, but as a rule children still need more sleep than parents. And parents need some time after a child is in bed for their own interests.

If the weekday bedtime routine is one of your most intimate times as working parents and children, make it a special event at your house. The routine is important as a low-key learning session. The components each take just a little time. Even a short bedtime routine can be filled with joy and love!

Parenting Point

No matter what has happened during the day, bedtime should reflect your unconditional love for your child. Remember the important line: "I love you no matter what!" Be sure to tell your child each night how much you love her. Step by step, work to establish a satisfying bedtime routine. A good night's rest makes for a more productive parent and a smarter child the next day.

Chalkboard for Chapter Twelve

Some parents and some children go along for many weeks feeling tired and in need of sleep. Others take too much time for sleep and thus don't have the time to do more important things.

How much sleep do you as a working parent need? We may think we know, but often we have just trained our bodies to accept a certain number of hours. It is habit, not need. Ideally, you should get approximately the same number of sleep hours six days of the week, and let one day be alarm free, letting you sleep as long as needed. The same is true for kids.

You can find your optimum number of sleep hours this way (and you can adapt this system for your child). The plan is to move your bedtime gradually later, making your sleep hours shorter.

How many hours of sleep are you currently getting each work night? _____ hours.

Deduct ten minutes, making your bedtime: _____ p.m.

Try this ten-minute-later time for one entire week. If after a week you don't feel any more tired than before, try deducting another ten minutes. If you *do* feel tired, add back just five minutes and try that for a week.

Second week bedtime: _____ p.m.

For the third week, try deducting another ten minutes if you haven't been tired, only five minutes if you have.

Third week bedtime: _____ p.m.

Do the same thing for another week.

Fourth week bedtime:_____ p.m.

Next, keep the same new bedtime for an entire month, without deducting any more time. Then, after a month, start again to take off five or ten minutes each week.

You will eventually find a weeknight bedtime that gives you the number of sleep hours that leaves you rested and ready for the new day. Some people have been able to cut back as much as an hour on their sleep time using this method.

Thirteen

The Wow! Weekend

Mike and Nancy work hard at their jobs and feel they deserve to sleep in on Saturday mornings. Their kids are up at dawn. By the time Mike and Nancy are awake, the dog is cleaning up left-over potato chips in the family room, the younger kids have seen three hours of cartoons and commercials, and it's almost time for lunch. Mike had plans to work on the car this morning, Nancy had some shopping she wanted to do alone, and they had promised the kids a picnic at a scenic hilltop about half an hour's drive away. The weekend had just started and it was already a mess. Then their older son, Tim, returned from soccer and asked if he could do his weekend chores later because he wanted to go out with the guys right away. Mike blew up (probably more angry at himself than at Tim). Nancy made a smart-alec remark and took the younger children to the grocery store as Mike *tuned in a T.V. sports event and Tim rushed from the house. So the day went—another disjointed, unproductive, and unmemorable Saturday.*

We all need time to kick back, and there is nothing wrong with sleeping a few extra hours on a Saturday morning, but working parents need to have a plan—beyond sleep—for the weekend. After all, you've been looking forward to these two days all week long. Now that the weekend is here, don't let it get away from you!

The basic question is how to get some chores and errands done and also to have important family time. Both are essential. Home maintenance is needed, but time with children is very much needed. More than any other period of the week, the weekend hours help build relationships, bring about memory-building activities, and educate. It's one-on-one time, boy-with-boy time, girl-with-girl time, boy-with-girl time, parent-with-child time. The many combinations of family members and togetherness activities are almost endless.

If a working parent is to have a smart child, the weekend hours are pivotal to success. During the weekdays, parents have held things together with the six touch-base times, and there have been after-supper activities that stimulate and educate. But there have not been opportunities to work and play together over long periods of time. This is what the weekend should provide.

So how does it all fit in during a typical sixty-hour weekend (from 6 p.m. Friday to 6 a.m. Monday)? Well, few weekends are typical! But there are some things that should take place almost every weekend so that on Sunday evening the family says, "Wow! It's been a terrific weekend!"

Components of a Wow! Weekend

Let's divide the activities into two categories: (1) Must Do and (2) Might Do.

If you were to make up a list of Must Do activities, you might begin with sleeping or marketing or housework. But actually, the number-one thing on the Must Do list is *family time*. Putting family togetherness first on the list gives it the proper priority. It may not be the first thing *done* on Saturday morning, but it is the one event that will be done no matter what else happens.

So, on the Must Do list, family time comes first—and it may be the *only* event. This family time includes a wide and wonderful range of things that can be enjoyed as a family: everything from hiking up a hill and attending church together to assembling airplane kits and having supper in front of the fireplace. We'll go into details on possible activities in a moment, but let's look first at the other list, the Might Do list. These are the things that you would *like* to accomplish before the next work week begins. You might want to do many of them, but you may not have time to do them all. These include:

1. Extra sleep
2. Home maintenance, including cleaning, paying bills, correspondence, car maintenance
3. Errands
4. Kids' weekend tasks
5. Sporting events—organized or personal, active or spectator
6. Social time for parents
7. Social time for kids

If your weekend plan skips one of these seven, it isn't the end of the world. There is always next weekend. But these seven deserve time almost every weekend, certainly twice monthly.

How to Get That Extra Sleep

If you are normally up by six or seven o'clock on weekday mornings, treat yourself to two additional hours of rest on Saturday. Don't set your alarm. Enjoy the luxury of catching up—you deserve it. And if you get sleepy during the day, take a nap before supper. Being good to yourself is important. Your children depend on your physical and mental well-being. And sleep is one essential.

If you have a baby or toddler and no older child to care for him during these extra sleep hours, spouses should take turns: one sleeping late one weekend, the other the next. If you are a single parent with a young child, take your nap while baby is napping.

Preschoolers shouldn't be left to mischief. A preschooler needs a child-safe room for morning play. (See chapter 11 for ideas on child-safe play areas.) If you're the kind who can go back to sleep, you may want to give him breakfast, start his morning play, and then go back to bed.

Most school-age children can be trusted to carry on by themselves, knowing that parents are nearby. But this shouldn't mean hours and hours of T.V. The children in our survey watched an average of *three* to *four* hours of weekend T.V. (However, 22 percent spent *five* to *six* weekend hours on T.V., and one family averaged *sixteen* hours!) Most of this is unsupervised Saturday morning T.V. That's far too much, and a waste of a child's time and intelligence.

Plan what your child should do when she awakens on Saturday morning. You should also do this for older kids, even teens, until you are sure they know how to manage their time effectively. For children who can read, make a little list of what you would like them to do. For children who cannot read, draw simple pictures to remind them of the activities. Together, go over the early Saturday morning list each Friday and try to vary the activities and the order. The list should include:

● *A simple breakfast.* Lay out as much as possible the night before. Juice, toast, cereal, fruit—choose things your child likes and can prepare on his own. For young children, avoid items that require sharp knives or stove-top cooking. Tell her you expect her to clean up after herself too.

● *Something useful.* Bed-making, dog-feeding, dishwasher-emptying—every child can perform a simple, helpful function that saves you time later.

● *Play time.* Select from a child's toys some very favorite ones and put them in "The Saturday Box." Keep the box out of reach on a top shelf. Before retiring Friday night, bring the box out where kids can easily find it. Change the contents of "The Saturday Box" every few weeks or as needed.

● *Reading time.* After some early morning play, tell a child that he can read as many books as he wishes. Put some new books from the library in a prominent place where he's sure to see them. Children with weekend homework can work on it at this time, too.

● *Video time.* Permit one hour (but no more) of television viewing. One Saturday, actually view the available shows and help your child choose the most worthwhile. Write down the time and channel of any show you and your child agree is worthwhile. Some parents record a video cassette, or rent one, for Saturday morning viewing and have it ready to run so that all a child needs to do is push "start."

● *Keeping safe.* Go over family safety rules specifically for Saturday mornings. Tell children what you expect concerning going outside to

146

play, leaving the yard, answering the phone, opening the door, using appliances, taking a bath or shower, using matches, and so forth.

● *Getting-ready time.* Depending on weekend plans, tell a child to prepare for the time when you'll be up. Perhaps she should get dressed, make her bed, and bring you orange juice in bed! This anticipation of being together can be significant in getting kids to accomplish certain morning tasks.

The Ever-Present Home Repair List

For most parents, home maintenance is a four-letter word. Keep a list on the family bulletin board of what needs doing around the house. Leaky faucets, locks that don't work, broken drawer handles—no house is exempt from maintenance tasks and we seldom catch up.

That's why it is important to do a few things from the list each week. A parent and a child make a good repair team. This is not solely a father and son event; mothers can take the lead, and daughters should learn right along with sons.

At our house, it was a tradition that a child's fourth birthday include the gift of a tool kit. Receiving your own metal case with a few basic tools inside was a sign of growing up and being responsible. Then, each year at Christmas, each child received one additional tool. Tools do fit nicely in Christmas stockings! Both our sons and our daughters knew what Phillips screwdrivers were and how to use them. And as the kids went off to college and careers, the tool boxes went right along.

Every child needs a tool kit. Then, the parent-child repair team is ready to work together. It's a learning experience that makes for a smarter child. This repair time should never last more than one hour.

Another part of home maintenance is house cleaning. Although a few working parents have the luxury of a hired cleaning person, most have to do it on their own. With child help, you can accomplish a lot in one hour on Saturday morning. Better yet, try the room-a-day system for tidying up, cleaning, and dusting. Then just vacuum all rooms on Saturdays. A clean house is important, but let's not let this activity consume too much time. Although bathrooms may require frequent cleaning to remain sanitary, some things can be cleaned every other week or even monthly. Working together makes it much easier.

Saturday Errands and Shopping

During the time that one parent is making repairs, vacuuming, washing the car, or accomplishing other at-home tasks, the other parent can be running an errand or two or getting groceries. As much as possible, fit short errands into weekday schedules. Doing them "in the cracks" on weekdays makes them take up less time because of less travel. But often, there's still an errand left for Saturday.

Grocery shopping should be a once-a-week project. Working from a list prepared during the week, go at a time when your store is less likely to be crowded with shoppers. If possible, take just one of your kids along. Make the drive easy-going fun with car games and conversation—it's a vital one-to-one opportunity to bond with your child.

Older children can be given half the shopping list. (This really does cut down on time spent at the market!) When children are old enough to drive, doing the grocery shopping can be an assigned task done each Thursday or Friday after school. This is good training for when they're on their own. Be tolerant and nonargumentative if some items aren't just exactly what you requested. Discuss their reasons for the change and your reasons (cost, brand, quality, size).

Grocery shopping with a child provides opportunities for him to learn. Young children can identify pictures and colors. Grade-schoolers can compare prices and values. Teens can estimate the total bill, deduct for coupons, and figure the proper change.

It's nice to shop alone, but that time will come later in your life. Right now, make the most of this time together and increase your child's knowledge while you shop together.

Kid-Help

Chapter 18 gives you plenty of ideas on things kids can do to save you time and also how to encourage them to do them.

Don't worry if tasks aren't done perfectly. A child will gradually improve with your appreciation, instruction, and encouragement.

When a child helps with shopping, home repairs, food preparation, laundry, younger child-care, and so forth, she learns worthwhile skills that add to her general knowledge and also to her self-esteem.

Sports Events and Practices

If your child is on a sports team, a big chunk of Saturday time is probably spoken for. This is usually seasonal and often both child and parent feel relieved when the season is over! Still, such team activities are important and provide lessons in sportsmanship, versatility, patience, coordination, and cooperation. Get whole-heartedly behind the sport and encourage your child to give it her very best.

At the same time, be sure that the sports schedule doesn't throw family life out of balance. Permit each child to be on one team with a regular practice. Unless you have a future Olympian, don't use up all of a child's free time with many different sports activities and practices. Make it clear that home responsibilities are to be finished before a child goes off to practice and that the all important Must Do family time will be the real highlight of the weekend.

When the team activity is a game, rather than practice, make every effort to be there. How the game went and your child's reactions when winning or losing are important topics for conversation. The time spent talking *after* the game can be as vital as the sport itself. Many of the skills and lessons learned in a sport carry over into social and business activities. You will want to help your child make these connections.

Social Events for Parents

Each weekend should provide togetherness time for parents. This can be as elaborate as dinner and dancing or as simple as a late-night living room supper with a video.

Like good recipes, good marriages have essential ingredients—and they both need stirring. Don't substitute or skimp on the togetherness ingredient—it's the leaven. And don't forget to stir the relationship regularly with creative activities. This stirring prevents a marriage from becoming boring or routine.

When working parents have such little time during the week, they need weekend time to talk, discuss, dream, plan, laugh, love, relax, and enjoy friends. This time shouldn't be in the category of "we'll do it later"; it is basic to both weekday and weekend life.

Besides the time a couple should have alone together, a social time with good friends is a relaxing change of pace. This can also be a time for sharing and learning. Good friends feel at ease with one another and can sometimes talk over parenting problems and benefit from one another's experiences. Getting to know other married couples can put your own marriage in perspective, too. And spending time with friends adds stability to a marriage; it's one more pleasant connection that both spouses have in common.

But social time should not be spent just with other couples with children. Couples without children and singles should be included. Their ideas are often most insightful because they can stand back and talk from a different perspective. The greater the variety of your friends, the better. Different professions, different religions, different races, and different ages bring broadening contributions to parenting.

Kids need to know these other adults, too. So, the friends of parents often become extended family.

This social time for parents means plans need to be made regularly. This isn't the prerogative of the wife; a husband should do his share of leading socially: planning a supper with friends, selecting a movie, ordering theater tickets, picking a place to hike, setting aside time to talk.

Kids Socialize Too

An intelligent child is one who is comfortable socially. Parents should provide opportunities on a regular basis for a child to be with her peers in social situations. This goes beyond day-care and school experiences.

Start early with children to encourage friendships and attendance at social events. Poise, openness, flexibility, and lasting friendships are marks of a truly smart child. These qualities are developed gradually throughout a child's social life.

Preschoolers have a great need to be social, but this takes a bit of arranging. You may know of a similar-aged child in the neighborhood or at child-care. It takes advance planning and your supervision for this social time, but it's worth it. For these children, one to two hours is a good length of time for socializing.

Grade-school children enjoy sleep-overs, going to movies, and active play together. With a hesitant or shy youngster, a parent should start by encouraging her to have just one friend over at first. When that is successful, another playmate may be added. Help her work up to having—and enjoying—a small party.

Teens usually have plenty of social ideas and opportunities and are capable of making their own plans. It is a parent's responsibility though to be sure that the activities planned and the friends included are wholesome.

You'll find plenty of party ideas for all ages in my book *1001 Things to Do with Your Kids* (Abingdon Press, 1988).

Weekends provide opportunities for parents to get to know a child's friends. Working parents should be sure they do their share of inviting young people to their home, "chauffeuring" kids to events, sponsoring social events, and acting as chaperones.

A child's social life doesn't just happen. Parents shouldn't ignore this important need for children to relate to their own peers.

Must Do Events

All of the activities above are secondary to the Must Do event of every weekend: the time the family spends together.

Why is this time necessary? Because we don't really know our children (or our parents, or ourselves) until we see one another "in action." Eating supper together, reading a book together, taking an evening walk together—all such weekday activities start to build a relationship of mutual appreciation, caring, and trust, while increasing a child's intelligence. These weekday events are the firm foundation for the weekend time together.

Remember how Mike and Nancy had thought about going on a picnic with their children? They knew there were other things to do—car maintenance, errands, Tim's practice—but they hadn't planned their weekend to include time for the Must Do family time.

Saving the Time

It is easy when children are babies to control where they go and what they do. It grows more difficult as children become more mobile—and extremely hard when they have wheels of their own. So start when children are very young to participate together in a weekend family time.

When babies become toddlers, they can take part in the weekday discussion regarding what events will take place over the weekend. Talk about the weekend *every* weekday. Decide on and plan the family event. Write the time and place on a piece of paper and put it on the bulletin board or refrigerator. Make it very clear that this is an important event and other things must be planned around it; don't let it be pushed into the background. Certainly, you should consider other weekend obligations, and occasionally change the time of the family event, but it should usually take priority.

Teens are the most difficult to include, so consult with them on the best time and you'll get better cooperation. Then emphasize that this one event is mandatory (and enjoyable). They may even want to include their friends from time to time.

Family Time Events

These occasions for togetherness need not be money-spending events. They may be free and even money-saving. The purpose is to bring the family together in an active way, so that members talk with one another, work together, play together, and learn together. In this way the family becomes closer, good memories are built, and caring is established as a priority.

With so much else to do on weekends, the family time events will vary in length. Sometimes they will take the entire weekend (a camping trip, for example). Sometimes they will be as short as two hours at the park. Since the time spent with one another is the highlight of the weekend, try to make it last at least two to three hours. You may split it into several different activities, but be sure not to so fracture the time that it has little meaning. Time is needed to establish rapport, to become comfortable, to accomplish an objective.

The aim is to be together and this can take place in a variety of environments as long as they're pleasant. This means that some of the time may be used for family work projects, but most of the time should be spent on recreational activities. Weekend activities may include work projects, outdoor events, indoor excursions, cultural events, and religious observances:

1. Work projects. A large family-project, particularly one that everyone is excited about, can be great fun. Making things for the home falls into this category.

One family actually built a large above-ground swimming pool together! They look back on it as one of their best summer activities. It provided tasks suitable for both younger and older kids, and carried the wonderful reward of many happy pool hours.

Building a tree house, a sandbox, a firepit, a screened porch, a jungle gym, or family room bookshelves improves family life. When everyone shares in the labor and works with good humor, the benefits—in addition to the worthwhile product—include camaraderie and bonding.

Washing the car is another project that one family does in a variety of unique ways. Sometimes they do it with lunch, providing pick-up foods set on a table by the driveway. Sometimes everyone wears swimsuits and there is quite a lot of hose play. Occasionally, one child sits on a stool and reads aloud from a book of riddles. Or, each participant gets five minutes of rest inside the car for reading alone while others work on the outside of the car. Sometimes there are contests to see who is the best window washer or which half of the hood gets polished better. When a work project is treated in this creative way, it becomes a memorable and happy time of being together.

2. Outdoor events. When you've been inside an office or school room all week, there is nothing like getting outside. No matter where you live, there are parks, fields, forests, mountains, shorelines, or waterways that provide places for activities.

Just because you have a young child, you needn't remain indoors. Today, babies are packed up mountainsides in safe carriers and taken on bike trips in special safety seats. Strollers bounce along park paths and through the zoo. Tiny tots roller-skate with their parents on the boardwalk. And toddlers are safely treated to the summer sun at the shore or bundled up for a winter walk along the river.

All-weather clothing lets us enjoy the outdoors in rain, wind, and snow. One grade-schooler looks forward to rain because his family's tradition is to go outside and play in puddles. They float small paper boats in rain gutters. They see who can jump into a puddle and make the biggest splash. They lift their chins for a rain-water drink. They return home for hot chocolate by the fire.

Keeping in mind the available facilities near where you live, compile a list of weekend outdoor excursions. Talk with friends and neighbors about their favorite places and add these to your list.

Younger children often need a rest from vigorous activity, so plan your outdoor excursion to include a quiet picnic, a sit-down game at a viewsite, even a nap on the ground.

Some equipment can make the outdoors more fun: binoculars for looking at objects far away, magnifying glasses for looking at insects, bags for collecting colored leaves or rocks, canteens for each family member. You don't need expensive ski equipment to enjoy the snow or expensive scuba equipment to enjoy the water. You can borrow or rent equipment until you're sure you want to invest in your own.

Sharing a sport with your child, whether it is jogging or tennis or skiing, is one more memory-building bond. And you will find that this joint love for the outdoors easily continues when your youngster becomes an adult.

3. Indoor excursions. The weekend edition of your local paper will provide ideas on special things to do indoors. Some stores and businesses offer free tours: to demonstrate ice cream making, water purification, light and power, and what goes on behind the scenes at large markets. Such tours can be very educational and springboards for conversation.

Museums that specialize are very popular and are often free. These feature one thing only: old railroad cars, airplanes, wildflowers, cheese making, coal mining, model railroading.

More traditional museums may charge fees but they are worth it. And please don't groan over the idea of museums! Nowadays, many have a new look that entertains and teaches at the same time. A few hours spent in an art or science museum is fun if approached the right way. In chapter 17, "Frosting on the Cake: Enriching Family Life," you'll find many ideas on how to make such visits meaningful.

4. Cultural events that cost. When you decide to buy tickets for a cultural program, make sure you get your money's worth by talking with a child about the event beforehand.

The circus, ice skating shows, and sporting events are better enjoyed when your child has an appreciation for the skills to be performed. Purchase tickets far enough in advance so that you can enjoy anticipating the event. Although such events are good for all ages of kids, they are especially interesting for young children since there is lots of action, and talking and moving about are permitted.

Nowadays there are very few movies that young children should see. The classics and full-length cartoon movies that are reissued every few years make for a wonderful afternoon, but children need to be able to sit quietly for a few hours in order to enjoy them fully. Make a movie a special occasion and require a rest or nap beforehand.

When a child enters school, it's time to introduce her to theater, classical music, and dance. Some schools include such excursions. Again, a parent and child will get more out of the event with advance preparation. Knowing about the author or composer, the plot, the stars, the various instruments, ballet steps, even listening to some of the music in advance, enriches the experience.

Children's theater is alive and well in many cities and provides excellent "live" culture. Kids especially enjoy seeing other kids on stage.

By exposing children to the arts, you may discover in your child new talents and interests in these fields.

5. Together at church. Part of every good weekend is the religious observance at church or synagogue. A basic understanding of God, the history and literature of the Bible, and a knowledge of your own religion can provide comfort and stability for the family.

There is much that is strange and frightening about growing up today, and now more than ever a child needs something to rely on beyond himself and family. The Bible stories provide examples of triumphs over fear, ignorance, disease, temptations, and all the other problems so common today.

The moral, ethical, and spiritual values taught in the Bible provide a child with a basis for right action in the many diverse fields of life. Don't deny him this knowledge because of your own beliefs, your desire to sleep in, or his preference for play instead of attending Sunday school. Find a church that is relevant to your family's life-style. Support it with vigor, and you'll find that it brings many blessings in return.

Attending church services or Sunday school should be a "given," not an option in family life. Start when children are babies to include them in church life and activities.

Associations with church friends provide a second focal point for family life. Churches and synagogues have wholesome youth activities that bring young people together. Many young people have commented that these church-related groups and the friendships made through them have kept them out of trouble.

If a family makes religious principles part of everyday life, not just a once-a-week ritual, the utility of religion will become apparent. This means that, as children become adults, they will continue to make religion a vital part of their lives.

Daily prayer in the morning or at bedtime, study of the Bible and the adventure stories told therein, living by the precepts of the Ten Commandments, the Beatitudes, the Sermon on the Mount give each family member tools to use when all ordinary means fail.

The trite old saying is still true: The family that prays together stays together. Statistics show that church-going families are less apt to break up and suffer the tragedy of divorce. That alone should make religion valuable to a family.

———————— Parenting Point ————————

Doing things together brings family unity and love into focus and provides opportunities for democracy, self-government, and learning. And that means wiser kids. You can do it! Get organized and start having Wow! Weekends at your house.

Chalkboard for Chapter Thirteen

This coming week, take time to talk with your spouse and family about putting together a dream weekend with time for many of the Might Do activities and the all important Must Do family time together.

Here is your time schedule to fill in:

SATURDAY	SUNDAY
9 A.M. _____	_____
10 A.M. _____	_____
11 A.M. _____	_____
12 noon _____	_____
1 P.M. _____	_____
2 P.M. _____	_____
3 P.M. _____	_____
4 P.M. _____	_____
5 P.M. _____	_____
6 P.M. _____	_____
7 P.M. _____	_____
8 P.M. _____	_____
9 P.M. _____	_____
10 P.M. _____	_____

If everything doesn't work perfectly the first time, keep trying for your Wow! Weekend. It *will* become a reality!

Fourteen

T.V. and Your Bright Child

Marie thinks that her children, Jessica and Travis, watch too much television. Husband Jim turns it on at breakfast and again at supper to catch the news. Then, after supper, the family just drifts toward the set. Marie **does** monitor what they look at together to be sure that it isn't too violent or sexy. The problem is when she isn't home. The kids turn it on after school before she gets home. They also turn it on first thing Saturday morning and those evenings when Marie and Jim aren't home. She knows she should set some limits, but when the kids were little she found T.V. a handy form of amusement, and so the habit has just continued. Jessica reports that the teenager next door is permitted to do her homework with the set on; in fact, she has her own T.V. in her bedroom and often goes to bed with it on. Now Jessica and Travis are campaigning for their own T.V.'s. Jim says *that this is O.K. since he was raised on television and he turned out fine. But Marie is not convinced that this is a good idea.*

A parent who wants control of television viewing is on the right track. A smart child needs a variety of experiences, and television should be just one of them. The time spent viewing T.V. should be a very minor part of growing up. Unfortunately, today it is the major indoor activity for young people in America.

Nation-wide surveys show that the average number of hours a T.V. set is switched on in a typical home is now about forty-five per week. We hope that some of the time it's on, it's just talking to itself! The parents in our survey reported that their children see an average of *two* hours of T.V. on weekdays and about *three* to *five* more hours over the weekend. This includes family viewing as well as the typical Saturday morning kid-viewing time. No matter how it is divided, it is far too much, and for these reasons:

- When the T.V. is on, it is difficult to have a conversation.
- When the T.V. is on, the body is inactive.
- When the T.V. is on, the viewer is rarely learning or being mentally challenged.
- When the T.V. is on, it is usurping time that could be devoted to more productive activities.
- When the T.V. is on, the viewer is an observer of life, not a doer.

What's a Parent to Do?

Getting control of T.V. viewing is not easy, but it is definitely possible. It is easier if you start when children are young, but you can gain control whatever the age of your child.

In a report from the United States Bureau of the Census (the 1982 Report on the 1980 Census), more than 98 percent of all U.S. homes have one or more television sets and 68 percent have multiple sets. What a wonderful communication tool it could be if the networks and the public could work together for higher quality programming. But until that happens, quality control is up to parents.

Denying a child extensive T.V. time is *not* some form of punishment. You aren't a mean and unfeeling parent. You want the best for your child. And if you want a child who is well educated and smart about a variety of things, you have to come to grips with the T.V. question.

So make up your mind that, as a responsible parent, you're going to take control or improve the control you now have. And, at the same time, you are going to learn some facts about television that will help you use it to your best advantage.

Television Is Beneficial

Certainly, there are wonderful things about T.V. When a parent is rushed, it can entertain rambunctious youngsters. When a child is not well, it can soothe. And, when there is a special program geared to children, it can both entertain and educate.

The medium often does this welcome job of entertaining and educating. It brings the world right into the home and shows us people, places, and things we might otherwise never see. What we view is memorable, etched in our mind for a long, long time. And for many children, television is their only window to the world outside their homes.

But it is a passive medium. It requires little interaction. It does not require much thought or the making of conclusions or the use of reason. It speaks with authority and what it says is generally believed to be true. Without other activities to balance television, the output of the T.V. becomes a major input into a child's mind. Sometimes this is good input, often it is trivial, often it is actually harmful.

So, it's a parent's responsibility to sort out the worthless and encourage the best T.V.

In the book *Television and America's Children: A Crisis of Neglect* (Edward L. Palmer, New York: Oxford University Press, 1988), the author says, "We have become the age of the flash and the zap, the hour-long epic, the thirty-minute encyclopedia, the five-minute explanation, the one-minute sell, the ten-second teaser." It is true that T.V. gives glimpses (often without depth) of many topics. Young children raised on T.V. find school, with its quieter atmosphere, which requires thoughtfulness and personal effort, "boring." They are hooked on only what is entertaining and what can be grabbed quickly. Palmer also says, "Our children must learn how to spot a stereotype, isolate a social cliché, and distinguish facts from propaganda, analysis from banter, and important news from 'coverage.'" He believes that the potential of television as an electronic teacher is boundless when it is in partnership with the school.

The Wall Street Journal reported in September 1988 that by the end of high school, America's children have spent more time watching television than doing anything else except sleeping—15,000 hours on average. With children so dedicated to viewing T.V., parents need to direct choices so that there is some benefit derived from those 15,000 hours of viewing.

Don't Ignore the Violence Connection

A few years ago, there was an R-rated movie that had a vivid scene depicting a game of Russian roulette. The movie was eventually shown on T.V. at an evening hour when kids could easily see it. In the seven days that followed, there were twenty-eight copy-cat Russian roulette shootings by children, including eleven fatalities! (Reported by KNX radio, Los Angeles, California.)

We are kidding ourselves if we don't recognize the connection between television and violence. It is a rare television program that shows a conflict resolved by nonviolent means. Over and over we are showing our children that violence has a useful place in society.

After a decade of research on the behavioral effects of television viewing (1972–1982), the National Institute of Mental Health reports that there is overwhelming scientific evidence linking television violence to aggression and violent behavior among children and teens. Each time such a report is made, there comes a rebuttal from network officials. But soon there is another report, and another, to the point that parents can no longer disregard the evidence.

Even cartoons and fairy tales that depict violent behavior can have an adverse effect on young children, who are not yet able to separate fact from fable. One study (reported by Richard Louv, *San Diego Union*, November 13, 1988) reveals that the "Transformers" children's cartoon program contains eighty-three violent acts per hour and an attempted murder every thirty seconds.

Yes, public broadcasting is out there offering great programs such as *Square One TV, WonderWorks, Reading Rainbow, DeGrassi Junior High,* and *3-2-1 Contact,* but these national shows are overlooked by most parents and their children as being "too wholesome or educational." One wise parent presents these shows as the only choices for her young family.

Children are imitators. When they see that anger and force bring desired results, they adopt similar ploys for their own use. Some even accept violence as normal behavior. In one research project (reported by Robert Reinhold, *New York Times,* Thursday, May 6, 1982), it was found that preschool children who often watched cartoons containing a great deal of violence were abnormally aggressive toward their playmates and cruel to their pets.

Grade-school children were part of another test in the same project. One group read books, then played an active game. A second group watched a violent television show, then played the same active game. This second group was more than 200 percent more aggressive both verbally and physically.

This same research also showed that children, particularly teens, who watch violent shows are less obedient, less outgoing and friendly, and less self-controlled. A separate survey of MTV programming reveals that 75 percent of the themes of MTV's rock videos deal with violence, drugs, or sex.

Heavy T.V. viewers have far less trust in other people and firmly believe that the world is a mean and fearsome place. Although for some the world seems oppressively cruel, violence is *not* so widespread as T.V. makes it appear to be. T.V. presents greater numbers of forceful men than women, and thus viewers form the assumption that being forceful and sometimes violent is manly, whereas calmness and kindness are weak, feminine qualities.

Aggressive behavior, disobedience, lack of trust: These are big prices to pay in return for the cheap thrills of violent T.V. shows.

Don't Ignore the Sexual Connection

Over and over, we establish with our children that television life isn't real life, but the message is not actually heard. Viewers in foreign countries think we live like the actors and actresses in sitcoms, and our own children think that sex is like what they see on T.V.

According to Victor Strasburger, Director of Adolescent Medicine at the University of New Mexico (as quoted in *Medical Tribune,* New York, 1988), the average adolescent hears and sees about 15,000 references to sexual intercourse on T.V. each year. Many of these references relate to casual sex between unmarried participants. Numerous acts are between teens, giving the impression that "everyone does it" and you aren't a part of modern life if you don't do it. Of the 15,000 references to sex, Strasburger says only 150 included any reference to birth control or abstinence.

Unless a parent watches the T.V. programs with a youngster, that parent may not be aware of the tendency to consider sex a casual part of every relationship. Here is where home training must take precedence. If you don't explain what you expect—or even what is nearer to reality—a child will just accept what T.V. teaches.

Where to Begin Your Control

A conversation with your child is a good start. Don't unilaterally make a plan and put it into action. You'll be far more successful if you work in a collaborative way. But remember, you *are* in control and you are the one responsible.

When your family initiates a new T.V.-viewing system, agree to give it a month-long trial, then meet again to discuss the results.

You can gain control in many different ways; some are gentler than others, but consider them all.

Cold Turkey

Selling the T.V. set and going without is one possibility. It has been done by many families without any dire consequences. Or, consider keeping the set and pledging not to turn it on. Some small towns and a few school districts have embarked on such stringent programs and have found profound changes in their young people (and often in the parents too): better grades, increased physical fitness, new skills. Later, when the T.V. viewing was restored, the families in these experiments continued to prefer other activities and watched much less television.

Short of selling the set, you can put a lock on it. There are various types of locks and switches for the cord and outlet that you can control. This is a good alternative for working parents who aren't home when children are likely to overdose on T.V.

These last-ditch means of control don't make much difference unless you fill the time now available with something better. So don't embark on such a program until you are ready with some attractive alternative activities.

Less Than Cold Turkey

Many families have found that the following methods make television viewing special and more beneficial, and free up time for other adventures.

- *Watching a "special."* Read the television guide and advance reviews when there is going to be an outstanding program, and announce it ahead of time. Put a note on the refrigerator door. You may want to let your child invite a friend, permit a later bedtime, darken the room, make popcorn.
- *Commercial talk.* During commercials, talk about the show so far, go over the plot or the objective of the show. Ask questions and answer questions.
- *Summary talks.* When the program is over, discuss what was learned. Did the show make its point? Was the plot interesting and plausible? Was it worth the time? Was it true to life?
- *The library connection.* If a program's topic is of special interest, find library books on the subject. Make them available before or after the show. Find other writings by the same author.
- *Bad news.* You can even learn from a poor show. Were the bad guys always of one race or nationality? Were women equally involved in the plot or only in subordinate roles? How were families pictured? Were drugs shown as glamorous? Were businessmen or blue-collar workers put down?
- *Suffering through sitcoms.* If there is a sitcom that is a must-see at your house, find some benefits. Are the characters portrayed realistically? Do they do wise or stupid things? How could the misunderstandings be avoided? Do they talk things over? Was there a moral to the story? Would we like to add some of the sitcom ideas to our family life? Since the word *sitcom* means situation comedy, was the situation truly funny?

Basic Rules

In keeping with your child's age and interests, actually write down some rules. Put them on the family bulletin board. For young children, go over the rules at least once a week.

1. No turning the set on without a plan of what to see.
2. No meal-time T.V. When the T.V. is on, family togetherness is off.
3. No T.V. during homework. Statistics show that homework done without T.V. is of a much higher quality.
4. No violent shows. See that your child's mind is filled with better things than gore. There are plenty of exciting adventure shows that are not filled with car chases, torture, rape, murder, and so on.
5. No cheating when parents aren't home. Make it very clear to sitters that you hold them responsible for seeing that kids don't watch junk T.V. or violent shows.
6. No school-night T.V. at all if any grade falls to an unacceptable level (such as a C-minus). This lasts for the quarter or semester, and if the grade is raised the next term, minimum T.V. will be reinstated.

When our children were in grade school, we kept tight control on what shows they watched. Certain worthless programs shown in the late afternoon were in the definitely "no" category. Two of the children always asked to play at a neighbor's in the late afternoon. It was a long time before I discovered that the forbidden T.V. show was permitted at the neighbor's house and our children were regularly viewing it there. Kids are clever!

Make Alternative Activities Attractive

You can't fight something with nothing. If you are going to wean your family from dependence on the tube, you have to offer some attractive alternatives. These have worked for other families:

● An after-supper sports activity—scrub baseball, shooting baskets, taking a walk, going for a swim. Some families enjoy aerobics together, especially with music or videos.
● An after-supper game (suitable to a child's age)—box games such

as Monopoly or Scrabble, old favorites like Chinese checkers and backgammon, card games such as Hearts and Pinochle.

And Then There Are Books

The smartest children are avid readers. Thirty minutes of reading can entertain and educate at four times the rate of T.V.

When it comes to quiet leisure activities, you want your family to think of reading first. To get your children started thinking this way, you'll have to set the example.

As a parent, initiate a time for reading. Encourage reading for fifteen minutes before even considering any television viewing. Keep plenty of books around the house—purchased as gifts and borrowed from the library. Don't let there be the excuse, "I have nothing good to read." Keep books in the car, take them into the dentist's office, over to grandma's. Don't waste any waiting time; read instead.

Make a deal: for every hour of T.V., thirty minutes of reading that same day. Make another deal: A cheerful child may read in bed for fifteen minutes after the "official" bedtime.

When you encourage reading in a variety of ways and places, it becomes a natural part of everyday life, and you won't have to enforce reading time.

What About Video Games?

Games can't be harmful, right? Wrong! A growing number of family psychologists and child development specialists are stepping forward to warn parents of the harm of video games. Many insist that video games shouldn't be categorized as toys.

When such games first came out, they seemed like a new variety of fun. When video game parlors sprang up in every community and kids began blowing their entire allowances in them, we should have gotten the message. Such games can be addictive and monopolize free time without any real benefit.

Now comes even worse news about many of these games. Not only are they addictive and obsessive, but also they are inherently frustrating and promote stress. Parents report that some video games trigger negative behaviors such as aggression, lying, tension, and sullenness. When a child loses, that child may react with frustration and even anger. Can it be considered "play" when a child cries, screams, or throws things?

Even if your child doesn't exhibit these overt signs, he may feel upset inside for not being able to get higher and higher scores or to win the contest. In an effort to achieve success, a child will play time and time again. One psychologist says that the need to score increasingly higher is akin to the chemically dependent person's obsession with "scoring" by using greater amounts of the addictive substance.

A game or toy should bring about a delight in learning and leave the participant feeling in control, happy, even relaxed. If video games are not having these effects on your child and you feel that they are increasing the child's anger and frustration, you may want to control the use of these games.

Of course, there are good video games, ones that don't have scoring or killing off the enemy as the main components. So when you buy a game, read the rules and strategy first.

Don't Let T.V. Rear Your Child for You

In many homes, family gatherings by the fireplace or around the dinner table have given way to pseudo-gatherings in front of the television set. A working parent has to work hard to be a greater influence on her child than the infamous box. Be sure that your own good ideas get a better showcase and more consideration than the ideas your child is accepting from T.V.

John Rosemond, a national columnist and family psychologist in North Carolina, says that watching television pacifies the growing child's intellect and imagination, and interferes significantly with the development of social, perceptual, motor, and language-communication skills. And it makes no difference what program is being watched. Children show significant gains in these developmental areas once television is removed or viewing time cut back. Parents should take heed!

Television encourages a child to be an observer, rather than a doer. It usurps the time a child could spend on more important things. Take charge and don't let this happen. Fill a child's free time with a variety of activities. You'll feel more successful as a parent, and your child will grow up happier and wiser.

The Couch Potato Test

One of the parents in our survey was quite outspoken on the subject of excessive T.V. viewing. She offered this quick quiz:

Do your children do homework in front of T.V.?
Do you eat with the T.V. on?
Have you committed to memory some of the commercials?
Are you depressed if you miss the end of a show—of an entire show?
Do you fail to hear family conversation because the T.V. talks louder?
Is the T.V. program-guide your favorite reading?
Does your entertaining include watching T.V.?
Do you watch a show but don't really know what it's about afterward?
When you think about relaxing, does T.V. viewing come first to your mind?

More than three "yes" answers indicates that you're a candidate for "Couch Potato" and you may want to rethink your free-time activities.

Parenting Point

There are only so many minutes in a day, so see that your child's time is balanced between T.V. and more important activities. A youngster's mind can absorb only so much; fill it with positive messages, rather than inane and violent ones that come from watching the wrong T.V. shows. Take charge of T.V.! Step by step, you can do it and have a brighter child.

Chalkboard for Chapter Fourteen

Try this T.V. test with your family to limit television viewing to quality shows. The chart below will help you.

Calculate the free time of each family member. First deduct from twenty-four (the hours in a day) the typical number of hours spent sleeping and in day-care or school or on the job. Then deduct two hours for eating and personal hygiene. Next deduct the time for homework and home chores. You will probably have left a number between two and four. That's the number of hours of unstructured time. Now keep a daily log of how much of that free time is spent in four categories:

Name: _____

Number of hours available for unstructured time: _____

	Mon.	Tue.	Wed.	Thur.	Fri.	Sat.	Sun.
T.V. hours:	___	___	___	___	___	___	___
Reading hours:	___	___	___	___	___	___	___
Outdoor fun hours:	___	___	___	___	___	___	___
Indoor fun hours:	___	___	___	___	___	___	___

Ideally, "free time" should be divided about equally between the categories, with T.V. hours, if anything, consuming the smaller amount of time. If this free time is out of balance, take steps to restore that balance.

Fifteen

Day-Care, School, and Your Smart Child

Baby Lowell is Judy and Lance's only child. They eagerly await each new development and each new achievement. Now that he's two, they're anxious about enrolling him in the best nursery school so that he can get into the best private grade school so that he can eventually get into the best college. Judy surrounds him with numbers and letters, and teaches him to put them in order. Lance buys him every educational toy on the market.

Right next door, Marci and Curt are raising three children: six, ten, and thirteen. Their daytime hours are so filled with their family business that they're trusting the public school to do a good job of educating the children. Son Johnny is having some problems with reading, but Marci says it's hard to make contact with his English teacher. Curt thinks the problem will solve itself in time.

Marci and Curt think that Judy and Lance are silly and overindulgent parents. Judy and Lance think Marci and Curt are lazy and negligent parents.

Who's right? Who's wrong? Sometimes there are fine lines between ignoring a child's educational needs and letting him learn at his own pace, or encouraging him to learn and overencouraging him.

At the same time, every parent must recognize that day-care providers and school teachers are usually the most important nonfamily influence on a child. What they teach, how they teach, and how they interact with your child can change the course of your child's life. The learning activities that take place in day-care and school take up the major portion of a child's day. They can either build excitement about learning or create apathy toward knowledge. With the help of modern technology in the schools, a child can enter the mainstream of today's fast-paced life or be left sadly behind. Today, more than ever before, parents need to be very much in touch with a child's educational environment. And that is sometimes difficult for a working parent.

Parental involvement at school along with encouraging learning at home can make the difference between a dull child, an average child, and a brilliant one. Parents need to know the right degree of concern, the right time to express this interest, and how to go about it.

Usually, a parent works at the job during the same hours school is in session, and this makes it extremely hard for a parent to keep in touch with a child's classes and teacher. It isn't like the old days when parents helped at school in the library, on special projects, or as room mothers. Sitting in on a child's class is no longer a commonplace parental activity. So today's working parent needs to be aware of today's means and methods for keeping in touch.

The 1988 edition of the Statistical Abstract of the United States shows that more than five million children under age five have mothers who work full-time. The children in our own survey were in day-care an average of *thirty* hours a week or in school and after-school activities an average of *forty-four* hours. How can a working parent see that a child makes the most of these hours?

This chapter will consider eight main areas of concern:

1. Selection of a day-care facility or school
2. Child-care in the work place

3. What to expect of your grade school and high school
4. Keeping in touch with a child's progress at school
5. Homework support, grades, and rewards
6. Challenging the gifted child
7. Looking ahead to college years
8. Day-care versus home-care

1. Selection of a Day-Care Facility or School

Sometimes there is no choice. A parent knows of only one day-care facility that is convenient and fits the budget. Or, the neighborhood school is the only option. In these cases, other methods of educational enrichment become even more necessary. (See chapters 13, 16, and 17 for additional information on this topic.) But, if there is a choice, certain important aspects should be considered when selecting the day-care facility or school.

Choosing a Day-Care Facility for a Baby

Babies do best in a facility that allows the smallest number of babies to each adult. Babies are learning how to attract attention, how to get needs satisfied, how to react to a variety of outside stimuli. Loving, individual, and consistent care is essential.

Depending on size, staff, and where you live, day-care facilities may or may not be regulated by law. Although I would strongly urge you to consider only those facilities that are licensed, don't depend on the law to make the place just right for your child. Go and carefully investigate for yourself. Except for considering cost, vacancies, location, and hours, here is a checklist that will help you:

1. Is there sufficient staff to give personal care?
2. Does that staff seem calm, interested, and loving?
3. Are the cribs and bedding clean and is the entire facility well maintained?
4. Are the diaper-changing tables sanitary? Does the room have a pleasant odor?
5. Is the kitchen clean and orderly and are the menus nutritious?
6. Is the play area clean, safe, and stocked with toys in good condition?

7. What are the activities offered? (Playpen play, music, swings, strollers for walks, floor mats, rockers for book time, and so forth.)
8. Are parents welcome to drop in unannounced?
9. Has there ever been a formal complaint filed against the facility or against an employee? (Yes, you have every right to ask this question.)
10. Is there a posted fire-and-other-emergency plan?
11. Is there a staff person with first-aid training?
12. Is staff turn-over too frequent to allow for quality care?

When you visit the facility, do not hesitate to inspect all the rooms and the yard. Ascertain whether the babies are cared for in a rushed or off-hand manner. Try to determine if this is the place you want your baby to spend her first important weeks and months.

Choosing a Day-Care Facility for a Preschooler

Caring for toddlers is quite different from caring for babies. They need the same loving and firm care, but they need a much larger place to play as they learn some of the basics of living.

Toddlers do not need schooling in the academic sense. Their education should cover learning to play and eat with a group, following directions, taking turns and sharing, learning to handle success and failure, obeying authority. Activities should encourage creativity and cooperation, joy and curiosity. Some activities could prepare toddlers for school, but in a very low-key way.

Schoolteachers say that preschools are best when they avoid teaching specific subjects and instead teach attitudes that encourage learning. The teachers appreciate children who have been taught to listen, who aren't afraid to ask questions, who have a lengthening attention span, and who can sit still for a period of time. They also want children to respect the property and rights of other children and the school materials.

Preschoolers should understand the basic vocabulary used in interacting with others. These words are: *yes, no, maybe, please, thank you, now, later, today, tomorrow, come, stay, sit, help, ask, tell, share, give, follow, quiet, pick up, left, right, hello, good-bye, red, yellow, blue, green.* If all children understood the meaning of these thirty words, the school room would be a happier, more efficient learning place!

Preschools have essential resting or nap times, and parents can help teachers with this part of the day by having the child observe a similar quiet time on weekends. Tell a child that she doesn't have to sleep, she only has to pretend to sleep. (Most pretenders fall asleep.)

Learning motor skills, practicing eye-hand coordination, and recognizing similar objects, are more essential for toddlers than attempts to learn to read. The joy of simple accomplishments, patience when things seem difficult, and a sense of success and self-esteem are more important than academic achievements.

Avoid the school that is pushing a child out of his playtime years. Learning in-advance-of-need often brings on academic burn-out later—and it also means that time has not been spent teaching the basic skills of coordination and socialization.

Before deciding on the school, be sure to ask how children are treated when they misbehave. Although children can live with various methods of discipline (isolation, deprivation), the different methods should not conflict. They should all respect the child's dignity and intelligence.

Some care-givers may not have sufficient child development training to handle discipline effectively. Unfortunately, people who work in day-care are among the poorest paid in the United States. Whereas a plumber must be certified, licensed, and registered, a child-care worker who is not breaks no law. What does this tell us about our reverence for children?

In considering a preschool, look for these assets (in addition to those listed for infant care above):

1. Small groups (four to seven children are ideal)
2. Two or more children the same age as yours
3. Clean bathroom and kitchen facilities
4. Nutritionally balanced foods, including snacks. Sweets only on special occasions and not used as rewards
5. No television viewing
6. Many good books and frequent story times
7. Outside play equipment keyed to this age group and in safe condition
8. Inside equipment for both active and quiet play
9. A teaching philosophy that has both a curriculum and opportunities for choice
10. Teachers who know the various stages of development for two-, three-, and four-year-olds

11. Teachers who teach at a child's eye level, instead of talking and supervising "from above"
12. Teaching social skills: bathroom etiquette, simple table manners, taking turns, saying please and thank you, alternatives to hitting and biting, tying shoes, fastening buttons and snaps, and so forth
13. Teaching basic educational skills: colors, some numbers and letters, writing one's name, knowing one's name and address, safety rules, using scissors, paste, and crayons, and so forth
14. No pressure to learn to read or compute, but rather emphasis on learning to think and express ideas clearly
15. An atmosphere that is happy and encourages a positive attitude and a spirit of adventure

Ask for the names of other parents and call them for comments and a recommendation.

Avoid premature education! Raising a smart child doesn't mean that you push him into learning modes at an early age. Research shows that the vast majority of children who learn to read at age three are not gifted children. They are usually children who learn to mimic quickly and have well-developed memories. By age seven, other children have caught up and the early achievers are no longer "ahead." However, by spending so much of their precious babyhood time on advanced academics, these children will probably have missed out on learning important interpersonal skills.

In his book *Miseducation: Preschoolers at Risk* (Alfred A. Knopf, 1988), author David Elkind of Tufts University lists many problems of premature education. He describes "superkid" as a precocious child who boosts parental ego and entertains guests. Such a child learns how to please others, but not herself. All reliable evidence shows that early education is short-lived and that long-term risks to the "superkid" are profound.

So when a parent or school disrupts a child's natural development it can backfire. Premature learners often have *more* learning problems in the upper grades. They often suffer from classic stress symptoms (headaches, stomachaches, and depression). They have neuroses and emotional disabilities, which stem from the conflict to please parents by learning, as opposed to enjoying learning for themselves and enjoying playtime with their friends. And, as a final blow, they often resent having been "used" by their parents.

Preschoolers learn best by imitation rather than by formal instruction. (This means seeing a skill performed by a teacher or peer instead of being told about it.) So, when they are instructed in academics too early in life, they become overly dependent on adult guidance and approval, and they are less apt to take initiative and risks when they're older.

When young children are asked to master skills before they are emotionally and physically ready, they develop a fear of failure and sometimes a sense of helplessness. A child given lessons in music, before his little hands coordinate with his eyes and brain, is more apt to want to drop the study. A child pushed into sports too early can do physical damage to his body because it has not developed sufficiently to withstand the strain—not to mention how his ego and confidence suffer when he can't "make the grade."

Childhood is brief. Let a preschooler enjoy these years to the fullest. Don't push. Let a child be a child.

2. Child-Care in the Work Place

At last the work place is becoming more attuned to parents with children. Some office situations permit parents to bring infants to work and have them right near their work station. However, when babies begin to be more active, they usually become a distraction to the parent and coworkers.

As common as working mothers have become, a recent survey showed that about 60 percent of women employees with children under twelve have great difficulty in finding suitable child-care.

Today, more and more large businesses are subsidizing child-care on-site or nearby. This permits parents to be with their children during commuting time, breaks, and lunch. This added time with a young child makes a big difference in parent-child bonding and provides extra time for casual talk and memory-building. Parenting is no longer postponed to a few evening hours or the weekend.

How well does it work when a business plays nanny? Companies with child-care facilities report that there is less turn-over among employees, less time off for child-care, fewer productivity slumps, and less absenteeism and tardiness. With such a good report card, on-site child-care should be more prevalent.

Although only about 10 percent of businesses with a hundred or more workers now provide child-care, the number is rising. Many employers are finding that they can hardly afford *not* to provide this benefit as we approach the mid-1990s, when two-thirds of all new employees will be women.

Paying attention to family life is one of the best lures a company has. Some programs are as simple as providing a room for an in-house nursery, others provide van service to nearby child-care. One Illinois company provides a summer day camp and another even has a special room at the work site where mildly ill children can be cared for by a nurse and checked on by the parent. Some corporate child-care centers operate around the clock to accommodate parents on late or night shifts.

Flex-time, part-time, and share-time jobs are also increasing in popularity. Many families don't need two paychecks; one and a half will do. If this could be an option for you, ask about it. You will never know if it's possible to share a job or work part-time unless you ask. The cost of training new employees has risen so high that many businesses will be accommodating in the effort to keep good employees.

Family leave may soon be law, requiring companies to grant parents up to eighteen weeks of unpaid leave to care for a newborn or a seriously ill child. Ideally, it would be grand if a parent could take several years of unpaid leave to be with a child until at least age five. These early-learning years are the most important for a parent and child to be together.

3. What to Expect of Your Grade School and High School

Whether you choose public or private schools will depend on your own circumstances and your child's needs. A good grade school has these assets:

1. A class size of no more than twenty-five
2. A pleasant but serious atmosphere for learning, free from disruptions owing to disobedience and crime
3. A stable and eager teaching staff composed of new and experienced teachers of both sexes
4. A school administration dedicated to teaching, not merely to maintaining order and keeping kids amused

5. Prime emphasis on the basics of reading, writing, and arithmetic, with special classes for reading encouragement. A child who can read can do anything!

6. Good equipment in sufficient quantity: computers, typewriters, library books, musical instruments, scientific supplies

7. Classes that introduce basic computer skills

8. Teaching the fundamentals of a second language by second grade

9. A rigorous physical education program with both indoor and outdoor facilities

10. Education concerning drugs and sex, taught and retaught in a way appropriate to each grade

11. Classes in art, drama, and music. A school band or orchestra with instruments available for all interested children

12. A *minimum* offering of light-weight courses (Basket weaving, tree planting, and Lapland culture should be part of an elective program only in the seventh and eighth grades after the more important basics are instilled.)

13. Participation in opportunities for learning beyond the school itself, such as spelling bees, speech tournaments, educational decathlons, statewide essay contests, science fairs

In addition to the above, a good high school includes:

1. Counseling for college and career, starting in the tenth grade

2. A closed campus (no coming and going during the day)

3. An extensive library and classes that encourage the use of it

4. Emphasis on extracurricular activities that tie in with academics: a science club, drama club, debate club

5. A varied athletic program for *all* students as well as competitive team play for students who maintain a minimum grade average of C

6. A strong administration that insists on a teaching plan from each teacher, emphasis on student excellence in reading and research, and a proper balance of school activities that reward knowledge and hard work

If you find that your school is lacking in certain areas, work to improve the situation—either through the school or by providing enrichment at home. Talk with parents of students who have been through the school to determine any weaknesses they may have noticed. Then, talk with teachers and administrators. One parent in our survey told of getting a choral music program instituted this way.

You are paying to have your child educated in a basic knowledge of many things and a mastery of some—whether through private tuition or public taxation. See that you get your money's worth.

4. Keeping in Touch with a Child's Progress at School

When the day is already filled to the brim, you may not feel excited about a visit with your child's teacher, but this contact is one of your chief ways of knowing whether or not your child is getting a quality education.

You may have to leave work early once a semester in order to attend a conference with your child's teacher, but it's worth it. Both academics and behavior will be discussed. Listen very carefully, ask questions, and find out what you can do at home to supplement the teacher's work.

This school visit used to be standard, but with working parents on the increase, some schools now provide alternative ways of keeping in touch. A few times each year, there may be evening meetings that let you see your child in action. At these you have the opportunity to meet many other parents and exchange ideas. You will also meet your child's school friends, and this can be quite an eye-opener, especially during the junior high and high school years.

To get specific questions answered, try a phone call to the school at the close of the regular school day. Or, you can send a note and ask that your child bring the answer home.

Some working parents ask a teacher to join the family for supper or a weekend lunch. Some teachers enjoy this social touch; others detest it as an intrusion on their free time. But just the same, ask.

One parent writes a note to the teacher at the beginning of the school year, describing the child's interests, and his strong and weak points. The face-to-face meeting with the teacher, however, remains the best. Parents should take turns going to these review meetings. It is here you really find out how well your child is learning, things that are going well, and any problem areas—and what you can do to help.

School officials say that these conferences are extremely valuable to a child's learning, and a parent should be prepared to ask some questions:

1. Is my child working up to the proper ability level?
2. What are her strengths? weaknesses?
3. What does the teacher take into account in grading?
4. Is the homework completed in a satisfactory manner?
5. Is the child self-disciplined, responsible, cooperative?
6. How does the child take suggestions and criticism?
7. Are social skills and self-confidence developing?
8. What can I do as a working parent to support the school?

Talking with your child each day about school is a good way to gauge his enthusiasm—or apathy—toward the varied events of his day. Be attuned to repeated remarks and complaints ("I hate geography." "I'm always chosen last for gym teams." "We had a great time in Mr. Bailey's class when he fell asleep at his desk.") and take action. These are signs of a growing problem—easier to correct sooner than later.

Be alert to the testing programs at school. Many of them are more important to the school system (better grades mean more state and Federal money) than to the child. But many tests also identify weaknesses, assess progress from year to year, and give some indication of teacher performance.

Ask your child's teacher when standardized tests are scheduled and talk about them with your child. Find out if only correct answers are counted and if there is no penalty for incorrect responses, thus making it a good idea to guess at answers when unsure. Encourage your child to ask the teacher to clarify instructions.

Since the areas covered on such tests are broad, there usually isn't a way to study beforehand, so it's best to encourage a child to relax and forget about the test. But do be sure your child gets a good night's sleep and eats a nutritious breakfast before that child takes such a test.

When test scores are known, give the child feedback. Be encouraging about areas that need improvement and matter-of-fact about weaknesses. And of course, give lots of praise for the effort.

Start a private notebook about your child. Write in it the facts you glean from conversations about school. In this way, you may note a repeated complaint, a trend concerning a particular subject, an especially liked activity. Only by keeping the notebook over the school year will you recognize certain subtle calls for help.

Don't let a day pass without talk about school. Appreciate the triumphs and be consoling about the miseries.

Use the refrigerator door or a bulletin board to display good work. Put special papers into the family's yearly scrapbook. Let a child call a relative and share good news about his school achievements.

5. Homework Support, Grades, and Rewards

No, you can't do your child's homework for her. Certainly, you would do a good job and get a good grade, but that's not the point. Homework is the proof of what a *child* has learned and can put into practice. It is the means of cementing new facts into thought. So, difficult though it may be, you have to let your child do it.

How *can* you best contribute to her good homework then? No matter what the age of your youngster, use the PACT System. This four-part system is one that many parents have put into use with success. Put a sign that says PACT on the wall near the place your child does homework. This will remind her that you have a pact with her to help her be smart, to succeed, to learn what's necessary for a happy career and life ahead.

PACT stands for four words: *P*lace, *A*sking, *C*hecking, *T*alking.

1. Place

Sorry, but research shows that homework done on a bed or with the T.V. on, isn't as thorough or meaningful as homework done in an educational environment. As a parent, you must create this environment for serious work.

In general, homework is best done in the same place each day. A teen may work at a desk in her room, but younger children work best at a table in the kitchen or family room where a parent is nearby. This place should have a large smooth working surface, good light, and few distractions. Radio music without lyrics is fine. (It can be a subtle introduction to classical works.)

The homework area can be shared by all youngsters in the family; in fact, it's good practice for kids to work quietly in the presence of siblings. An older child helping a younger one fosters appreciation and caring. Being able to concentrate on your work in the same place with others prepares a youngster for research in a busy library and also for studying in a small dorm room with a college roommate.

Gather the supplies needed and keep them in a drawer, on a shelf, or in a box nearby. These supplies should include: pencils with erasers, a sharpener, pens, clips, a stapler, lined and unlined paper, and an up-to-date dictionary. Buying a new dictionary every three to four years is a good investment. When children start grade school you'll want to consider the purchase of an encyclopedia, one that is supplemented annually with updated volumes so that it is useable through all the school years.

The trend in the past decade to give minimal homework until junior high school has proved to be a mistake. Children under that system have been overwhelmed by lack of organization and need for routine skills normally taught at an earlier age. Research now shows that children who are given homework early in the grade-school years do better homework throughout school.

Educational consultants recommend that the amount of time children study on weekdays should be no less than ten minutes times their grade level. (Thus a first-grader would study ten minutes a day and a twelfth-grader at least two hours a day. Even if they don't have homework, this is reading and quiet time.) It is unfortunate that today's average high school student spends more hours each night on television than on homework. It is a parent's responsibility to change this imbalance.

2. Asking

It may sound boring, but there is a question you have to ask every school day if you want a smart student. The question is this: "What is your homework today?"

The question serves several purposes. First, it shows a youngster that you care about his education. Second, it can be a subtle reminder to the child that he *does* have homework to do. (No parent or teacher wants to hear that "I forgot" line.) And third, it keeps you up-to-date on what he's currently learning. This last point is necessary since it gives you topics for discussion.

There are other important questions to ask: "How did your report go?" "Did you have the test today?" "Is your math getting any easier?" "What is the plan for the field trip?" "How did the game go?" "Did the new band music come?" "Have you been given a long-range assignment?"

A long-range assignment is one that is due in a week or a month. The tendency can be to forget about it until the last minute or to forget about it entirely. A book report, a scale model, a research paper: For quality work, these just can't be created in one short evening.

For such projects, use my forty-eight-hour rule. On the family calendar show that the assignment must be finished at least forty-eight hours in advance of the date it is due. Another notation a day or two before that will remind the student to get going and finish the project. Also, if it is "due" to you forty-eight hours in advance, you have the opportunity to look at the project and suggest improvements, instead of making last-minute suggestions at breakfast on the due-date.

3. Checking

Editing and correcting a child's homework doesn't help him truly see the mistakes. If you merely correct mistakes, they will probably be repeated. Your job is to make a general suggestion or indicate that there is an error. The child does the correcting work.

For example, in a composition you can say, "The adjectives are trite; try for more colorful words." On a page of math problems, you can say, "Number six is wrong; try again." For a misspelled word, you can give a hint how the word begins and then let a child look it up in the dictionary. Certainly, this method takes more time than just correcting the work yourself, but in the long run it makes for a smarter student.

When a child must do a large project or long composition, discuss it while driving in the car or at supper. Let the whole family share ideas and suggest topics to cover. If the student makes a list of these ideas, she has a place to start her work.

Encourage a student to do homework in this order: math and computer work, nonfiction reading, science projects, fiction reading. For the majority of students, this will put the most exacting homework first while they're most fresh and eager. The tendency is to do the easy things first, but it is far better to tackle the hard jobs and save the easier ones for a reward. Check on your student during the homework time. A snack or a ten-minute walk at the midpoint may be a needed refresher.

When there is a volume of homework to do, it helps to have a child set smaller goals and see how accurate he is at estimating the time required. Instead of thinking of ninety minutes of homework, consider it three projects: thirty minutes of math, forty-five minutes of geography reading and map drawing, fifteen minutes of reading for a later book report. This method makes the homework seem less overwhelming. When a child has a lot of homework, talk about which assignments are easy and which are difficult. Then help him write a schedule to get the work completed.

4. Talking

One of the best educators is conversation. Choose an academic subject you'd like to share with your child. Perhaps it's a topic you already know something about. Or perhaps it's one you've recently read about in a newspaper, a magazine, book, or encyclopedia. Or you may talk about your job and the economy, a childhood trip, how to get a business started, or your favorite author. Let the talking go both ways. Your child may talk about computers, racism at school, heroes, or soccer rules. And at appropriate times you'll talk about drugs, sex, dating, owning a car, leaving home, and marriage.

In talking with your child each day, don't forget to be appreciative of what she has already learned, and of what she is striving to achieve. In many different ways show that you have a great respect for knowledge. You do this by sitting down and talking together, establishing eye contact, actually taking time to look at work in progress or completed work, and never making fun of her ideas.

You also show your respect for knowledge by your own example. Continue your own learning through self-education and by taking adult courses. Research shows that the reading habits of parents are passed on to their children. Having good literature in the home and setting a time to read it is one of the best educational methods.

Should You Pay for Grades?

For some decades, paying for term-end grades was frowned upon. Then the argument was raised that one gets paid for a job so why not pay for schoolwork, which is really a child's primary job. For many kids this system works quite well, especially if the "pay" is sufficient.

Set up a decreasing sliding scale for grades from A through C (not C minus). Also set a fee for a grade raised, and a deduction for a grade that falls. Make small bonuses for good character ratings if the report card lists these. In private with each child, go over the entire report card, discussing both the good and the not-so-good grades. Have cash on hand for immediate payment. If you have set your pay scale high, you may want to agree with your child in advance that a certain percent goes into savings, the remainder being his to spend in any way he chooses.

Do this for each middle-of-term and end-of-term grading period for a year, then discuss the system with your child to see if you both feel that it has encouraged better grades.

6. Challenging the Gifted Child

Poor grades, boredom with school, an apathetic attitude: These may be signs of a child in need of academic tutoring. But they are also signs of a bright child who is not being sufficiently challenged. Although some gifted children shine so brightly it is easy to identify them, others may keep their light hidden.

A generation or two ago, the answer to educating a gifted child was double promotion. This often resulted in a child who was socially and physically out-of-step with her classmates. Today we have become wiser and recognize the need for children to socialize and work with their peers. Enrichment programs for grade-schoolers and advanced placement classes for high school students provide educational challenges for bright children while letting them enjoy social and sports activities in keeping with their age.

A most important role for parents is the identification and nurturing of a gifted preschool child. Here it is not a question of "superbaby" but one of perceiving the child's needs for activities and materials that can support development of talents without pressure, tension, or fear.

According to the book *Your Gifted Child* (Joan Smutny, Kathleen Veenker, and Stephen Veenker, New York: Facts on File, 1989), these are qualities and characteristics of gifted young children:

1. Expresses curiosity about many things
2. Is observant and asks thoughtful questions
3. Has extensive vocabulary, uses complex sentences
4. Expresses himself or herself well
5. Solves problems in unique ways
6. Has a good memory
7. Exhibits unusual talent in art, music, creative drama
8. Has an especially original imagination
9. Is able to order things in a logical sequence

10. Discusses and elaborates on ideas
11. Learns quickly and puts previously learned things in new contexts
12. Takes initiative and works independently
13. Exhibits wit and humor
14. Has persistence in working on challenging tasks
15. Has a sustained attention span
16. Can make up stories and tell them
17. Enjoys reading

In most cases, although it is the school that identifies and educates the gifted child, the home does have an equally important part. Being a parent of a very intelligent child requires special effort, but the most important gift for such a child is the parent's time. Although the parent may not be able to challenge the child academically, there are extremely valuable lessons for the parent to teach at home:

- Creativity
- Effective time management
- Decision making
- Responsibility
- Social skills
- Goal setting
- Accepting both failure and success
- Distinguishing between worthwhile and worthless activities

This list alone is a sufficient challenge for a parent without getting into the academics.

To stimulate a gifted child, begin by providing an environment that appreciates knowledge and promotes reading. Books will have many of the answers that you don't have, so make the library your second home. And since you may be wholly nonconversant with your child's special interests, teach him how to find the answers. Research skills are essential to the gifted child. Make up your mind to ignore a gifted child's work area, which may be creatively untidy.

Encourage your child to tell and write stories. Provide toys that can be taken apart and put back together. Provide time for lots of hands-on activities and experiments. See that you satisfy a child's need to know "how things work." Take your child to a variety of cultural places—ones that tie in to her interest and ones that may develop a new interest. Above all, love your gifted child. And love your average child just as much.

A wealth of information on books, seminars, creative summer programs, and hints on raising a gifted child is available free from Joan Franklin Smutny, Director of the Center for Gifted, National College of Education, Evanston, IL 60201.

7. Looking Ahead to College Years

The years go fast—and suddenly, your child is off to college. Will you have shared all the information you feel she should have before setting out on her own? Once a child is off for college and career there are never the same opportunities for learning together.

Today a college education is more valuable than ever. According to the Bureau of the Census, the number of years it takes to recoup four years of tuition (and lost earnings while attending college) is now just eleven years, and it's getting shorter. So, you want to encourage your smart child to get all the education he can.

Sometimes a year off before or during college is useful as a maturing time, but, in general, encourage your child to hang in there and finish. Of course, going back later in life for a degree is a possibility, but most often those good intentions are never realized.

Starting in junior high school, work with your youngster and her school counselors to plan a program that will prepare her for several likely colleges. Academic requirements differ from school to school and from major to major, so it's good to check entrance requirements a few years in advance.

8. Day-Care Versus Home-Care

The results of research are just beginning to come in on children and day-care. Jay Belsky, a Pennsylvania State University psychologist, has been studying this subject and cites a 1984 study showing that infants and toddlers in day-care for twenty or more hours a week have increased insecurity and "weak and insecure bonds."

A 1985 study from the University of North Carolina found that five-year-olds who spent a lot of time in day-care were more anxious, aggressive, and hyperactive than their parent-raised counterparts.

Another study found that children who began day-care before reaching eighteen months of age were more likely to cry and misbehave at ages nine and ten.

There are also studies, however, that show that children who spend entire days in day-care are more outgoing and trusting. Tiffany Field, a professor of pediatrics and psychology at the University of Miami's Mailman Center for Child Development, says of the Belsky report, "I think it's bunkum," and that Mr. Belsky and his allies are either relying on bad research or misreading good research.

Nationally known psychologist Lee Salk says that women must insist on better child-care centers to avert a generation of children with problems (and parents with guilt). He feels that present day-care facilities actually harm children and that they won't improve until parents demand quality care. He would like to see the highest standards and credentials for the professionals who would care for children during their first years.

Speaking of bonding, Dr. T. Berry Brazelton, pediatrician, lecturer, and author, says we must protect that postnatal period in which the attachment process between parents and baby is solidified and stabilized. He would like a new mother to feel free from the demands of the work place for at least the first four months. The younger the child, the more critical the environment is for the future of emotional and cognitive development.

A parent should remember that in addition to meeting her own needs, a child has needs that must also be met. What a child learns through being close to a loving, caring, responsive, and nurturing parent cannot be replaced by anyone else. A parent must be aware of this when he is turning over the job of parenting to other people.

Many youngsters come home to empty houses and minimal contact with parents in the evening. Weekends are spent in which family members each pursue their own activities. So if a parent is not "there" when a young child needs him, the teenager may protest to his parents: "Why should I listen to you now?" How to fill this gap is the question that every working parent must answer.

Since many parents have no choice about whether or not to use day-care, they need to be very observant of their child's behavior and do as much as possible at home to compensate for any inadequacies.

Children vary and day-care situations vary. Many working parents are so aware of their time away from their youngsters that they double their parenting efforts when they are with their children. They become far better nurturers than they might have been had they had the opportunity for more at-home time.

When both parents work, a vacuum is created by the lack of time they have to transmit ethical values, social skills, and responsibilities to their kids. The vacuum has to be filled—but how? Unless parents reclaim their rights, the Federal or state government or the public school system will be taking over that job.

Perhaps we need a new work environment that discourages the headlong rush toward workaholism—a work environment that values the family. We need to start questioning our need for so many *things*. Is working so very hard and being away from a child so much really worth it?

There needs to be a better balance between home life and career. Couples who choose to have children need to accept the commitment to raise those children. This means long hours and hard work if both jobs are to be done well. In some cases it may mean a five-year sabbatical for one parent and less-affluent living for the family during those years. However you choose to work it out at your house, your child should come first.

Parenting Point

Love, self-esteem, knowledge: These are the best gifts you can give your child. Help your youngster become well educated by showing that you value learning. Step by step you can do it, if you find the proper balance in your dual job as both a career person and a parent.

Chalkboard for Chapter Fifteen

Select an area in which your child needs academic support. Try the contract method using this form as a guide:

THE CONTRACT

Hereby let it be recognized that _____ known hereafter as the Student, and _____ known hereafter as the Parent, have willingly entered into the following contractual agreement.

The Student agrees to achieve the following:

_____

In return, the Parent agrees to grant the following to the Student:

_____

The length of time to complete this contract is from _____(date) to _____(date).

The terms of this agreement include no reminding or shouting by the Parent, and no cheating or grumbling by the Student.

Signed this _____ day of _____ (month), 19___.

_____ (the Student)

_____ (the Parent)

Sixteen

Extracurricular Stuff and Your Happy Child

Monica wanted all the best things of life for her preteen daughter, Julie. Being the single parent of an only child made Monica feel the need to be not just a good mother but also a father and a playmate. Since the neighborhood where they lived was a safe one, Julie enjoyed coming home most afternoons after school. She'd have a snack and then go outside to ride her bike and play with a friend until the five o'clock deadline to start homework. But when Monica's salary increased, the after-school plan changed. She wanted Julie to have every social and educational advantage, so she happily worked out this extracurricular schedule: Monday—ballet, Tuesday—Scouts, Wednesday—piano lessons, Thursday—a computer class, Friday—horseback riding lessons, Saturday—soccer. Just thinking about all these things Julie was doing gave Monica a satisfied feeling! Then late one Friday afternoon when she picked up

Julie at the stable she got a surprise. Julie said, "I want to quit riding and ballet and maybe piano, too." Monica protested, "But Baby, I only want the best for you!"

Just what is "best" in the way of extracurricular activities? What helps make a smart and well-rounded child? Certainly, clubs and other after-school activities contribute to a youngster's know-how and make him more knowledgeable in areas different from school-day academics. And to Monica the whole smorgasbord of activities seemed best.

Striking the right balance between structured and unstructured after-school time is a parent's job, but it should include regular consultation with the child. Even teens can succumb to peer pressure and overextend themselves. A parent knows his child much better than teachers, coaches, and club and group leaders, whose job it is to encourage participation. But a parent should also know that every youngster needs some free time. Thus, the parent must guide a child in picking and choosing from that rainbow of activities offered young people these days.

Each autumn when school starts, clubs and other activities start organizing too. Most are worthwhile, but a child can't do them *all* in one year, so you have to help her make good selections. What isn't done this year can be tried next year. The family budget comes into it, too. Sports equipment, uniforms, instruments, dancing costumes, dues, and special excursions: They all add up, so you want to be sure your child gets real value in return for what you must pay.

Commitment is a major element. An extracurricular activity requires the commitment of both parent and child. Be sure to consider this before you sign up. Is the parent committed to being supportive and arranging the way his child will get to the activity and home afterward? Is the parent willing to give the time to attend games or recitals? Will the parent begrudge the extra money needed?

And what about the child's commitment? Is she willing to stick with the activity for the school year or at least a semester? Sometimes the benefits aren't immediately apparent, so it's important to establish the idea of giving an activity a fair try—a minimum of three to four months—and then deciding whether or not to continue. A team may seem very exciting when the uniforms come, but rather boring or frustrating a few months later. A club may take some time to get organized before the friendships and events become really worthwhile. A child who wants immediate success might want to join and quit, join and quit, rather than give an activity a real chance.

Popular Activities

The parents in our survey shared with us those activities their children found most enjoyable and educational. The top ten were:

1. Soccer and baseball teams
2. Gymnastics classes
3. Groups such as Scouts, Camp Fire, Indian Guides
4. Music lessons: drums and brass instruments
5. Dancing lessons: ballet and tap
6. Music lessons: piano, guitar, violin
7. Craft and art classes
8. Science and rocketry clubs
9. Horseback riding lessons
10. Reading classes

High on the list also were ski lessons, magic clubs, cooking and sewing classes, swimming lessons, foreign language groups, and computer clubs.

Don't overlook the unusual. One child begged for harp lessons, which the parents thought an absurd idea. After giving in and renting a harp, they found that the music was delightful and their daughter was very talented. Another youngster didn't want music lessons but instead wanted mountain climbing lessons. This eventually led him to a useful and satisfying career in the outdoors.

Parents willing to pay for lessons should also be willing to subsidize a child's special interest class or group. Once, our youngest son pointed out the cost of his sister's piano lessons and asked if he couldn't have a lesser sum to pay for the fuel he needed for his rocketry group. This reminded us that talents come in all varieties, not just musical, so we agreed to underwrite his scientific interest. The same should be true of sewing materials, books on magic, computer disks, brushes and canvas, and so forth.

As you become supportive of an assortment of childhood interests, you'll quickly find that some of these time-takers are also big money-takers.

Extracurricular Means Extra Costs

Weighing the cost of joining an activity is part of a child's maturing process. Start young to teach children how to spend money carefully. Being money-smart is an advantage all through life.

Work together to make a very specific list of all the expenses involved in a chosen activity. Sometimes costs seem small on a weekly basis, but large when added up for the year. So talk about it: Is this the best way to spend the money? Will there be enough new things learned, unused skills exercised, and friends made to make it worthwhile? Is your youngster really eager to take part?

Many youngsters who want to be in a group can earn all or part of the cost of joining, and older grade-schoolers and high school kids should be encouraged to contribute what they can. For some large fees, you may want to go fifty-fifty with your child. When everything in a child's life is a gift, the gift may not be appreciated as much as when a child is using hard-earned money for the project.

Many kids spend savings or summer earnings for their extracurricular activities. Keep a list of jobs that you're willing to pay for. See chapter 18, "S t r e t c h i n g Your Time," for more ideas. Help your child also to consider these business opportunities for young people: pet care for travelers, dried flower arranging, babysitting, rubbish hauling, car washing, lawn cutting and weeding, minor repair service, cupboard cleaning, party help, errands and marketing for senior citizens, gift wrapping. A smart child *can* earn money and in so doing he learns and becomes even smarter.

Just How Many Activities?

Participation in organized activities every afternoon is actually harmful for a child. Of course, there are exceptions when sports team practices take priority, but a life of solid routine and structure can be boring and constrictive. Everyday organized activities leave no time to unwind from school, no choices on what to do with free time, and no time for spontaneous creative thinking or play.

First, consider what your child would be doing if not in an organized after-school activity. If after school she's cared for at home or responsible enough to be at home alone, choose only about two activities. This is especially true if you live in a neighborhood where children can play safely. This will give a balance between structured and unstructured play. If you live in an unsafe neighborhood and your child must remain indoors five afternoons a week, you may want to increase the extracurricular activities to three.

Perhaps your youngster stays in day-care every afternoon. This is most usually unstructured play, so an organized activity once or twice weekly would be a good change of pace.

Boys' and girls' clubs offer a safe place for after-school games (unstructured time) and some organized activities (structured time). Some of these groups act merely as caretakers and the time spent there can be wasted. Other clubs offer a true home away from home with a good variety of options. Before signing up, a parent and child should go several times to observe the activities.

Another possibility is after-school tutoring or reading clubs. Although these may sound dull, they do augment a child's education, especially when the material is presented in an interesting and attractive way. And if they help a child surmount a learning difficulty they can be extremely worthwhile. Be sure to sit in on a lesson before deciding if this would be beneficial and stimulating. Because these can be so similar to school, a contrasting organized activity may be needed on another day: something that is physical, something that is completely fun.

Two or three organized activities a week are sufficient, leaving time for a child to engage in solo creative play, neighborhood play, and play with friends at their homes or at yours when you are present.

When considering the two or three activities that your child will participate in, encourage a variety: one sport (soccer, gymnastics), one club (Scouts, Camp Fire), one cultural (music, dance). Don't let a child become lop-sided; let him experience many different activities during grade-school and high school years. Some activities will be dropped like a hot potato; some may be enjoyed for several decades. Some may lead to careers; some will provide lifelong friends. All will contribute to the general body of knowledge that makes a smart person.

So the key word is *exposure*. Tell your child, "You won't know if you like something until you try it." At the same time, don't force a child into an activity, and don't promote something that was your own heart's desire. There are thousands of unhappy children dutifully taking piano lessons because of their parent's unfulfilled dream to play with the symphony!

The Importance of Group Activities

Teams and clubs teach lessons that go far beyond their advertised scope. These group activities carry social, physical, and emotional benefits for the only child but also for kids from large families.

Being on a losing team teaches the importance of good sportsmanship this time, the desire to try harder next time, and grace in defeat. Being on a winning team also teaches good sportsmanship as well as diligence, team spirit, and generosity in victory.

Setting up a tent and cooking an outdoor meal teaches ingenuity, self-sufficiency, and the ability to follow instructions.

Dancing with three other "bumble-bees" teaches coordination and cooperation.

Selling cookies teaches manners as well as salesmanship.

Being the treasurer of a group teaches math and honesty.

Being the president or chairman of a group teaches leadership and humility. Not being the head of a group teaches one how to follow—an equally important talent—and self-control, which leads to self-esteem.

Earning badges or beads teaches the wonderful feeling of achievement but also the willingness to investigate a spectrum of subjects.

Playing in a recital teaches memorization and poise.

Training a horse teaches precision and patience as well as care for an animal.

Being part of a large group teaches democracy in action and leads to the appreciation of the beliefs and desires of others.

Unless you plan to let your child grow up to be a hermit, she'll need to know how to work effectively with others. A group activity can be a useful microcosm of society, one that teaches your child valuable character traits while expanding her knowledge base.

At What Age?

Don't worry that your child will miss out on being a prodigy if you fail to start piano lessons at age three. If the talent is there, it won't go away!

Age five or six is certainly soon enough to start most of the activities listed above. Starting earlier may be pushing a child into physical and social situations that can be very damaging. Yes, three-year-olds are darling in soccer uniforms and ballet tutus, but the pleasure is mostly in the eyes of the parent. All the child gets is burn-out on an activity she might have really enjoyed later.

Remember, you're in charge. Just because other parents are rushing their toddlers into violin lessons doesn't mean you have to.

Saying "no" is an option you should exercise when life gets too busy with activities that are just time-fillers as opposed to things that are mind-fillers.

So help your child choose well—at the appropriate time. You have many years ahead for all these valuable activities. Some may be worthwhile at age four, others at age fourteen.

What About Practicing?

"Practice time!" can be one of the dreaded phrases of childhood. So when considering activities with your child, be up-front about the possible negative aspects. A baseball team may mean tedious batting practices and then hours of sitting on the bench. Trumpet lessons require daily practice sessions. Scouts need time during the week to earn badges.

If you are willing to arrange the transportation and pay the fees, your child should be willing to accomplish the necessary practice with zest.

Some parents use the pro-and-con method of helping a child choose after-school activities. Seeing the benefits (pro) and also the work involved (con) in each possible activity, helps a youngster make a decision. Don't be discouraging but do be realistic about the need to practice, the time it will take each day, and other activities that may be missed while practicing.

Certainly, hitting a home run in the bottom of the ninth, dancing the part of the swan in "Swan Lake," or rope-climbing a tall mountain sounds wonderful. But before those things can happen there has to be a lot of background information learned and put into practice.

According to a Gallup survey, each year more than fourteen million kids from age five to seventeen take up an instrument—and quit during that first year. So before you buy an instrument that might end up in the attic, consult your school's music teacher, who can explore your child's ability to distinguish rhythm and pitch. Then to save you money and a lot of nagging, try renting the instrument.

Most schools have low-cost instrument rental arrangements with a local store. Often the rental money goes toward the purchase price and you have the option of returning the instrument (in good condition) at any time. If your child's enthusiasm is still strong after three months, you have the option of buying.

When you embark on an activity that requires practice, save yourself arguments and watch-dogging by setting a minimum time for practice and providing a small notebook. In it the practice-person puts the day, the time the practice starts, and the time it ends. Provide also a timer so that the practicer doesn't have to keep checking on when she is finished. When the timer rings, the practice can be over.

A Working Parent's Involvement

Nonworking parents complain that working parents are often freeloaders when it comes to helping with kids' activities. The stay-at-home parents are the chauffeurs, the coaches, the Scout leaders, the cookie-drive chairpersons, the overnight chaperones, the snack bakers and costume makers. Although this may be the way it has to be for some of these tasks, a working parent should strive to be helpful in some tangible way. A frank talk with those in charge will uncover possible contributions that a working parent can make without disrupting his work schedule too much.

Of course your time is short, but since the best defense is a good offense, you may want to just tell the adult leadership the ways you can and can't participate when your child signs up. Let those in charge know that while there are many things you can't do, you'll be happy to drive on Saturday, make a casserole, take kids to visit your interesting office, staff the concession booth for the evening or weekend games, paint scenery or make costumes.

You'll benefit yourself by participating. Through your youngster's activities, you'll get to know parents of similar-aged children. Some will become new friends and some may be worthwhile business contacts. So don't be standoffish.

Youngsters like it when their parents show interest and take part in their activities. That's why you'll want to attend games, performances, and ceremonies as much as possible. And that's not just moms' work! Involve dads and siblings as cheering sections for your outfielder or tap dancer.

The Importance of Time Alone

Don't let schedules and supervision replace spontaneity—one of the fleeting joys of childhood. Many educators and psychologists worry that the currently popular rigid regimens are producing passive and pressured kids.

Instead of exploring on their own to find things that give pleasure and satisfaction, kids are being told what to like and how to perform. Like a puppet on a string, the child is controlled from above: Parents, teachers, and activity leaders are pulling the strings.

When a child is given constant direction in school, sports, and lessons, he can become afraid to take a risk. Adventure is no longer an option for that child. In keeping with common sense, we need to encourage spontaneity and adventure. And we have to make adventure possible in an environment where children are often pawns and where neighborhoods may not be safe.

In just a generation, childhood has changed. The important hours of leisure in which a youngster could do nothing, think about any old thing, and nurture creativity by experimenting with his toys are now filled with planned activities and television. Today few children have a chance to unwind after school. The motto is "On to the next activity!" And if he returns home to a frenetic pace for homework, supper, television, and bed, he might be so tired that there's not a moment for thought before sleep comes.

How to be alone and enjoy aloneness is a seldom taught but indispensable asset. Most people can function when told what to do, but the smartest people know what to do on their own. Getting used to being alone starts with a baby playing in a playpen. It continues with a toddler in a child-safe room. And it should continue with school-age children spending at least half an hour alone each day in a play environment at home.

What are the lessons a child learns when alone? To make do with what is at hand. To make something out of nothing. To make something different out of something. To combine several games and toys into a greater game or toy. To repair what is broken. To invent a new method or toy. To accept a failure and to keep trying for success.

Wonderful qualities of diligence, patience, and creativity are exercised in time alone. And most vital, a child learns what he can do and thus more about his real selfhood. He comes to appreciate himself: his abilities and possibilities. "I did it myself" is a great esteem-builder. And when a child likes himself and values his life, he will be less apt to waste that life or purposely destroy it.

Don't take away from your child this precious solo time for self-knowledge.

Overprogrammed children can experience burn-out. Then, even a few activities seem like too much. Apathy can set in and spread to the school hours. Overorganized children can become nervous and anxious. And saddest of all, they forget how to have fun!

In this era of superprogrammed kids, peers can ostracize a child who resists being completely engulfed by organized activities. Wise parents will support that child's need and desire to just "hang out" at home, ride a bike, play with building blocks, or stretch out on the bed and look up at the ceiling.

Let me repeat: Being alone teaches a child independence, self-government, self-esteem. So try to provide several afternoons of unstructured activity each week. You'll be pleasantly surprised when you come home from work. Your child will be happier, less rushed, eager for company, willing to take direction, and ready to be part of family activities.

Having Your Child's Friends at Your House

There is playing alone, and there is playing in an organized group. And between those two is the happy option of playing with a friend or two. The shared intimacy, the stress-free ambience, and the casual camaraderie of playing with a friend should be an important part of childhood. It makes a child abler in the important asset of knowing how to get along with others.

Having a child's friends at your house isn't always easy. You have to find the time in your own busy schedule and your child's schedule, and sometimes you have to make transportation arrangements if the kids don't live in your immediate neighborhood.

Urbanization of neighborhoods and the increase in the number of working parents have silenced some of the sounds of former childhoods. That back door call, "Can Chris come out and play?" has been replaced with phone calls and written invitations—or nothing at all.

But fight back. Help your child find some nearby friends who are available for play on the spur of the moment. Or set up a time late Saturday afternoon or for an hour after supper.

It's your job to create a comfortable playtime environment at your home. When the home is an attractive gathering place, there is less tendency for kids to wander away into trouble. If your home is just being used for eating and sleeping, you have work to do!

In keeping with your child's age and the space available in your home, provide a place where kids can freely play without fear of making too much noise or breaking something. Toys should be readily available on shelves or in boxes so that the players can pick and choose without bringing everything out at once. Plastic wash baskets and easy-to-carry cardboard "bankers' boxes" help keep component parts and similar toys together. Creative toys, action toys, and outdoor toys are good, as well as the more quiet box games.

For older children and friends, privacy is important: a place to listen to music, look at magazines, or talk without interruption. Or, they may need a place to work on a hobby or play on skateboards.

For all ages, keep on hand snacks the kids enjoy. These shouldn't be junk foods, but nutritious and appealing things to eat or prepare. While they eat, take this opportunity to really talk with your child and her friend. You can learn a lot by just listening, so give some thought on what you hear and learn. Teach kids that you expect them to clean up after themselves.

Occasionally a parent may have to step in to settle an argument, but it's better to teach kids how to do so among themselves (by sharing, taking turns, using a timer, talking out a problem, or by sometimes giving in to another's wants). Of course, you should always be aware of what activities are taking place in your home. Be sure they are safe and legal!

You'll be a popular parent if you remember these points:

1. Once you've met the friends, don't intrude on play. When a child has a friend over, he doesn't need or want you for play.

2. Find out what time the friend has to go home. Remind him about fifteen minutes ahead so there can be some last minutes of play and enough time for pick up.

3. Don't be a grouch. Loud music or a few crumbs on the floor beats worrying about where your child is and what he's doing.

4. Be prepared with ideas, but hold back. Certainly, you are capable of settling arguments or suggesting new games, but wait it out. Usually the playmates will come up with something on their own and that's a great learning experience. If they don't, then make your suggestions.

5. Never, *never* discipline your child in front of a friend. If possible, wait until the friend goes home. If you must say something, take your child aside and talk quietly.

6. Be happy! Your child has a friend! Be sincerely pleasant to the friend—compliment him on something, tell him you hope he'll come and play another day.

7. Make play better. After your youngster has had a friend over, ask

her what was good about the time together. Find out what each of you can do to make it even better the next time.

A child's free time diminishes with every passing year. The time to play, to "goof off," to just be a child is soon gone. Working parents, fast-track parents, and parents who live in unsafe neighborhoods have to work harder to bring about a balance between a child's structured and unstructured time. But the things learned *after* school can be just as advantageous as the lessons taught *in* school.

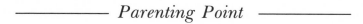 *Parenting Point*

The happiest child is the well-rounded child. Although your child may never grow up to be a football star or a famed guitarist, he learns much by being exposed to varied activities. Don't let after-school hours and weekend days be frittered away. Help your child choose each year those organized activities that are the best, and save out some time for spontaneous fun. Step by step, you can introduce your child to all the wonders of active living.

Chalkboard for Chapter Sixteen

Make a list of five activities *you* would enjoy if you had free time (aerobics, tennis lessons, a book club, pottery making, etc.)

1.
2.
3.
4.
5.

Next, make a list of five activities you believe your child would enjoy in free time. Then ask your child for five favorite after-school activities which that child would like to continue or try in the future.

YOUR LIST	YOUR CHILD'S LIST
1.	1.
2.	2.
3.	3.
4.	4.
5.	5.

How well did you guess your child's interests? Using these lists, talk about the differences. Circle the activity that seems most interesting to your child now. When it's time to choose a new after-school activity, refer to these lists, remembering to include time for the adventure of unstructured play, playing with friends, and playing alone.

Seventeen

Frosting on the Cake: Enriching Family Life

The school district where Carrie and Andrew bought a home had a reputation for not being the greatest. Yet, they wanted to support public education—and anyway, they couldn't afford private schools. They weren't discouraged; they figured that they could find time to increase their kids' knowledge by enriching their home life. Carrie's job let her be home by 3:30 in the afternoon and Andrew had made the commitment when Sarah was born to devote extra time to the children each weekend. So, they started their enrichment plans when Sarah was an infant. Now she is 14, Jonathan is 11, and Kim is 6. Through the years Carrie and Andrew have developed a closeness with their children that includes meaningful conversations, worthwhile excursions, and varied activities. Sometimes it is hard to find the time, but they agreed before they had a family that they wouldn't be apathetic parents—there *would be time later for their other projects and dreams. Until then, the kids would come first.*

Enriching family life is easy to talk about and sometimes difficult to accomplish. For parents who want intelligent children, however, it's an absolute necessity. School, extracurricular activities, and television are today's major channels for learning. Wise parents will make the home an additional learning center, second only to schooling.

Cake is O.K.; cake with frosting is better. The school your child attends will provide the cake. It's up to you to put on the frosting—the extras that make the difference between an average-educated youngster and a truly cultured one. And although the word "culture" may turn some people off, it doesn't mean "snooty," it means "broad-based understanding in music, literature, drama, and so forth." And who wouldn't like that!

In a 1988 *People* magazine story on illustrious parents who have well-balanced offspring, these artistic and scientific families were polled on the greatest influences on them during growing up years. Almost without exception, these were the five leading comments:

1. *Dinner talk*—conversations were held on every imaginable subject.
2. *Books and word games*—leisure time included reading, reading aloud, and intellectual box games.
3. *Role models*—parents were "doers" and provided opportunities for the children to be with other intelligent adult friends.
4. *Consistency*—parents meant what they said, their word was good, they frequently showed affection.
5. *Encouragement*—they didn't push, but they provided challenges and opportunities that built their offspring's self-esteem.

The Renaissance Child

Earlier in this century, a cultured person was sometimes called a Renaissance Man. (Today we'd have to say a Renaissance Person.) The Renaissance was a time of revival in art, literature, and learning in Europe. Beginning in the fourteenth century and extending to the seventeenth century, it marked the transition from the medieval to the modern world. The term originally meant someone who had a profound knowledge or proficiency in more than one field. Today it means someone who is knowledgeable about a variety of subjects.

Instead of being one-sided, children should have an acquaintance with many subjects. They should be Renaissance Children, ready to live in a universe and a world that is bringing all people and places closer each day.

On what subjects should a Renaissance Child have a conversational knowledge? Art, literature, theater, music, business, budgets, economics, world history, politics, travel, geography, science, the environment, religion, ethics, computers, and language. He should also have an understanding of home upkeep, auto maintenance, and personal health care. That's quite an assignment!

And who's going to help teach all this in a child's eighteen years at home? You, the parent! This chapter will help you get started. You'll be teaching in a number of ways: by example, by demonstration, by conversation and discussion, by reading, and by excursions and travel.

And how do you teach something you yourself know little of? You can learn right along with your child. Home enrichment needn't be dull, it can captivate both you and your child.

Our survey asked parents what weekend activities their families participated in most often. The top five were:

1. Television viewing
2. Visiting friends and relatives
3. Watching a sport
4. Playing in a sport
5. Going on a picnic or hike

Do you notice something missing from this list? Although these are all acceptable activities and some of them improve skills or entertain, none of them are strong educators. They do precious little to increase a child's general education toward being a whole person—a Renaissance Child.

Let's consider the dozen most important areas where you can help educate your child:

1. Art
2. Literature
3. Theater
4. Music
5. Business, budgets, and the economy
6. World history and politics
7. Travel and geography

8. Science and the environment
9. Religion and ethics
10. Computers
11. Language skills
12. Home care, health care, auto care

As an example, the first topic, art, will be dealt with in more depth than some of the others so that you can see how self-education works.

1. Yuck, an Art Museum!

The museum is the all-time most boring excursion, right? Wrong! To illustrate how a parent and child can truly enjoy art, let's go into some detail on art and visiting an art museum—one of the more difficult enrichment subjects. Then, you'll be better prepared to transfer these ideas to visiting other museums, the zoo, or the cathedral, or attending a symphony concert.

After a busy week at work, it's understandable that many families head for the park or the mall rather than to a stuffy old art museum. But today's museums are no longer stuffy and today's children are capable of enjoying visits starting at a young age.

Often a parent's hesitant and doubting attitude is the biggest obstacle to overcome. Remember, a family doesn't *have* to go, a family *gets* to go to a museum!

At what age will a child benefit from a museum? It can be a wonderful excursion with a four-year-old—or any older age. But even younger children with good manners and attention spans can be included.

It doesn't matter whether you're close to a major art museum or just a small local one. There will be plenty to see and do. Check your nearby college or university for art museums and galleries, too.

Most of the following information is suitable for grade-school children, but can be adapted for older or younger ones.

First, don't just spring the art museum trip on the family one Saturday morning. There are five things to do first:

1. Call the museum and ask about hours, strollers, cameras, places to eat, free admission days. Choose an art museum that specializes in paintings. Sculpture, crafts, glassware, and antiquities can come later.

2. Decide who gets the privilege of going. Three or four make an ideal group: parents and two children, mom with grandpa and two

children, two dads each with a child. Don't take an entire Scout troop on the first trip!

3. Visit the library and look at or borrow some art books. Don't ponder each page! Let kids look through the books at their own pace and share pictures they find interesting. Nonreaders especially like to do this.

4. Plan your take-alongs: camera, lunch, snack, notebook and pen for each child, and an eighteen-inch ribbon or string per child (more on that later).

5. Announce the date in advance and put it on the calendar in red. See that everyone has a good rest the night before. Plan for no more than two hours at the museum, and then add to that your driving and eating time.

On the way to the museum, keep the conversation light and happy. Talk about colors: What is each child's favorite color? What is a bright color? A dark color? A pale color? What do artists draw with? Crayons? Ask a child to remember something she saw in an art book: a mountain, a boat, a battle, a baby. Which of these does she think we'll see today? Cover the three museum-trip rules: no running, no shouting, no touching the art work.

When you arrive, sit on the steps out front and have a granola bar or fruit snack. Explain that paintings are very precious and that guards will be inside to keep them safe and also to help people. If there is an employee near the entrance, introduce yourselves and let the kids ask a few questions. Next, locate the bathrooms and get that necessity over with.

As a first quick stop (you'll come back later), visit the museum gift shop—if there is one—or find the place where postcards of the paintings are for sale. Let a child choose and buy one postcard he likes. Now, attach the postcard to the ribbon you brought along by making a small hole in one corner. A little child may like to hang her postcard around her neck. Others can keep it handy in a pocket or bag. Parents should choose a postcard too. Ask in which room each of these paintings is displayed.

Now it's time to see actual paintings. Don't sign up for a museum tour; that's too regimented for this visit. And remember, you don't need to see every room in the museum. Leave some for another time.

Choose rooms that seem most interesting or least occupied. Move at a leisurely pace and don't give a running commentary—just look and listen. Remind each one to be on the lookout for his postcard picture.

After about ten minutes of viewing, you're ready for some observations. Ask a child to find the favorite color he mentioned in the car. Are the paintings with bright colors the happy pictures? Are there mysterious looking paintings made with dark colors?

Don't skip the modern art. Sometimes kids, especially teens, relate to it better than parents do. Ask what the artist might have felt when he painted the picture. Does the painting's title give a clue?

When children become a little restless, try one of these ideas:

• Where do artists sign their works? What are some artists' names? Is there more than one picture by the same artist? Who are the most famous artists? Look for paintings by Rembrandt, Picasso, El Greco, Monet, Renoir, Wyeth, Cassatt, and Seurat.

• Sit down on the bench or the floor in one room. Using the tablets, let each child list the subjects of the paintings in that room. For example, paintings of landscapes, rich people, buildings, water, biblical characters, battles. Compare the lists.

• Look for people and animal paintings. Are there paintings of children? grandparents? soldiers? angels? moms and dads? What animal gets pictured most often?

• Play the game "I'd Like to Live There." Let everyone point out places that look interesting for play, living, working, or visiting.

• Ask which pictures depict real events, and which depict fantasy or dreams. See if anyone can point out some differences.

• See who can find the biggest picture. Read the description and find out where it was originally hung.

• Play "If I Were a Millionaire." Let each child point out a painting he'd like to take home if he could afford the no-doubt huge price.

• Look for a funny painting, a serious painting, a sad painting. Does everyone in the family agree?

• Play "That's Me!" Encourage each one to find a picture she thinks she could fit into or would like to be a part of. Would she like to be Renoir's stylishly dressed girl with a watering can? the horseback rider? the queen? the warrior?

After about an hour of walking and viewing, it's time for lunch and a bathroom break. Let each person tell what picture she likes best so far. How many have found their postcard picture?

After lunch, continue viewing but be sure to find the postcard pictures. Then let each person return to his "favorite" picture. Make a note of the painting's name and artist. If permitted, photograph each person with his "favorite." (If photography isn't permitted, take photos outside so that this excursion can go in the family memory book.)

Finally, return to the museum shop and investigate books, games, and other artistic gifts. Listen for comments which may give you ideas for birthday and holiday gift-giving.

On the way home, talk about what you saw: the colors, the best paintings, the artists, the postcard pictures. Look out the car windows for scenes that an artist might draw.

Back home, put the postcard pictures on the family bulletin board or let the children send them to grandparents, telling about the excursion. Talk about what made these paintings special. Without your leading the discussion, let children share with others what the museum visit was like. In the following days, encourage an art project at home. Supply plenty of paper, crayons, paints, and markers. Don't suggest, just see what the child paints, and let him explain it to you. Display the finished pictures.

If you approach the art museum visit this way, you won't be met with resistance when you suggest a follow-up trip later. Museums of all varieties will no longer be intimidating places. And with the growing number of "hands-on" museums, art and artifacts will take on new life and relevance.

As children grow older, discussions on technique, history, religious art, patrons, the Masters, and so forth can be part of the experience. A tour led by a museum docent will also be valuable.

Books you may want to look at together or read include: *Visiting the Art Museum* (Brown; Dutton, 1986) and *The History of Art for Young People* (Janson; Abrams, 1987)—both good for young children; *The National Gallery of Art* (Walker; Abrams, 1984)—a magnificent picture book; and *Children Are Artists* (Mendelowitz; Stanford U. Press, 1963)—a good book for every family.

Encourage art in the home. Go to an art fair. Let a child select an inexpensive picture for her own room. Give a child an art object as a gift. Provide opportunities for artistic expression: everything from a soap-carving contest and collages made of fabric scraps to making a wall mural on shelf paper and adding texture to pictures with sand, cereal, or glitter.

Check on the art program at your school. Sometimes arts and crafts are given low priority and all that is taught is the "doing." The "appreciating" is just as important. Encourage school trips to art museums, the purchase of good art books, and the display of art prints on the classroom walls.

Art teaches many things: history, design, zoology, architecture, botany, costuming, perspective, and more. A visit to an art museum should be on your family's excursion list at least twice each year. That way your child will know something about art, and when she is grown she'll continue this important learning with her children.

Now that we've considered an art museum visit in depth, let's go on to the other subjects for your Renaissance Child.

2. Literary Literature

As your child grows up, he'll read many wonderful books—books assigned at school, books chosen from the library, books suggested by you, books received as gifts. He'll also be exposed to literature that isn't too literary. You want your child to know the difference between good literature and trash.

Some of the contemporary books for young people will eventually become classics. Some will fade as fickle society changes its interests. But there are enduring books—ones that evoke pictures, ideas, adventures—that should be read by every educated person.

You'll want to see that your Renaissance Child reads these classics—a few a year until he is launched into independent adulthood. (But even when your child is grown, you can still give books as gifts.) Lists of classic books abound and few agree on what should be included or excluded.

After consulting with librarians, English teachers, and other well-educated readers, I've prepared two lists for you to use through the years. One is for grade-school children, one for high schoolers. If *you* haven't read some of these books, you may want to read them at the same time. Stimulating conversation comes from such a joint experience.

The smart child is the one who reads. If you read you can do almost anything. Literacy is the ability to read and write; it is the key to a full life. The love for reading starts when a parent first reads to an infant, and is nurtured by the wise parent.

How do you stimulate reading? First by having good books in the home and providing the time to read them. Next, by your own example of being a reader and taking a sincere interest in your child's reading.

You'll find more than fifty ideas (incentives, games, and projects) to encourage your child to read, in my book *1001 Things to Do with Your Kids* (Abingdon Press, 1988).

Magazine subscriptions for young people are another good way to stimulate reading. Some good ones include *Highlights for Children, National Geographic World*, and *Ranger Rick*.

Don't consider the following book lists definitive, but do use them as good outlines of books that most educated people have read.

Classics for Grade-schoolers and Middle-schoolers

The Adventures of Tom Sawyer	Samuel Clemens (Mark Twain)
Aesop's Fables	Aesop
Alice's Adventures in Wonderland	Lewis Carroll
Andersen's Fairy Tales	Hans Christian Andersen
Anne Frank: The Diary of a Young Girl	Anne Frank
Anne of Green Gables	Lucy Montgomery
The Arabian Nights' Entertainments	ed. Andrew Lang
A Bear Called Paddington	Michael Bond
Black Beauty	Anna Sewell
The Boys' Sherlock Holmes	Arthur Conan Doyle
Caddie Woodlawn	Carol Brink
The Call of the Wild	Jack London
Charlie and the Chocolate Factory	Roald Dahl
Charlotte's Web	E. B. White
A Child's Garden of Verses	Robert Louis Stevenson
A Christmas Carol	Charles Dickens
Don Quixote of La Mancha	Miguel de Cervantes Saavedra
East of the Sun and West of the Moon	Peter Asbjornsen
Grimm's Fairy Tales	Jacob and Wilhelm Grimm
Gulliver's Travels	Jonathan Swift
Hans Brinker or the Silver Skates	Mary Mapes Dodge
Heidi	Johanna Spyri
Hitty: Her First Hundred Years	Rachel Field
Island of the Blue Dolphins	Scott O'Dell
The Jungle Books	Rudyard Kipling
Just So Stories	Rudyard Kipling
The Lion, the Witch, and the Wardrobe	C. S. Lewis
Little House in the Big Woods	Laura Wilder

The Little Prince	Antoine de Saint-Exupery
Little Women	Louisa May Alcott
Mary Poppins	Pamela Travers
The Merry Adventures of Robin Hood	Howard Pyle
Mother Goose	Mother Goose
National Velvet	Enid Bagnold
Paul Bunyan Swings His Axe	Dell McCormick
Peter Pan	James Barrie
The Phantom Tollbooth	Norton Juster
The Pilgrim's Progress	John Bunyan
Pinocchio: The Adventures of a Little Wooden Boy	Carlo Collodi
Pippi Longstocking	Astrid Lindgren
Rebecca of Sunnybrook Farm	Kate Douglas Wiggin
Rip Van Winkle and the Legend of Sleepy Hollow	Washington Irving
Robinson Crusoe	Daniel Defoe
The Secret Garden	Frances Burnett
The Story of King Arthur and His Knights	Howard Pyle
The Swiss Family Robinson	Johann Wyss
The Tales and Poems of Edgar Allan Poe	Edgar Allan Poe
Tales from Shakespeare	Charles and Mary Lamb
Tanglewood Tales	Nathaniel Hawthorne
Treasure Island	Robert Louis Stevenson
Twenty Thousand Leagues Under the Sea	Jules Verne
The Velveteen Rabbit	Margery Williams
Voyages of Doctor Doolittle	Hugh Lofting
Watership Down	Richard Adams
The Wind in the Willows	Kenneth Grahame
Winnie-the-Pooh	A. A. Milne
The Wizard of Oz	L. F. Baum
A Wrinkle in Time	Madeleine L'Engle
The Yearling	Marjorie Kinnan Rawlings

Classics for High School Students

The Adventures of Huckleberry Finn	Samuel Clemens (Mark Twain)
The Age of Innocence	Edith Wharton
The Alexandria Quartet	Lawrence Durrell
All Quiet on the Western Front	Erich Maria Remarque

The Ambassadors	Henry James
Babbitt	Sinclair Lewis
The Bridge of San Luis Rey	Thornton Wilder
The Call of the Wild	Jack London
Candide	Voltaire
Crime and Punishment	Fyodor Dostoevski
Cry, the Beloved Country	Alan Paton
Doctor Zhivago	Boris Pasternak
Emma	Jane Austen
Ethan Frome	Edith Wharton
The First Circle	Aleksandr Solzhenitsyn
For Whom the Bell Tolls	Ernest Hemingway
The Forsyte Saga	John Galsworthy
Germinal	Émile Zola
Gone with the Wind	Margaret Mitchell
The Grapes of Wrath	John Steinbeck
The Great Gatsby	F. Scott Fitzgerald
The Heart of Midlothian	Sir Walter Scott
The Hobbit	J. R. R. Tolkien
Human Comedy	William Saroyan
Jane Eyre	Charlotte Bronte
Les Miserables	Victor Hugo
Look Homeward, Angel	Thomas Wolfe
Lord Jim	Joseph Conrad
Madame Bovary	Gustave Flaubert
The Mill on the Floss	George Eliot
Moby Dick	Herman Melville
Moll Flanders	Daniel Defoe
My Antonia	Willa Cather
1984	George Orwell
A Passage to India	E. M. Forster
Pere Goriot	Honore de Balzac
The Portrait of a Lady	Henry James
Pride and Prejudice	Jane Austen
The Red and the Black	Stendhal (Marie-Henri Beyle)
The Red Badge of Courage	Stephen Crane
The Rise of Silas Lapham	William Dean Howells
The Scarlet Letter	Nathaniel Hawthorne
Sons and Lovers	D. H. Lawrence
The Sound and the Fury	William Faulkner
The Sun Also Rises	Ernest Hemingway

A Tale of Two Cities	Charles Dickens
A Tale of Two Cities	Charles Dickens
Tess of the D'Urbervilles	Thomas Hardy
Tono-Bungay	H. G. Wells
Ulysses	James Joyce
Vanity Fair	William Thackeray
War and Peace	Leo Tolstoy
Wuthering Heights	Emily Bronte

A child who reads well will also speak well and write well. Observing the way words are put together (and how they are spelled) helps in composition writing, conversation and speech-making, debate, essay-writing in examinations, and in other tests. And books provide a link to the past, present, and future. The characters in books become friends, and the ideas in books become catalysts for a child's adventuresome life.

Theater—Front Row Center

A child's wonder at seeing a live production, perhaps with Peter Pan flying across the stage, upstages anything that movies and television can offer. Good live theater requires a child's commitment of mind and body. The child eagerly leans forward in her seat and follows every word and action. Soon she is drawn into the plot. The characters become real people and she cares what happens to them. Their words ring in her ears and are long remembered after the final curtain falls.

Being at a live production versus seeing it on television is as different as being at a live circus versus looking at a picture book of animals. The third dimension makes a more vivid and lasting impression. It makes the situations, the characters, the point of view more real and relevant to everyday life.

A good place to begin a knowledge of the theater is with school productions. Make it a family tradition to attend even the simplest of programs presented by young children, and then continue with support of high school and college-level productions. The first purpose of school theater is to encourage child participation and the skills of memorization and speaking in public. The second purpose is to introduce the idea of sitting, watching, listening, and learning as part of the audience. But don't limit yourself to school productions.

Children's theater is the next step. Most cities have a thriving program for young actors and actresses. Seeing other children act can encourage a child to be more comfortable speaking in the classroom or on stage. Actually taking part in a play is a great poise and esteem builder.

When children are young, borrow some plays from the library to familiarize your child with the format. When children read well, borrow a play, assign roles among family and friends, and have your own play-reading session.

Along with your encouragement of book reading, add play reading, from Euripides to Shakespeare to Neil Simon. Discuss the strong points and the weak points of the plays and playwrights suitable for your child's age. You don't have to like them all! Show how settings and characterization are described for the reader, leaving much to the imagination of the reader or the interpretation of the director.

Through your newspaper, find plays being presented by local theater groups. Although the acting style may not be quite ready for Broadway, take in plays at "little theaters" and nearby colleges. As a special treat, attend a really professional play at least twice yearly.

Before attending a play, use the encyclopedia or make a trip to the library to bone up on the plot and the playwright. Keep an eye on your local newspaper for a review. Sometimes it may help to borrow the text of a play and read it beforehand. (A public or school library or book store will be good sources.) Go ahead and share the plot with the child. This takes away some suspense but will help build comprehension. The child will be free to appreciate more of the spectacle of the overall performance if she doesn't have to be concerned only with the plot.

The following playwrights can form your basic list:

Edward Albee	T. S. Eliot
Maxwell Anderson	Euripides
Sir James M. Barrie	John Galsworthy
Philip Barry	Gilbert and Sullivan
Bertolt Brecht	Jean Giraudoux
Anton Chekhov	Ben Hecht
George M. Cohan	Lillian Hellman
Sir Noel Coward	Victor Hugo
Russel Crouse	Henrik Ibsen
Alexandre Dumas	Ben Jonson

George S. Kaufman
Howard Lindsay
Clare Boothe Luce
Carson McCullers
Christopher Marlowe
W. Somerset Maugham
Arthur Miller
Clifford Odets
Eugene O'Neill
Harold Pinter

William Saroyan
William Shakespeare
George Bernard Shaw
Robert Sherwood
Neil Simon
Sophocles
Voltaire
Oscar Wilde
Thornton Wilder
William Butler Yeats

This list may look a bit formidable at first, but remember that you have many years to cover it. There are forty names on the list, so if your child is eight years old and will leave home in about ten years, you will want to read about four a year. Now that's not too taxing, is it?

A Renaissance Child should have some familiarity with great actresses and actors too. Look up these names in an encyclopedia and learn about them:

Tallulah Bankhead
The Barrymore family
Sarah Bernhardt
Marlon Brando
Katharine Cornell
Sir Noel Coward
Hume Cronyn
Marlene Dietrich
Eleanor Dusa
Sir John Gielgud

Sir Alec Guiness
Helen Hayes
Katharine Hepburn
Walter Huston
Charles Laughton
Eva Le Gallienne
Sir Laurence Olivier
Will Rogers
Sarah Siddons
Jessica Tandy
Orson Welles

Your Renaissance Child will want to be familiar with theater words and terms: the difference between the producer and the director, plotting, "flying" scenery, prompters, blocking, costume design, make-up techniques, Broadway and Off-Broadway, summer stock, tragedy, comedy, Greek theater, Kabuki plays, "Theater of the Absurd," theater-in-the-round.

Beyond reading plays and attending the theater, you can occasionally see good plays on television. This may be the only way you'll still be able to see some of the well-known stars. Make home viewing special by placing chairs theater-style. Observe intermissions (commercials) by standing up and enjoying a snack and conversation. After the play, let viewers share their reviews (their opinions) on why this play was important.

In the summer, when kids have more time, you can encourage your child and her friends to stage a production at home. In keeping with ages and talents, the children can write, make scenery and costumes, direct, act, and be the audience.

Marionettes or hand puppets are other excellent ways to encourage a child's interest in theater arts. Encourage informal nonscripted plays by just suggesting a situation (a million dollars has been found, a hurricane is coming, the queen is invited to a birthday party, a little boy won't talk, or a tree is growing five feet each day). Then let the puppets extemporize on the plot idea. This is creative and often hilarious. Children who are normally shy will often become very bold and vocal when speaking on behalf of a puppet.

Movies are also part of the theater. There is quite a difference between seeing a movie in your living room and seeing it on a big theater screen with a large audience that laughs or gasps at the turns of plot. Although some movies lend themselves to a cozy home situation, others are best seen in a theater. Select only the best for home or theater viewing. In advance, talk about actors and actresses, plots, settings, and so forth. Read the reviews and talk about why you agree or disagree with them.

Live theater is a very real extension of a child's "let's pretend" play. In general, plays present much deeper ideas than do T.V. sitcoms. Many plays have lasted for generations because of their unique production possibilities and the ideas they present. Like books, plays cause children to think, and that's good.

4. Music—Charm and Sometimes Chaos

We like the music we grew up with. As for the music our children like? No way! Still, there is something to be learned about all kinds of music, from rock to opera and from Sibelius to Springsteen.

A Renaissance Child doesn't know just one type of music. Even though he may prefer one kind of music, he is familiar with the entire menu. Since music is a basic cultural and social activity of humans, a child should be introduced to various types of music and musicians at an early age. Music in the home can be from a good FM station, cassettes, and records, or can be self-produced on rhythm instruments at first, and on more professional instruments later.

Starting with infants, expose children to a variety of music: in the background during the day, at naptime, suppertime, homework, or playtime. While riding in the car, play music and tapes and keep simple songbooks in the glove compartment for song sessions on longer trips.

As kids begin to show strong musical preferences, be willing to listen to their style if they will give equal time to yours. Symphonic music, ballet music, opera, musical comedy, choral music, dance music, rock, ballads, soul, country and western, reggae—these are just some of the varieties you'll want to listen to in your home and car. Most libraries have music collections that can be borrowed for home use.

Attendance at musical events is sometimes organized by the school, but in any case, outings to musical events should be a regular part of family life. Like planning for museum trips, advance planning when going to a concert makes it more enjoyable.

The composer, the plot (if any), the musical instruments to be used, classical music forms, outstanding performers: These are subjects not generally taught in school. So if your youngster needs to know the difference between a sonata and a symphony, it's up to you to know and share. The library has many up-to-date books on music suitable for each age group.

Love for music starts early in life with lullabies and rhyming songs. Musical games are taught in nursery school. Unfortunately, many grade schools ignore music with the exception of a little choral singing. Your child's participation in vocal and instrumental music groups should be encouraged when possible.

Music appreciation courses are sometimes offered in high school, or as adult evening classes. A parent whose music education has been slim may want to take such a course to round out her own knowledge.

How to read music is something everyone should know, because it helps us to appreciate the most difficult orchestral piece and the simplest hymn. Many toy-style instruments teach the scale in relation to the notes printed on the staff. When a child has music lessons he will learn this, but many young people never master the treble and base clefs. It's up to the parent to either help a child learn to read simple music or find someone who can share this information.

Before attending a symphony, talk about the various instruments and the differing sounds they make. Your encyclopedia will have pictures and descriptions. Listen to a classical piece and see who can identify some of the sounds. *Peter and the Wolf* is a perfect beginner piece for this exercise.

Before attending a choral music event, learn the various voice ranges (soprano, mezzo-soprano, contralto or alto, tenor, bass). Depending on the music you'll be hearing, you will want to define special terms such as *a cappella* (without accompaniment). Be prepared to look up aria, recitative, appoggiatura, basso buffo, and other terms.

Although there are hundreds of truly great classical composers, you can't go wrong if you choose from this list for your initial introduction. These are names that should be familiar to the educated person, along with at least one of their compositions. This list covers composers of symphonies, concertos, and operas over the last four centuries:

Johann Sebastian Bach	Wolfgang Amadeus Mozart
Ludwig van Beethoven	Sergei Prokofiev
Georges Bizet	Giacomo Puccini
Johannes Brahms	Maurice Ravel
Benjamin Britten	Nikolai Rimski-Korsakov
Frédéric Chopin	Gioacchino Rossini
Aaron Copland	Franz Schubert
Claude Debussy	Jean Sibelius
Anton Dvorak	Richard Strauss
George Handel	Pëtr Ilich Tchaikovsky
Franz Joseph Hayden	Giuseppe Verdi
Franz von Liszt	Vaughan Williams
Felix Mendelssohn	

"Painlessly" introduce musical terms by incorporating them in daily family living. For instance, instead of saying "Come quickly," say "Allegro." For slowly, use "largo." "Con brio" means with great liveliness. "Speak loudly (or softly)" can be "Speak forte (or sotto) voce." To pick up toys, "vivace" means with lively speed. When a child is about to take too large a helping of ice cream, say, "non troppo," which means "not too much."

Many symphonic pieces appeal specially to young people. *Peter and the Wolf, The Sorcerer's Apprentice, Pictures at an Exhibition, Afternoon of a Fawn*, the *Alpine Symphony*, and *Also Sprach Zarathustra* (the theme used for *2001: A Space Odyssey*) are some easy-to-find ones to start you off.

Before going to the opera, you should definitely discuss the plot. Otherwise your child won't have the slightest idea of what is happening. When we first introduced our children to grand opera, we chose a production in English so that they could better understand the action. At the first intermission, one son complained: "But you said this was in English!" We had to agree that it was so difficult to understand that it could just as well have been in Italian.

Television has provided a showcase for many opera stars. In the program guide, look for operas, musical comedies, and concerts. Choose some of these performances to view with your children. Then, when you go to a live production, it will seem less strange.

One of the most pleasant forms of music for all the family is the musical comedy. Whether done by a high school theater group or a national company from the original Broadway show, the music, lyrics, and plot combine for a very enjoyable evening.

Since hearing the music in advance won't spoil the plot (and it will help you understand the words), listen to a tape of the songs before going. Cassettes of musicals make good car-listening, and many families sing along on the most popular songs.

Choral singing is one form of music your child can most easily participate in. School choral groups, high school and church choirs, holiday carol singing, and the popular *Messiah* sing-alongs get young people singing.

When your child is old enough to attend, buy recordings and spend money on popular music concerts. Help her to be selective. Discourage interest in pop stars whose music tends toward explicit sex, explicit violence, and explicit substance abuse. This isn't easy, but it's your right as a parent and there are plenty of acceptable modern musicians to choose from. Be willing to listen, rather than just rule out all heavy metal music.

Let your kids know that they are not to spend their money on music that has destructive values. Tipper Gore, author of the book *Raising PG Kids in an X-Rated Society* (Abingdon Press, 1988), says: "We should be deeply concerned about the obvious cumulative effect of this cult of violence that has captured the public's imagination and pervaded our society. Few parents realize how much the angry brand of music that is part of it has presented suicide, glorified rape, and condoned murder. The message is more than repulsive—it's deadly."

She continues, "Parents need to be as tuned in to music as they are to television or the movies. We want to bring this material out into the public eye, where it can be judged in the free marketplace and not hidden away where only children know where it is and what it's about."

"Music that makes my toes wiggle" is one way a child described ballet music. Nowadays both girls and boys take ballet and tap dancing lessons. Don't start dance lessons too soon, before muscles are ready to be stretched. And when you have a dancer in the house, encourage the entire family to attend his performances.

But even if your children are not interested in learning to toe dance or tap, you can still expose them to good dance music as a background for other activities. Choose from favorite ballets, dance music of your own era, ballads, and marches. When toys must be picked up or an entire house cleaned, try it to the tune of a stirring ballet or a soaring Sousa march. You'll be surprised how much faster the work gets done.

5. Business, Budgets, and the Economy

Business and industry make the world run. Although you can't instruct your child in the technicalities of all the various jobs, you can talk about business in general. Even with young children, you'll find an interest in how things work, how products are made, how services are provided.

Your own job is a good starting place. How does it fit into the nation's economy? Why is the product or service needed? How are the earnings divided? What happens to the profit? What is the future for your company?

If possible, let your child visit your work place. Saturdays and school vacations are often good visiting times. Let your child be useful by cleaning out a drawer, making copies, running an errand in the building, filing, looking at business magazines, or accomplishing other suitable tasks.

If you subscribe to *The Wall Street Journal,* you can recommend to children the page-one column "What's News" for a succinct summary of world happenings. Find and share other short newspaper articles on the economy. In kid-terms, explain the stock market, the gross national product, and the trade imbalance.

Talk also about your own family budget. When it is out of balance, elicit the family's help. You may be pleasantly surprised at the results when young people are included in money management. Set a family goal of staying on the budget, use everyone's ideas and help, and plan a small monthly reward for success.

The smart child knows how to handle money—how to spend and how to save. When a child is four or five years of age, start her on an allowance. Be definite on what it should include (lunch money? gifts? Sunday school collection?). Provide a systematic way for a child to save for special things. A cash gift might be divided into 25 percent to save and 75 percent to spend.

Open a savings account in a child's name. Actually take her to the financial institution so she can see how the account is opened and where her money is invested. This can be an impressive event for a child and the beginning of a lifelong good habit.

When your child is eleven or twelve, he is ready to have his own clothing allowance, separate from his regular allowance. (Usually, this allowance is kept on paper and not given in cash.) This gives him the opportunity to make choices—one of the lessons you want to teach. He can spend the budget on one expensive item or several less expensive ones. Give your views, but don't be insistent. If he makes a poor choice, he may have to wait before being able to make another purchase. But that's a good learning experience too.

One of the most important lessons for youth is an appreciation of what hard work, business, capitalism, unionization, and democracy have achieved. Although the work ethic has been abandoned in recent years, the pendulum has now begun to swing the other direction. In many families, both parents spend long hours on the job and consequently neglect family life. Workaholic parents is a new problem that adversely affects children. Although the Renaissance Child needs to see the benefits of hard work, help your child—and yourself—find a good balance.

6. World History and Politics

History is more than dates. It is the story of humankind's progress. But a few dates as reference points are helpful to the smart child.

Recent surveys of high school students show that they have little knowledge of when major world happenings occurred and indicate the need to strengthen history teaching. (One grade-school student thought Moses lived in the time just after Disneyland was founded. A high school student thought World War I freed the slaves.) Although it isn't important to commit to memory hundreds of exact dates, a smart child needs to know some dates so he can envision the long flow of history, rather than fragmented parts of it.

A unique and not-too-expensive aid in understanding historical events in context is the large book *The Wall Chart of World History* (Dorset Publishing, ISBN: 0-88029-239-3). The price is modest for the wealth of information provided in pictures and words. The fourteen connecting panels trace history in a timeline from biblical days through the 1980s, showing what was going on concurrently throughout the world at any date.

Since teaching students to memorize important historical dates is not currently popular in many schools, here is a list of dates that educated people know. They're useful in marking divisions between major events that have shaped history and affect both the present and the future.

Cover the right-hand column and see how many you know. Have a family contest to see who can remember the most. Make the dates more memorable by putting them in context. A history book or encyclopedia will help.

230,000,000 B.C.	Age of dinosaurs begins
2,500,000	Pleistocene Ice Age begins; lasts until about 10,000 years ago
3100	Unification of Egypt; first national government in the world
331	Alexander the Great defeats the Persians
55	Julius Caesar invades Britain
0 A.D.	The birth of Jesus
32 A.D.	Christian era begins
476	Approximate date Rome falls; the end of ancient history, beginning of medieval history
622	Mohammed's flight; the beginning of Moslem calendar
1000	Approximate date Leif Ericson explores North America
1066	The Battle of Hastings
1215	Magna Charta signed

1271	Marco Polo begins travels to Orient
1300–1600	Renaissance
1440	Gutenberg invents movable type for printing press
1492	Columbus discovers the new world
1519–1522	Magellan's voyage around the world
1533–1603	England's Queen Elizabeth I reigns
1564–1616	William Shakespeare writes
1620	Plymouth Colony established in America
1768	Captain Cook sails around the world
1769	James Watt's steam engine
1776	U. S. Declaration of Independence
1815	Napoleon Bonaparte defeated at Waterloo
1860s	Lincoln is president; the Civil War
1893	First successful American gas-powered automobile
1903	Wright brothers' first airplane flight
1914–1917	World War I
1920	Panama Canal opened
1939–1945	World War II
1944	First digital computer
1946	Television era begins (first telecast made a decade earlier by NBC)
1950–1953	Korean War
1957	Russia launches Sputnik I, first satellite
1965–1973	Vietnam War
1969	Man walks on the moon

Dates in themselves mean nothing until they are placed in context in the long story of humankind. See that the school your child attends teaches world history, not just Western world history.

World politics is as important as world history. A Renaissance Child won't be able to understand present-day politics without some knowledge of world events such as what caused the Magna Charta to be signed, the social repercussions of the French Revolution, life under communism, and the unrest in Central America.

Include young people in political discussions and encourage them to listen to campaign speeches long before they are able to vote. Have family talks about what seems important and necessary to change in local, national, and world governments—and how a citizen can go about doing it.

Preteens and teens can follow one current political issue, such as Polish labor unions, Apartheid, unrest in China, and child-care in the U.S. Conduct a once-a-week supper update on the topic.

Encourage a youngster's participation in school politics. Managing a campaign, discussing issues, and taking part in student government teach practical lessons in democratic action. Many politicians got their start in school politics. Being a part of the governing process at an early age helps a child see the proper way to improve society and its laws.

7. Travel and Geography

Tests of grade-school and high school students show that although the nations of the world can communicate instantly, kids have little idea of where other countries are and what life there is like. How can we be ready for space when we don't understand our own planet?

Relating to the community, country, and world should start early in life. With a simple atlas, you can use lines such as these:

"This is a map of our town. We live here and the grocery store is there."

"This is a map of our state. We live here and Grandma lives over there."

"Mommy is going on a business trip from this city on the Atlantic Ocean to this city on the Pacific Ocean."

"A new president has just been elected in this tiny country named _____."

"Grandpa fought in a war that took place in this European region."

"The fighting we read about in the newspaper is in this part of the world."

"Uncle Joe builds machines to be used on an expedition to this continent."

"Our vacation will take us from here to here."

When children are toddlers, purchase a large globe of the world or a good atlas. By the time children are in school, have a world map tacked on the wall so that places in the news can be located and discussed.

Once a child understands the places, he can better understand the people. Travelogues on television or presented in the school or community can show life in the remotest corners of the world.

Come even closer to world neighbors through pen pals. This is a wonderful idea to start when a child writes well enough to communicate ideas—usually by age eight or nine. Your friends with overseas contacts, church groups, and pen pal clubs can put your child in touch with a child of similar age in another country. A correspondence over the years can bridge the differences and make "foreign" seem friendly.

Stamp collecting interests some older children. Beautiful stamps of various countries can help educate a young person and provide a special focus. Start inexpensively; then, if your child shows a real interest in this collectible, purchase more supplies.

School excursions are an enjoyable method of teaching about other places and other ways. These excursions may be just in your own state, but some schools provide excursions to nearby states and even across national borders. One New York school has an exchange of fifth-grade children with a Canadian school. A California grade school offers a three-week trip to one area of Mexico when children have learned the basics of Spanish. High schools and colleges provide semesters of study in foreign countries. Taking part in such travel contributes to maturation and education and is well worth the cost. You may want to make a deal with your student that you will pay a portion of the travel expenses if she earns the other part.

Opening your home to an exchange student is an in-depth way to learn of another's culture and language. The American Field Service program is just one that has been a dependable source for goodwill and understanding between young people. The friendships that come from hosting—or being—an exchange student often last a lifetime. The student truly becomes one of the family, an added blessing for a large family but a unique experience for an only child.

Family travel is one of the most pleasant learning experiences. When children are young, start talking about places to visit on vacations. You may want to start a list and add to it through the years. There are many wonderful choices beyond Disneyland! A trip to a travel agency can give you good ideas in keeping with the age and interests of your child.

Travel posters and folders are an education in themselves. When you've picked a destination, write the Visitor's Bureau and get all the information you can. In the weeks before the trip, spend time learning about the place or places you'll visit. Be frank about how long the travel time will be and start a list of bring-along diversions for boring moments. A once-a-week trip-talk session is ideal and builds anticipation.

At these pretrip get-togethers, talk about more than just the popular tourist attractions. Include the size and terrain of the area you'll visit, the climate, business and industry, political history, dialects or language, regional foods, products to buy, plants and animals, and so on.

Give each child a file folder or envelope for his travel material. Decide together how far to travel each day, which sights to see, where to stay overnight, how much money the trip will cost. The more involved the child is in the pretrip planning, the more he will benefit from the trip.

When you are on a trip, encourage a child to keep a diary or a scrapbook. See also that a child has her own simple camera so that photographs can be added to the record later. Take along the scrapbook, glue, and scissors so that the book can be put together while the enthusiasm is high and the details easily remembered.

On a car trip, stop often to stretch and observe life in a new area. Buy the elements of lunch in a local shop, picnic and walk in parks and woods, look at the schools and try the playground, attend a church service, take in a sporting or cultural event—put yourself into the local life.

When you return home, spend an evening or two looking at the photos and other memorabilia. Finish the scrapbook. Talk about the best parts of this trip—and the things you'd do differently. Parents who do more listening than talking here gain some good ideas on how to make the next trip even better.

Then, talk about the destination for the next trip and start looking forward to it!

8. Science and the Environment

Sensitivity to the world around him is the sign of a Renaissance Child. Not just a user, he is also a protector and a preserver of the environment.

This sensitivity starts when a toddler is taught to care for his possessions and when he belongs to a family that doesn't litter when hiking or driving. It should be a family practice to recycle paper, cans, and bottles. But beyond this caring approach to the environment, a child should be knowledgeable about the sciences of botany, marine biology, astronomy, physics, and chemistry. The latter two are taught in high school, and a youngster should be encouraged to take a basic course in each. Chemistry sets and physics kits for the grade-schooler will whet her appetite for these fields.

The life sciences can be taught even to very young children. Botany is the scientific study and categorization of plants. The making of leaf or flower collections is often part of the grade-school curriculum. But parents can point out elms, oaks, maples, eucalyptus, or pines when outdoors. The names of the more common flowers should also be learned. Planting and tending a small garden is an enjoyable spring and summer project.

The physical science of astronomy is a fascinating one, even for toddlers. Before actually learning the names of stars and constellations, he can glimpse some of the magnitude of the universe just by stretching out on a blanket on a clear evening and looking up at the stars. Make this a family activity to be enjoyed often. On a cool evening have hot chocolate and popcorn and snuggle together.

Ask questions: What is the brightest star? The largest star cluster? Is there a star that blinks? Later, teach the more easily recognized constellations, stars, and planets: the Big Dipper or Ursa Major (the Great Bear), the Little Dipper or Ursa Minor (the Little Bear), Polaris (the North Star), Venus (Earth's sister planet), and the Milky Way (our galaxy). Talk about meteors, "falling stars," black holes, eclipses, and space travel. A visit to a planetarium should follow when a child understands some of these basic concepts.

Watch the newspapers for notices of meteor showers and let children stay up that night to watch and count the meteors. One night when there was a heavy meteor shower predicted, our family had a contest. We divided into teams, stretching out on sun chaises clustered together but facing different directions. The idea was to count the meteors and see which section had the most. Watching a comet or an eclipse can be a memorable event if gently mixed with facts on causes and frequency.

In recent years, marine biology has become a popular academic subject. A child's first introduction to marine life is often the traditional bowl of goldfish. But don't stop there; go beyond this stage with regular visits to an aquarium.

Older children can enjoy snorkeling and even scuba diving for closer views of marine life. Some schools offer marine biology as a course, now that there is increased interest in the preservation of marine life and in learning what the seas can offer us.

Scientific tools make excellent and lasting gifts. Give a young child a magnifying glass. Older ones will enjoy a microscope, telescope, camera, or binoculars. You can't just give such expensive gifts; you also need to show how they are cared for and used. A few hours of encouragement and participation by the parent, along with the joint reading of books on science experiments and photography, will keep this equipment from ending up on a shelf gathering dust.

The intellectual curiosity of a child needs to be encouraged and stimulated. Learning about how things work doesn't have to be a destructive activity. Provide toys that can be taken apart and put back together again.

Don't let those "why?" or "what?" questions get you down. Be willing to take time to look up answers. Inexpensive books on birds, flowers, and trees should be kept in a handy place at home and tucked in the backpack when going hiking or picnicking.

Teach your child to be observant of the sights and sounds of nature. Watch a hawk wheeling in the sky. See who can find another bird. Compare the structure of different leaves. See the effect of fertilizer by planting two identical flowers and fertilizing one and not the other. Walk in tide pools and observe the minuscule life. Point out the phases of the moon and start the tradition of taking a family walk on the night of each full moon.

It doesn't matter if you live in a city apartment or on a remote farm. Nature is available in parks and arboretums, rivers and oceans, fields and forests. It's sometimes temptingly easy to raise an "indoor" child and figure she'll discover the outdoor world later. Why not discover it with her now?

9. Religion and Ethics

Stability is added to the child's life when he is taught that there is a Supreme Being. Perhaps you were raised in one religion and your spouse in another, or perhaps you had absolutely no religious training at all. Many young parents are now realizing that there is something missing in their lives, something to give reassurance through difficult times, something to add stability and continuity to life. You can provide that missing element and enrich family life through religious study.

Find a place of worship that provides both adult services and childhood education. Basic religious education helps develop the Renaissance Child. If you are not already a follower of one religion, visit various churches and synagogues. Listen to the speakers and observe the traditions; then ask about basic beliefs. Attend several services and see if you are comfortable with the teachings and want your child to learn more. (You may want more religious education yourself.)

The Ten Commandments and the Sermon on the Mount (which includes the Beatitudes and the Lord's Prayer) can form the basis of an ethical, moral, and therefore satisfying life. These concepts have stood time's test and can be a valuable framework for behavior. Some of the words may need explaining, but the ideas are very pertinent to current life.

A wise child, no matter what religion, knows something about the major characters from the Bible, including: Moses, Jesus, Abraham, Adam, Daniel, David, Elijah, Elisha, Eve, Hagar, Hannah, Jacob, John, Jonah, Joseph, the Virgin Mary, Mary Magdalene, Naomi, Noah, Paul, Peter, Priscilla, Rachel, Ruth, Sarah, Solomon.

There are many other religious words and concepts that should be familiar to a Renaissance Child. See how many you know; look up the others. They make for good topics while in the car. Some of these are:

Amish	jihad
apocalypse	Koran
apocrypha	Latter-Day Saints
atonement	Messiah
Babel	Methodists
baptism	Passover
Baptists	patriarchs
communion	Pentecost
Congregationalists	Pharisees
Episcopalians	Presbyterians
Gentiles	Psalms
gospel	Rosh Hashanah
Hanukkah	sacraments
Holy Spirit	Torah
Jerusalem	Yom Kippur

Children should have a basic understanding of the great religions of the world: Christianity, Judaism, Islam, Confucianism, Taoism, Buddhism, and Hinduism. The difference between Protestant and Catholic, atheist and agnostic, should also be explained to children. An encyclopedia or Bible dictionary will help.

Being conversant with the names of religious leaders is helpful: John Calvin, Francis of Assisi, Martin Luther, Mohammed, the current Pope, Billy Graham, Mary Baker Eddy, Joseph Smith, John Wesley, and others.

Religious studies form the basis of a child's ethics, that branch of philosophy that teaches the difference between good and evil, right and wrong. Ethical teachings start in infancy and remain an important part of a parent's education of a wise child. Ethics is taught in the home by example; thus, the importance of honesty, fairness, and kindness in dealing with children. Since the molding of a child's character is of prime importance, you will find an entire chapter on this subject: chapter 19, "Eight Great Traits of a Smart Child."

10. The Computer—Tool and Toy

A smart child needs to be adept in computer technology. Because computers have become the door to so much other learning, computer skills are now taught even to toddlers and kindergartners.

Many schools start computer use at an early age so that it becomes as natural to learning as an encyclopedia or an atlas. At the same time the technical and manual computer lessons are taught, thinking and reasoning skills should also be taught.

Children are not robots. They need to be instructed in how to write, compute, and make decisions completely on their own. They need to know how to reason, evaluate, and make good choices. A parent must be sure that her child has the necessary computer knowledge without letting the computer take over all the child's free time.

Computer training is like learning to ride a bike: The skill is valuable only in that it can let you do certain things more easily and rapidly. You don't teach a child to ride a bike so he can just go back and forth in front of the house on training wheels. You teach him so he can exercise his body while enjoying the freedom of going places. With a computer, you also give basic training, but the real worth comes from the freedom to do writing, research, and computing tasks with greater ease and efficiency.

A computer is an asset in the home provided its major use isn't for computer games. Although some games are fun to have, they're no substitute for active play. The main use for the computer will be for other tasks.

Begin by letting a child sit in your lap or right next to you when you are using the computer. A good first lesson is letting a youngster help when you are making a simple list. Next, show how correspondence can be handled with accurate spelling and no cross-outs.

Let the computer be a central part of family headquarters, keeping lists of tasks to be done or outings planned, providing a place for the calendar of events, and serving as the message and reminder center. Let each family member learn to log on, find his file, and read his computer "mail."

Before your child adopts the "hunt-and-peck" system on the computer keyboard, teach the proper fingering. This takes time at first, but is much faster once learned. Since the computer keyboard is much like a typewriter keyboard, the learning has a dual purpose. This basic teaching, done before wrong habits become ingrained, will save your child time and increase accuracy in all the years ahead. A book can help if you don't know proper fingering yourself.

As a youngster gets older, the use of the computer for school assignments will make her a smarter student. Research can be added to a partly completed paper and then edited, spelling can be checked, and word usage can be expanded by way of the word processing program's thesaurus. A generation ago, revising or recopying a paper or project was boring and time-consuming. Sometimes a student settled for mediocre work, instead of taking the time to do it over. Today, the tedium is gone and the result is much higher quality, thanks to word processing software.

Daughters should be taught that the computer is genderless, as are all other mechanical devices. It's unfortunate that education and business still seem to favor boys with disproportionate work opportunities. This gap between the sexes will close when parents and schools treat girls as equals. There is nothing so technical that it is beyond the grasp of the female mind!

Take a genuine interest in computer use at your child's school. If there isn't a good program, start a campaign for one. If that fails, try to work up an all-volunteer program with parents teaching the computer skills. Summer camps and special classes in computer are also available.

By the time today's toddler goes off to college, a computer will be a standard take-along, much as a typewriter was in past generations. Don't hobble your child by failing to see that he has acquired this skill. Basic school learning used to be the 3 R's: reading, writing, and arithmetic. Now the essentials include a fourth skill: computer use.

11. Lasting Language Skills

One mark of a Renaissance person is the ability to speak correctly and clearly. During the Renaissance era, this meant skills in at least three languages. Today, even in a "shrinking" world, few people are competent in more than their own tongue—and many aren't even competent there.

Language is a mirror of a person's education, culture, and background. Although we can't change our background, we can learn the language of the educated and cultured person. For the Renaissance Child, this skill is a necessity.

Speak clearly and properly to infants, because much about language is mimicry. A baby repeats what he hears. If you speak incorrectly (no matter how much good usage is taught in school) your child will pick up many of your inaccuracies.

A parent should expect proper grammar to be taught in school, but shouldn't count on it. For many years, topics such as the "parts of speech" were not specifically taught. And many teachers found it easier to speak like the kids rather than set an example. In composition writing, content was all-important and grammar was overlooked as irrelevant. See that grammar is taught in both speech and writing classes at your school. If it isn't, wage a campaign to change that.

You can brush up on your own language and writing skills by borrowing a grammar book from the school or library. These are the seven most common faults to correct:

1. Pronoun use. If you say "Give the paper to Mom or I" (instead of me), you can expect your child to say "He and me want cookies" (instead of he and I). Go over the simple rules and get it right, remember it, and if you hear it wrong, gently correct it.

2. Troublesome verbs. Knowing the proper use of lie-lay, teach-learn, bring-take, and others will add to a youngster's confidence in both writing and speaking. If you don't know the difference, look these words up and practice them together.

3. Non sequiturs and run-ons. These are thoughts that don't logically follow what has just been said or that are connected like railroad cars. (The Latin *non sequitur* means "It does not follow.") Children often think so rapidly that thoughts spill out randomly; for example, "I fell off my bike and when is supper?" The problem with permitting non sequiturs is that they often lead to run-on sentences. Teachers say this is a major problem in writing. Help a child to slow down when speaking. Point out how each sentence has one subject. Show how run-on sentences are improved when broken into several sentences.

4. Agreement. Too often we fail to match the correct pronouns. We say, "Everyone must mind their manners," but since the pronoun "everyone" is singular, the possessive pronoun must be singular: his or her, not their.

5. Adjective and adverb misuse. We should know that adjectives modify nouns and adverbs modify verbs, telling how, where, when, or to what degree. Thus it is correct to say, "That is a good story. She told it well" (not good). You can spot adverbs since many are formed by adding -ly to the adjective (perfect-perfectly, beautiful-beautifully, smart-smartly). Bone up on these with your youngster.

6. Similar words. Do you know when to use principle and principal? What about capital and capitol? Or who and whom? Your grammar book will straighten these out. Simply defined, principle is a concept, principal is a person; adjectivally, principal means "chief." Capital is the principal or most important, or the large form of a letter, or the foremost or capital city. But Capitol is the building in which a state or national legislature meets. Got that? "Who" is a pronoun and "whom" is a pronoun in the objective case. Read up on that one and get it right. Another trouble spot in writing is "it's" and "its." This is an odd one, but easy to remember. "It's" is always the contraction of "It is." "Its" is always the possessive of "it," even though, unlike other possessives, it has no apostrophe.

7. Profane words, mispronounced words. Profanity is usually used to show anger or frustration, or to hurt. The words are usually meaningless to the point being made. These inappropriate terms, used originally to shock and gain attention, are now so common that they've lost even that value. An educated person doesn't have to resort to uncultured language or street slang. As a parent, take a stand against profanity. Help your child find more exact words to show feelings of amazement, success, disappointment, or failure. Research shows that children pick up profanity mostly from peers, but they won't use it unless they also hear it in the home. So clean up your own act and you'll find that your child follows suit.

Mispronunciations abound in today's world. Many newscasters say "nucular" instead of "nuclear." Most people forget that the "l" is silent in calm, balm, Psalm, palm, and so forth. We say "gotta" and "wanna" and "becuz" because we talk so quickly. But when mispronunciations and sloppy speech are permitted in the early years, they have a way of sticking through life. Try to improve your standards as an example for your kids. And gently correct mispronunciations at home but not in public.

Along with the mastery of English, encourage the use of a second language. Help a child choose another language that will be useful in his daily life. If you live near eastern Canada, encourage French. If you live along the southwest border of the United States, encourage Spanish. If a child is interested in world affairs, encourage her to consider Russian, Chinese, or Japanese.

The study of Latin is regaining popularity. High school students who have had a year of the "dead language" of Latin find that it increases their English vocabulary to the point that it improves their comprehensive test scores and writing ability.

Foreign language skills are useful when traveling. Before your family visits a foreign country, learn enough about the language to cope in common situations. There are plenty of books available, but cassette lessons or evening classes are usually more effective.

Foreign terms abound on restaurant menus. So as not to feel stupid, your child needs you to explain a few of the more basic terms.

Antipasto (Italian), Hors d'oeuvre (French)—appetizers
Beef Bourguignon (French)—a beef dish with a thick sauce, usually served with bread for dipping into the sauce
Bisque (French)—a thick soup of fish or game
Blintze (Jewish), crêpe (French)—a thin, filled pancake
Borscht (Russian)—beet soup
Buerre (French)—butter
Chateaubriand (French)—tenderloin steak
Chutney (East Indian)—a spicy relish
Creole (American south)—dishes made with tomatoes and peppers, or more generally regional specialties

En papillote (French)—meat or fish cooked and served in paper

Escargot (French)—snails, usually an appetizer

Flambé (French)—food served in flaming liquor

Fricassee—to cook meat by braising, then stewing in a white sauce

Goulash (Hungarian)—a beef and onion dish usually served over noodles

Marzipan—cookies and candies with almond flavor

Mit schlag (German)—with cream or whipped cream

Mousse (French)—a dish (appetizer, entrée, dessert) made with whipped cream as a base, sometimes stabilized with gelatin, then chilled

Niçoise salad (French)—a salad of many ingredients including beans, peppers, tuna, red potatoes, olives, tomatoes, and eggs

Paella (Spanish)—a main dish of rice, chicken, shellfish, vegetables, and seasonings

Pâté (French)—a smooth mixture of meat and spices, usually an appetizer

Pepparkakor (Swedish)—spicy gingerbread cookies

Prosciutto (Italian)—spiced or smoked ham cured by drying, and sliced paper-thin

Sauces: Béarnaise—a creamy, spiced sauce for broiled meat and fish

Bordelaise—a brown, beefy sauce for hearty meats

Hollandaise—egg and butter sauce for vegetables, poultry, and fish

Mornay or Velouté—a cream sauce, often with cheese, for eggs, vegetables, fish, croquettes.

Spatzle (German)—small flour dumplings

Sukiyaki (Japanese)—a main dish made with thinly sliced beef, soy sauce, bean curd, and greens

Sushi (Japanese)—raw fish used as an appetizer

Sweetbread—a main dish made of the pancreas or thymus gland of a calf or lamb

Tripe—a dish made of the stomach tissue of lamb or beef

Wiener schnitzel (German)—breaded veal cutlet

Yorkshire pudding (English)—a popover made in drippings and served with beef and gravy

Although these are just a few terms, you will find it educational fun to go to a restaurant with a foreign menu that also shows the English translation. See how many foreign terms your family already knows.

Young people are very comfortable in fast-food restaurants, but parents should help them feel equally at home in a restaurant that serves food from other countries.

12. Home Care, Health-Care, and Auto Care

A child can grow up to be academically brilliant but wholly unable to cope with everyday living. Consequently, along with the other forms of enrichment, you need to teach your child—boys and girls alike—the basics of maintaining health, home, and, home away from home, the auto.

Our survey of working parents showed that most parents included children in cooking and cleaning, but less than 5 percent taught home repair, automotive maintenance, or sewing. These three are probably ignored because working parents have little time to give the lessons and maybe feel that one can get along without these skills. They do deserve a place in a child's upbringing because hiring someone else to maintain clothing or make minor home and auto repairs can be very expensive.

A toddler can be taught the names of tools and given a few for his very own repair box. Boys as well as girls should be instructed in the use of a sewing machine. And future car owners need to know how to maintain their investment.

Here's a list of home skills that you should teach over the years:

1. Kitchen skills: cooking nutritionally balanced meals, measuring and baking, using appliances safely, knowing the refrigerator, freezer, and shelf-life of perishable foods.

2. Cleaning skills: dusting, mopping, vacuuming, scrubbing, disinfecting, polishing, cleaning the oven and refrigerator.

3. Home repair skills: using hand and power tools, changing a washer, determining the right wattage and safely changing a light bulb, using a plunger, resetting a circuit breaker, lubricating a hinge, gluing broken objects, repairing a frayed cord.

4. Laundry and wardrobe skills: sorting laundry, removing common spots and stains, using bleaches and special cleaners, ironing, mending, sewing buttons, using a sewing machine for major mending and the making of clothes.

5. Gardening skills: lawn cutting and care, planting, watering, pruning, fertilizing.

6. Automotive skills: filling the gas tank, changing a filter, adding oil, testing tire pressure, changing a tire, changing a fuse, checking a battery.

7. Health-care: knowing first aid, caring for common health problems, recognizing when to get professional help, exercising regularly, getting proper rest.

Certainly, you select skills in keeping with your child's age, but you must start when your child is young to introduce all of these subjects. It's mandatory that you teach safety at the same time since children should learn respect for appliances, caustic substances, power tools, and so forth.

Most of these skills are taught with your child right beside you. As you work together, mention the importance of doing the task properly. Regularly remind your child that these everyday skills are just as necessary to the Renaissance person as are the more exotic subjects.

Parenting Point

Enrichment doesn't require riches. Many of the cultural advantages you'll give your child over the years are free of cost except for your input. Step by step, you can enjoy your Renaissance Child and at the same time become wiser yourself.

Chalkboard for Chapter Seventeen

Where should you begin? Here are some sample ideas in each of the categories we've discussed. Choose the ones in keeping with your child's age.

	Pre-schoolers	Grade-schoolers	High-schoolers
1. Art	Make a paper mural to hang on a wall	Visit an art museum	Go to an art gallery
2. Literature	Go to the library weekly	Have a book reading contest	Read and study one author
3. Theater	Act out 5 nursery rhymes	Read a play aloud at supper	Go to a play
4. Music	Make an instrument out of an old pan	Visit a store to look at instruments	Listen to Bach
5. Business-Economy	Learn the names of coins	Follow one issue in the news	Make a clothes budget
6. History-Politics	Talk to Grandpa about olden days	Read a book about ancient Rome	Follow a political issue
7. Travel-Geography	Look at a world globe	Visit a travel agency and get folders	Plan a summer trip
8. Science-Environment	Play with a magnifying glass	With friends, clean up a vacant lot	Look at the moon with a telescope
9. Religion-Ethics	Take a friend to Sunday school	Practice living the Ten Commandments	List the most needed ethics
10. Computers	Play a computer game	Make a computer list of things to do	Do one entire project on a computer
11. Language	Memorize a poem to tell Grandma	Learn five words from different languages	Go one week without swearing
12. Home-Auto	Learn the names of five tools	Learn to use the sewing machine	Work one hour on auto maintenance

For more ideas, see my book *1001 Things to Do with Your Kids* (Abingdon Press, 1988).

Eighteen

Stretching Your Time

Silence and bitterness started creeping into Danielle and Justin's marriage when she returned to work after their second daughter was born. One Saturday after an argument—when they regained control of their tempers—they talked about what was bugging each of them. Justin began by saying he missed the hot supper being ready when he arrived home. Danielle countered by saying she'd like to go out once in a while to a real restaurant with friends instead of only to fast-food places with the kids. Justin said he missed the camaraderie of his bowling team friends but felt he should be home with the kids in the evening. Danielle said she felt that, besides the duties of her career, she was burdened with all the work of running the home and had none of the benefits. As they talked, they made a list of the various problems and then started to find solutions. Just writing the list and having *the discussion made them feel better, because they started learning how to juggle the two jobs each one had: career and parent.*

After making their priority list, Justin and Danielle started enjoying a wider variety of activities that included time with their youngsters and with their friends. Talking with other parents, they found many time-saving systems that let them accomplish household tasks more efficiently and thus have more time for this family fun. At the same time, they discovered the benefits of working together as a family. Even toddler Ashley had certain tasks she did each day—and she loved doing them! Their organization plan was contagious, not only to their two older children, but also to other friends and neighbors, who began to adopt some of their methods. In fact, they all formed a parent support group to share their best ideas.

There are only twenty-four hours in the day, and when a parent has two necessary jobs to do, prioritizing is important. Some things aren't going to get done in a perfect way and some things aren't going to get done at all. There is nothing wrong with that, provided a parent chooses the right things to eliminate.

And what does this have to do with a happy child? A youngster's relationship with her parents is the most influential framework she has. Do not underestimate the effects of a good role model in parenting. If the home is disorganized, a child has a more difficult time coping with homework, hobbies, and extended play. If there is constant bickering in the home, it affects the child's emotional stability. If there is no outreach beyond the home into community life, a child can become insular and selfish.

A well-run home based on the spirit of cooperation, an atmosphere of mutual respect and love, and time for activities that go beyond the routine of daily living give a child a sense of security and self-esteem. He feels part of a continuing adventure, with happy home life as the central focus.

But how can busy parents juggle their time to provide this all-important home and community environment? Shouldn't parents concentrate on just work and home and forget all other activities until the children are grown?

Hobbies, sports, friends, and church and civic activities need to be a part of every adult's life. They are a necessary bridge to the years ahead when the children are grown and launched. Single parents, especially, often find themselves lonely and unproductive when there is no longer a child on which to focus attention. And many married couples find that the years they looked forward to—with children educated and on their own—become years of restlessness and nonproductivity that sometimes split up the marriage.

So, while focusing on parenting, a successful working parent has to nurture secondary interests. Certainly, when there are infants in the house, child-care and career are nearly all-consuming. But gradually a parent must broaden the scope of his or her life. Becoming a whole person should be your continuing goal through life.

Managing the Home

If parents are going to juggle their time to include more than job and family, they have to manage the home efficiently and equitably. When greater numbers of women began entering the work force, they assumed that the work of managing the home would be shared by their husbands, so that each partner had one job (a career) and half a job (home and child-care). But as it turned out, most women who returned to work ended up with two jobs and the men continued just as before.

In addition, the myth that home management was an easy task was perpetuated by a few men *who left their jobs* and took over the home and child-care while their wives worked. These men wrote books on how fulfilling home and child-care were—and then they returned to their full-time office jobs!

Although there are a few fathers who do all the home management work, and some who do their fair share, most, unfortunately, do far less than a full 50 percent.

Some of the most heart-rending answers on our working parents survey came in response to this question concerning managing the home: Do you feel that you do more than your share? Not one father answered affirmatively, yet 76 percent of all working mothers said "yes." Many commented how this inequity hurt their relationship with their husbands. Others said: "He doesn't seem to notice that while he's endlessly looking at T.V., I'm still working around the house"; "I wish he'd ask what he could do!"; "He does one little thing and then quits helping"; "He pretends that he's not good at certain tasks."

When questioned further about home responsibilities, participants in the survey revealed that men selected certain home activities and stuck only to them: reading or playing with children, handling home finances, and making repairs. Many wives accused their husbands of choosing the easier and more pleasant tasks. One said, "I clean the bathtub while he reads the bedtime story." Areas that were jointly covered in some marriages were meal preparation and general child-care, although matters of discipline, transportation, and homework supervision usually fell to the mother. And those areas that were invariably presided over by mothers included care of a sick child, shopping, entertaining preparations, correspondence, and house cleaning.

There continues to be a great imbalance between a father's time spent on home activities versus a mother's. Working fathers contribute about one-fourth as many hours as working mothers do. Something has to change! And if it doesn't, we're going to have burned-out moms, confused kids, and broken marriages.

Here's the fairness rule: When two parents work full-time, the home tasks should be equally divided. Sometimes it helps to make a list of the jobs (cooking, repairing, infant care, shopping, cleaning, homework supervision, etc.) and the typical time each consumes. Then divide the work with the understanding that after a month you'll switch off. No typecasting permitted! Some jobs are more fun (or more difficult or more boring) than others, but both parents can learn to accomplish the entire list.

Remember that just because your mother cleaned the refrigerator each week or polished floors every Saturday morning is no reason for you to have to do likewise. In keeping with cleanliness, consider doing some jobs every other week or monthly. Make a chart for cleaning so that everything gets done on a rotating basis.

Social Times

Essential to a good marriage—and thus good family life—is a parent's social life. Unfortunately, this is often the first aspect of a marriage to be eliminated when babies come. What a mistake this is! Most parents in our survey said they wanted more time to be with friends but found this difficult to accomplish. In response to the question of how many nights parents spent out (without children) each month, the average was 2 1/2. Most felt that once a week would be ideal.

And what do working parents enjoy doing? The survey showed that the most common diversions were going out for a movie or dinner, attending a sporting event, or playing cards or party games at friends' homes. Other parents enjoyed playing in an orchestra, going bowling, singing in a barbershop quartet, playing tennis, attending a play series, and taking a class together.

Often a community project connected with your child's youth group or your church is a change-of-pace outlet for a parent. Just as your youngster's free-time activities include variety, so should yours. Parents, too, need to be willing to try new things.

Most away-from-home activities involve both parents, but when only one parent participates in an activity, that gives the other the opportunity to be alone with the children—a time that can be special and creative. Although mom's or dad's solo night out is beneficial for both, just remember that such activities should be balanced with ones that involve both parents together.

Most families in our survey expressed the desire to entertain at home about once a month. They said they especially enjoyed entertaining when they felt they didn't have to fuss with fancy foods or have the house in perfect condition. Home entertaining is a money-saver too. Potluck suppers spread the cost and the work, but even if you do it all yourself, casseroles and salads are very acceptable fare. It needn't be an entire meal either. Having friends over just for dessert or a variety of finger foods can be equally enjoyable.

Entertainment at home can range from an evening of conversation to what used to be called "parlor games." Popular games are cards, charades, play-reading, and newer ones such as "Pictionary," and mystery games that provide character descriptions and clues. Theme parties are fun and require some extra work but are worth it for special occasions such as an anniversary, Valentine's Day, July 4th, or Halloween.

Sometimes you may just want an excuse to be with other adults. The need to socialize doesn't have to be based on who owes whom or an invitation to a grand function. Sometimes you can have a "just because" party. Or, you can celebrate a birthday, a job promotion, the arrival of a new neighbor, or your child's entrance into first grade. One neighborhood has a party the first Sunday of each month.

No matter what you decide to do for your weekly social time with your spouse and friends, be sure that at least once a month the social event is just for the two of you. A romantic dinner, a quiet walk, or a stirring symphony performance contributes to the broad base of shared activities that keep a marriage strong.

Give a high priority to this social time with your spouse. Start when children are infants to have a sitter look after them several times each month. You can make these nights without you special for them by providing a favorite supper and a new game or loved book as part of the evening activities.

When our children were young, a favorite supper of theirs was macaroni, cauliflower, and apple sauce. We called it the all-white meal. Since my husband and I weren't too fond of macaroni and it was quick to prepare, I usually made it when we were going out for dinner. When the kids saw the fixings, they knew it was the folks' night out, but the prospects of the all-white meal made it a happy time for them.

Don't feel that because you are gone five days a week you must be home all seven nights a week. Of course you will plan for weekend and evening times with your child, but also plan ahead for times with friends or just your spouse.

Research shows that failed marriages—which are usually so damaging to children—most often stem from the failure to maintain the mutual interests that brought a couple together in the first place. Failure to have fun together, failure to find time to communicate, failure to talk over money problems, failure to build a network of supportive friends—don't let these failures spoil your marriage. Juggle your time to include social times with each other and your friends.

Something New

The time will come when your little ones are no longer little. They'll be off to college and careers of their own. And suddenly you will have more time for yourself.

In your child's growing years, keep learning new things, keep investigating new ideas, keep sharpening your skills. Whether you like soccer or sewing, world affairs or woodcarving, boating or bowling, keep your interests alive. Enjoy them when you can. Try new things to see if you can uncover any special talents.

Juggle your time to include a slice of the big world of enticing activities out there. Don't wait until you're middle-aged to test them; start now. Perhaps you'll only be able to do so on rare occasions, but you can look forward to the time when you can become a real pro.

Parent activities are important to kids too. Because these projects relax you, they make you a patient and more interesting parent. And talking about your activities provides one more opportunity to share information with your youngster.

Sometimes you'll find an activity to enjoy together. We started extended-family volleyball games when the kids and cousins were in grade school. The net is now regulation height and there are third-generation kibitzers on the sidelines, but the game continues to be an occasion for enjoying one another in the outdoors.

Don't skimp on your own personal enrichment time. Let it make you a better parent!

The Blessings of Outreach

Why would a parent with a job, a home, children, friends, a hobby, and a sport need anything more to do? You do need one more thing to do because without it you could become a selfish person. The last ingredient I would recommend for you to juggle into your schedule is time for outreach.

Outreach is any activity that you do to help those outside your immediate family. It can be advising a youth group, teaching Sunday school, raising funds for a worthy cause, working in a volunteer job, delivering meals to the elderly—the list of needs is long. You will probably engage in this activity without your children, but be sure to talk about it at home. Remember the effects of a good role model in parenting.

Sometimes there are service projects you can do together. One family has the tradition of working at an urban shelter each Thanksgiving Day, serving meals to street people. The kids say it is one of the best events in their family life. Another family adopts a needy family each Christmas and shares toys, a decorated tree, clothing, and food.

Find an outreach project that fits your family and your busy schedule. Many groups are happy to have your help on an irregular basis, as little as once a month. Although it may be physical work you'll be doing, you'll find yourself amazingly refreshed by it.

You bless others when you share with those who have less. At the same time, you find that *you* are satisfied and blessed—blessed with new friends, new talents, new insights, and an increased understanding of the goodness and peace that really exists in this world.

Efficient home management, as well as family cooperation, lets you enjoy this outreach time.

Two ways to save time at home are by:
1. Establishing a home headquarters
2. Using kid power

The Home Headquarters

Running a home is big business. Consider the cost of shelter, food, clothing, education, health-care, sports, and entertainment. Analysts have estimated that it costs about a quarter of a million dollars simply to raise a child from birth to college graduation. And many parents are trying to run such a business from a stack of clutter on the kitchen counter!

Establish a home headquarters, preferably a desk in the kitchen or family room. Equip it with desk supplies, file folders, an expanding bring-up or "tickler" file, a monthly calendar, and a bulletin board.

● *Desk supplies.* A ruler, stamps, tape, stapler, scissors, tablets, paper and envelopes, pens, pencils, markers, rubber bands, clips, tape measure, a box for keys and tags to label them, and a telephone and card file of addresses and phone numbers. With today's mobile population, the card file is more efficient than a book since a card can be updated more easily. Other niceties include an adding machine, typewriter, or home computer. Make this your central family management area.

● *File folders.* Use a big desk drawer or buy a bankers box (a cardboard file box). Establish files for these (and other) categories: Equipment warranties and guarantees, the budget, home ownership or rental papers, insurance, copies of wills, correspondence, charge receipts, vacation ideas, gift buying ideas, entertaining, community activities. Also make a file for each child and include in it a copy of his birth certificate, health record, school report cards, and those special papers he brings home that you can't possibly toss out.

Include the kids in the establishment of file folders—perhaps buy them in different colors for each person. Let each child make a file for her own activities and important papers. When a child has her own desk, she can move her files there.

The mother of one of our youngster's friends called one day to ask me a question. She had been talking with her daughter about possible eighth-birthday gifts and the daughter had mentioned she'd especially like to have some file folders like those the Krueger kids had. She couldn't quite understand what her daughter meant. She said to me, "Why should my daughter have file folders when I don't have any?" I couldn't think what to answer!

● *An expanding bring-up file.* This is the file that will keep you sane. At a stationery store, buy the accordion-like file numbered 1 through 31 for the days of the month. You may also want to buy the one with slots for the 12 months of the year.

In the 1–31 file, called a bring-up file, place items that must be attended to on certain days of the month. For example, if you pay bills on the fifteenth and thirtieth of the month, put the bills in the slots for those dates. If you have tickets for an event, or an invitation to a party, file them under that date. Select a date, such as the twentieth of the month, to be your correspondence day and file letters to be answered there. Notes on when to feed the plants, clean the carpets, decide on camp, change the car oil, renew a license, make cookies for a meeting, go shopping—whatever must be done on a certain date—should be filed under that date.

Items for other months can be stored in the monthly file and moved into the 1–31 bring-up file on the first day of each month. Get in the habit of looking into your bring-up file once each day.

● *Monthly family calendar.* Above the desk, tack a very large monthly calendar. Put on it all the regular events for the month: church, dental appointments, lessons, group meetings, and so forth. Then add the special events: birthdays, trips, shopping days, parties, and entertaining. Encourage kids to add their important events to the calendar: due dates for large school projects or reports, club meetings, camping trips, and birthday parties. When you have prepared the calendar for the new month, look it over and be sure that there is time for *family* events each weekend. You may have to move some other things around to make room for this most important time.

When family members ask questions that could affect scheduling (if they can go for an overnight, entertain some pals, have a party, if you can drive them somewhere, etc.) refer them to the family calendar. This lets you both see how the event will fit in and avoids confusion and social overdosing.

Start when children are young to refer to the calendar each day. Always point out something to look forward to: "This is today and in three days we go to Grandma's house." Or, "We have four easy days, but a very full weekend." "Nothing is scheduled for next Saturday or Sunday afternoons, so what would you enjoy doing?"

Depending on how complex your schedule is, you may also have a pocket or desk-top calendar that reminds you of additional things that don't involve the family but that you must do on certain dates.

Reserve one desk drawer as the scrapbook drawer. In it put programs, greeting cards, school papers, photos—all those things you want to save to remind you of the year. Let one child regularly paste these into a scrapbook, adding his own descriptive comments.

● *Bulletin board.* Hang it near the desk. Since purchased bulletin boards are often inadequate in size, it is more economical to buy cork material and just glue it to a large section of the wall. The family calendar can hang on the board.

Also on this board go the following important lists: emergency telephone numbers, often-used phone numbers, approved T.V. shows, repair list, grocery list, lent-out list, photos, good school papers, family weekly menus, school lunch menus, family rules, and so on. You will also want to have an area on the bulletin board for a list of needed tasks and your incentive plan to get the family to do them.

Keep the bulletin board fresh and up-to-date with new photos, drawings, and current lists. Older children can be in charge of changing the bulletin board each month.

Using Kid Power

One of the best time-stretchers is the use of kid power. This has several excellent results aside from taking work off your shoulders. When kids do tasks around the house, they learn how things work, they learn patience and cooperation, they become more responsible about the home, and they become house-smart.

Many parents deprive their children of these lessons out of misguided love. Perhaps a parent had to work very hard as a child, so he doesn't ask his child to do chores. Perhaps a parent thinks a child is too young or too old or too busy. Or perhaps a parent thinks that only she herself can do the job right. How sad to deny a child this important learning experience.

For many of the things that need doing around the house, perfection isn't necessary. For example, let a child dust the living room (unless of course the Queen of England is coming for tea). "Good enough" can be your motto in many areas.

Start including a toddler in helping around the house. She'll find it fun. When introducing a new task, you'll have to spend a little time to show how it is done, and again to show how it is done, and again to watch the child do it. But the more things you teach her to do, the more time you'll have to spend on fun with her.

How much time should a child spend doing tasks? Preschool children should spend about fifteen minutes each day and older children should contribute thirty minutes. Over the weekend, a total of two hours of work can be contributed by each family member.

You can see that if you have two children, you will have about nine extra hours each week to spend on something special! So, it's worthwhile to take the time and patience to teach children to help.

The time spent during chores is certainly not wasted. The skills learned are invaluable for living on one's own. In addition, when working together, you can have a good discussion (or horseplay) with your child, thus accomplishing two things at once and providing more time for closeness. Sometimes music can be enjoyed in the background, or a suitable book-on-tape played. Or, if only one person is working, another can read aloud to him.

Change tasks each month. Changing any more often is confusing and there are benefits to doing the same job over the longer period of time (you learn to do it better and faster). List each family member's chores on the bulletin board as a reminder.

Parents in our survey usually made the mistake of not assigning different and more challenging tasks for the weekend. Divide these bigger jobs into increments and never work more than two hours at a time. It's important to let children know what you expect in the way of weekend work so that you and they can then also plan the more adventuresome activities that come when work is finished. And that should be a given: Chores first, play second.

Avoid sex stereotyping in assigning tasks. And remember to let kids work occasionally in teams. This teaches cooperation and also appreciation for the talents of the sibling.

Each home will have different needs, but these are some tasks kids can do:

For young children: emptying wastebaskets by collecting the contents in a large plastic trash bag, cleaning wash bowls (kids love to play in the water), setting the table (make a diagram of a place setting), brushing the dog, delivering laundry to the rooms, picking up toys, bringing in the newspaper, making beds, opening curtains, picking up trash in the yard, dusting.

For older children: cooking a meal, sorting the mail, feeding pets, dusting and vacuuming a room, watering plants, polishing silver, painting a fence, doing laundry, washing a car, cleaning out a cupboard or closet, weeding the lawn, shining shoes, washing windows, repairing toys, loading and emptying the dishwasher, wiping countertops, pasting in trading stamps, making flower arrangements, raking leaves, cleaning bathtubs, changing light bulbs, running errands on a bike, washing piano keys, taking the trash to the curb, doing simple mending, keeping the family scrapbook.

For the oldest children: (In addition to the preceding list) changing an oil filter, reorganizing the garage, making a shelf, changing faucet washers, cutting the grass, putting up storm windows and screens, babysitting, running errands in the car, serving at and cleaning up after a party, defrosting the freezer, cleaning the refrigerator, sewing and mending.

A typical task list for a grade-school child is this:

Morning: Feed the dog, make the beds
Afternoon: Set the table, make a salad
Evening: Wipe the kitchen counters, pick up the family room
Weekends: Water the house plants, make Saturday lunch, participate in a family project of building a fire pit.

Some children do their assigned tasks with little reminding. Others respond to a star pasted on the chore list for each day the work is done. Still others require incentives and reminding and more reminding.

For variety, use incentive systems some months and not others. Here are some simple motivators:

1. The good month award. Let a child paste up a star or other sticker on each day her tasks are completed. Give a small reward for a month where there are twenty-five stars on the chart. Give a larger reward for a perfect month with a star on each day.

2. Seasonal gimmicks. On the bulletin board put a simply drawn picture: a Valentine heart for February, a bunny for the month in which Easter falls, a firecracker for July, a pumpkin for October, a turkey for November, a Christmas tree for December. Using colored paper, cut out small hearts, bunny tails, turkey feathers, round ornaments, and so forth. For a day when tasks are done without reminding, the child gets to add one of these to the picture.

3. Long-range goal. Let a child decide on something he really wants—a portable radio, for example. Put a sealed jar on the counter with a slit in the lid. Label it "radio fund." Put a dime in the jar for each day that chores are completed, a quarter for the weekend. See how long it takes to achieve the goal. This "payment" method is an exception to the rule that daily chores are done without pay.

These will get you started, but if you are interested in more inventive incentives, you'll enjoy all the ideas in my book *Six Weeks to Better Parenting* (Pelican Publishers, 1985).

Should a parent pay a child for accomplishing these regular tasks? No, this is the child's contribution to the family. When a youngster needs extra money a parent should have a ready list of other tasks he's willing to pay for. A child's allowance is entirely separate. It is not pay for regular tasks and is not withheld if the child doesn't accomplish his work. However, if a child is disobedient, the privilege of spending any of his money may be withheld for a certain period of time.

Time Tips

Here are some additional time-saving tips:

● *Desk projects.* If writing, phoning, figuring, and reading need doing, most people will do best to tackle the writing first, then the math, reading, and phoning. Make all the phone calls at one time so as not to interrupt other projects. Use small stick-on notes rather than clips when you want to bring an article or message to the attention of another family member. At the end of the day, look over your list of things to do and re-list those items not finished. Spend at least five minutes at the start and end of each day handling the most important items on your desk.

● *Car time-savers.* Have a hidden key firmly attached to your car's exterior. Make a habit of filling your tank when one-quarter empty. Each year, reorganize your glove compartment with a new map, hand wipes, paper, pencil, flashlight with fresh batteries, a granola bar, a deck of playing cards, simple bandages, a small supply of change, and a hidden $5 bill. Clean out your car trunk at the same time.

● *House cleaning.* Working together as a family, do one room each day. One person clears things off the furniture while another dusts and then puts the objects back, another vacuums, another takes misplaced items to the correct locations. Write out a schedule of things that can be cleaned monthly (like picture frames or the refrigerator) and things that can be cleaned every other month (like windows or book shelves).

● *Laundry.* Do a load whenever you choose instead of having a laundry day. Label plastic bins for jeans and socks, light-colored wash-and-wear, towels, and so forth. Nothing gets washed that isn't in the bins. When a bin is full, run the load. Read care labels when you buy clothes and keep special instructions handy in a large envelope. Use only no-iron table cloths and napkins.

● *Spring housecleaning.* Avoid it as much as possible by keeping up with your work all year. Using stick-on notes, put a price on each cupboard and closet (25 cents up to two dollars). Let family members sign up on the sticker if they want to clean the cupboard within a week. Give the rules for unloading it, washing it out, and putting down fresh shelf paper. You may want to return the contents yourself.

● *Repairs.* A parent and a child should work together, particularly when repairing broken toys. Teach a child the names of the tools and how to make simple repairs. Time is saved by having one repair day a month, instead of bringing out tools and supplies repeatedly.

● *Finding time to read.* Read ten minutes before bedtime. Keep a book under the seat of your car so you can read while waiting to pick someone up or for an appointment. Read in the bathtub. Listen to tape-recorded books while driving or doing household tasks.

● *Doing two things at once.* Make supper and test a child on spelling. Have a family cooking night when everyone works together to make casseroles, sandwiches, desserts. Jog with a child. Read to a child while he cleans up his room or bathes. Have a child read to you from a book, or from a book report he has written, while you drive. Do your nails while telephoning.

● *Keeping close to a spouse.* To avoid wasting time and creating confusion, make opportunities for good communication. Be sure to have breakfast together. Make one daytime "I love you" call. Meet for lunch. Sit down before supper and just talk for five minutes. Take an after-supper walk and let the kids run races ahead of you as you just talk or quietly enjoy one another's company. When driving together, use the time in the car for discussing important topics—actually keep a list. Take a class together. Work on a house project together. Cook together. Play a game together.

● *Cutting down on kitchen time.* Empty the dishwasher as you set the table for the next meal. Always make two of a casserole or dessert and freeze one. Make part of supper—clean vegetables or make salad fixings—as you prepare breakfast. Make a lot of sandwiches at one time and freeze them. Store left-over foods in divided trays so that each tray eventually becomes a complete meal.

● *Cutting down on preparations for entertaining.* Enlist kid help! You can have a weekend dinner party easily by working at it a little each day: planning the menu on Monday, making and freezing the cake on Tuesday, making the seating plan and the salad dressing on Wednesday, setting the table on Thursday, preparing vegetables or salad ingredients and storing them in tight containers on Friday, and preparing the main dish on Saturday.

● *Cutting down on shopping time.* Make an outline of the market where you usually shop (or ask if the store has one; many larger ones do). Then make a list of items you usually buy, aisle by aisle. Make copies of the list. Prepare your marketing list at home by checking off the items needed. With your list you'll find you can move very quickly through the store. Combine several errands on one trip and go at low energy time (when more challenging activities might be difficult). Take one child along for conversation, shopping education, and games. For hard-to-find items, call first. Consider occasionally shopping by catalog.

● *Cutting down on clutter.* Create storage places for items to be recycled—cans, bottles, newspapers—and get rid of them once a month on your way to or from work. Once a year collect items for rummage sales or charitable groups. Sort the mail daily and get rid of the junk. Put non-urgent reading and catalogs in a bin for weekend perusal. Don't store unusable clothing, because few items will look as good when the style returns or you get back into the same size. Establish a boo-boo box in the front hall closet; anything that is left where it doesn't belong is put in the box once a day. Assign a child to empty and deliver the contents each weekend. For the young child who is slow in picking up toys and clothes, use the timer challenge: Set a timer for a reasonable amount of time and say, "I bet you can't get everything put away before the bell rings." Once a year before school begins in September, spend an hour or two with each child in her room—making stacks of out-grown clothing, unwanted toys, and rubbish, and getting rid of these items. Try not to build more and more shelves—this only encourages clutter! Follow this rule: If it hasn't been used this year or last year, give it away.

Parenting Point

Keep your marriage alive and well by wisely dividing your time between your children, your spouse, your home, and your career. Try not to slight any of the four! Then go one step farther and reach out and share.

Chalkboard for Chapter Eighteen

Make a list of important things that you are overlooking or neglecting because of your dual job as career person and parent. See how you can work these into your schedule over the course of a month. Some suggestions are: social events, entertaining at home, attendance at church, reading, home repairs, excursions with children, outreach to the community. Put a star in front of those you think need the highest priority and start with those.

1.
2.
3.
4.
5.
6.
7.
8.
9.
10.

Look over the list in a month and see how you're doing. Try each month to add one of these important items to your calendar.

Nineteen

Eight Great Traits of a Bright Child

Lauren and Cam felt that their kids were quite smart—in fact, too smart sometimes! Matthew was able to lie quite effectively by age six, and preteen Debbie would clam up and refuse to talk whenever she didn't get her way. With these ploys they managed to confuse and anger their parents. Once when Cam asked Lauren if Matthew had lied about taking candy, she found herself lying to protect him! Another day when Lauren told Cam of Debbie's unwillingness to communicate, Cam refused to talk about it! So, they just let the bad habits continue, hoping they would go away. But they didn't. It was a long time before they realized that many of their own bad habits were being mirrored by their children. Eventually they decided to make a list of the character traits they wanted to instill in their children. They agreed to teach these patiently but diligently each time there was *an occasion. They saw that the traits of a happy child are built little by little from infancy onward and that their own example was one of the most important educators.*

Recognizing the need to build good character in children is a great beginning. When you make the decision to become a parent, you are also making the decision to help your child grow into a person with good qualities.

Character-building isn't a term young children understand. When I once told a disobedient son that I was going to help him mold his character, he protested, "I'm too young to know what character I want to be!" Today's kids are wonderful characters!

Many of a child's traits come from observation; kids observe their parents, accept what they say as fact, mimic what they do as the right way to act. Or, they subtly test us with a new attitude to see if we will permit it or reject it. So, a parent has to be alert to first set a good example in actions and words, and second, be aware when a child is trying out a new idea to get that parent's reaction.

Parents in our survey selected the traits they most wanted to instill in their children. These eight great traits are:

1. Self-esteem
2. Love
3. Intelligence, creativity, inquisitiveness
4. Self-government, orderliness
5. Responsibility, poise, leadership
6. Honesty, ethics, religious faith, patriotism
7. Ability to communicate
8. Cheerfulness

Wouldn't it be wonderful if a child were born with these traits built in! Some good traits do come naturally, but others require work. The important news is that you have eighteen years in which to teach them, gradually, while your child is under your roof. Even if your child is a teen, it's never too late to start!

Self-esteem was at the top of almost every parent's list. Since every family would order the other traits differently, let's consider them in reverse order, with self-esteem last.

8. Cheerfulness

We want our child to enjoy life, to have a sense of humor, to be flexible, to be optimistic. This can be summed up as a cheerful attitude. Certainly, cheerfulness makes family life go more smoothly. It's nice when kids are happy!

Often we set an example for gloominess by emphasizing the wrong things. For example, a child spills milk. You go into a rage as if it's the start of World War III, and so your child thinks that the spilled milk is something really important. Thus you are wrongly teaching that little mistakes should depress him and make him feel put down. Your better reaction would be to teach him how to quickly clean up the mess and find a safer place to put his glass.

If every little upset in daily life brings on shouting, tears, or guilt, the sweeter, happier times are overshadowed and a cheerful family environment is lost. Kids pick up on a parent's pessimistic remarks and body language and mimic these. They too will have a downer attitude when they constantly hear lines such as:

"Nothing ever goes right."
"There's not a thing I can do."
"I'm so upset."
"I'll never be happy again."
"The world's a mess."
"This is hopeless."

How much better to encourage an upbeat tone in the home. If a child is having difficulty learning to ride her bike or tying her shoes or picking up toys, a parent should learn to comment more constructively and cheerfully:

"That's not so bad."
"I had trouble too, but I finally got it."
"It's not the end of the world." "Let's try again."
"I know you'll do it."
"Let's work on it together."

Such lines make us all feel happier.

Helping a child gain a sense of perspective can make the difference between a cheerful and a gloomy child. This often starts when a parent can laugh at his own mistakes. I once served beef with a dish of what we found to be whipped cream, which meant I'd already heaped the horseradish sauce on top of the gelatin dessert! At first I wanted to cry, but then I laughed, and the others did too. And so the event became an oft-told family story. It made the children better able to accept and keep in perspective their own silly mistakes without tears or anger. Teach your youngsters that some things in life are truly important events, but many things are just everyday happenings without long-range consequences.

Do you hear laughter at your house? If you do, encourage it. To smile and laugh come naturally to a baby, but adults often wrongly suppress joy by failing to appreciate and encourage it.

Start with little children by smiling at one another, by giggling, by making funny faces, by laughing aloud at humorous rhymes and stories. Then, as children get older, appreciate funny jokes and the repetition of amusing stories. Learn tongue-twisters, celebrate April Fools Day with harmless pranks such as hidden alarm clocks, short-sheeting beds, placing small, paper cups of water on door tops, or adding food coloring to the milk.

Be sure to emphasize the difference between harmless and dangerous pranks. Discourage sick or hurtful humor. Talk about truly funny things in movies, books, and on television. And even when there is work to do, keep a light attitude and try to find something cheerful about it.

Provide humorous books and look at funny cartoons. Be sure that *you* laugh aloud. Teach this laughter early. Too many children are afraid to laugh. Many think that a smile will suffice. Have a laughing contest so that children can hear laughs and not be embarrassed at the sound of their own laughter.

And, when something funny has happened, reminisce about it later. If the butt of the story is comfortable with the teasing or joking, let the story be told again and again.

Flexibility also connects with cheerfulness. Are you an inflexible parent—do you think you already know the one and only way things are to be done?

Be flexible enough to accept a new idea when presented by a child. Change plans when possible. Make family life more adventure than routine. Encourage flexibility in schedules, in chores, in room arrangements, in eating places, in study areas. Sameness is so boring!

Flexibility means that you may occasionally let a child stay up beyond his normal bedtime so he can see the full moon or a T.V. special. This means you may eat supper by the fireplace or out on the porch. This means you may have a weekend night when each family member sleeps in another's bedroom.

If you're flexible and want to teach flexibility, you may occasionally want to make a deal. "If you do this, I'll do this." Kids usually respond to deal-making with willingness and flexibility.

Most important, show a child that there are *several* good ways to do things right—not just one perfect way.

Being positive and joyful and hopeful often comes out in our language. Which of these lines sounds more like you? (The first line in each pair is obviously wrong; the second line is a better response.)

"That's impossible for you."
"Let's see if we can figure out how you can do this."

"I guess you should give up."
"If you want to try again, I'll stand by you. I'll help."

"Be realistic; you can't jump off the roof."
"You can jump from this tree branch. I'll be right here."

"That's a stupid idea!"
"That's one idea, but have you thought of this . . ."

"It doesn't look as if you're going to get your homework done."
"Let's divide your homework into small segments; it will seem easier."

"I don't think you'll ever be a great speech maker."
"Remember how you had trouble learning to ride your bike, but you practiced and did learn? The same will be true of your speech."

Don't make it a disgrace to give up on something. It may be a right idea at the wrong time. Make "Let's try it" a family motto, but remember that "Let's try it next year" is O.K. too. Don't worry about your child's failures. Worry about the chances your child misses when she doesn't even try. Her successes will outweigh her failures. So when there is a failure, remind her of other successes she has already had.

For a happier, smarter child:

• Provide opportunities for fun and laughter
• Make light of silly mistakes
• Create a home atmosphere that is flexible
• Speak with hope and cheerfulness
• Plan surprises and adventures

7. Ability to Communicate

You remember that Debbie clammed up when she didn't get her way. She didn't know how to communicate her needs or her dissatisfaction. And we can see from the opening story that she'd learned this from her dad. Good communication is built on trust and love. When you're close, when you know others care, you want to share your feelings.

Parents can turn off communication so easily. Here are some turn-off lines and their turn-on opposites:

"For goodness sake, will you just shut up."
"Let's find a time when I can really hear you out."

"What a dumb idea."
"Can you explain how that's going to work?"

"You two—Quit the arguing!"
"Sit down here for a moment and let's talk it over."

"Not now! I'm too busy."
"That sounds like quite a story; would you tell it at supper?"

"Your comments were really out of line at the party."
"Was that the only way to make your point?"

Be available for listening when a child wants to communicate. When that isn't possible, set up a time to have a private chat. If the atmosphere in your home is busy, you may want to go for a walk in order to get that one-on-one opportunity.

When you must put off a child's question or topic, remember to bring it up at a better time. When putting off a young child, give him a piece of paper that says, "Talk time with Dad at 7." This shows him that his communication is important and that you do care.

Provide a home forum for trying out new ideas. Encourage talk at supper or at the family meeting. This practice with loving family members makes it easier for a child to communicate at school, with friends, at assemblies, at Scouts.

Remember that often the idea a child voices is just a trial balloon. Don't overreact or she'll learn to keep ideas to herself. Be open to new ideas. Listen carefully for the real or underlying message, which is sometimes hidden. Encourage a thoughtful, nonjudgmental discussion of the pros and cons of an idea.

Don't make a child fearful about sharing. Learn this line and use it often: "I'm so glad you told me about it." Hearing something bad that your child wants to share is better than being in the dark. When you're in the dark, you can't help. Let your child know that you want to hear the problems and that you'll love him "no matter what."

You stifle sharing if you shout, punish mercilessly, or make fun of a child's ideas. You also stifle sharing when you take over the conversation or finish a child's sentences. Sometimes you have to wait out the silence to give her the opportunity to tell her story her own way. Appreciate what she says and try to help her solve the problem.

If some family members are more vocal than others, which is almost always the case, make sure that they don't monopolize conversation time. Each family member deserves to be heard and it's up to you to see that he gets the opportunity. Include these less vocal ones by asking questions such as, "Do you agree?" "Would you do it the same way?" "Have you ever experienced anything similar?"

Help a child to be communicative at social functions. Suggest something she can talk about at Grandma's supper. Ask her what might be a nice thing to say to the hostess when leaving the party. Practice intelligent conversation at your own supper table. (Remember, if the T.V. is on, it competes with supper talk, so don't get in the habit of T.V. at mealtimes.)

Our family had the practice of each person thinking of five topics he could speak on at social events. For a holiday open house one little son had his list (a school excursion, a new tool, a riddle, a question for Grandpa, a book he'd read). When we said it was time to go home, he said to the hostess, "Oh good; I've just used up my fifth topic!"

Use written forms of communication and encourage kids to do the same. Leave an "I love you" note on a pillow. Help a child write about a special trip. Encourage both boys and girls to keep diaries. Insist on youngsters sending written thank-you notes for gifts and special occasions. Most important, see that your child has varied experiences so that he has things to share.

If his life consists of the morning rush, sitting at school, doing chores and homework, eating in front of the T.V., and then watching T.V. until bed, you are not giving your child time to read, time to learn new skills, time to play, time to be creative, time to think, or time to communicate.

6. Honesty, Ethics, Religious Faith, Patriotism

These can be some of the more difficult traits to teach. And they aren't taught in a single day; they are taught every day in bold as well as in subtle ways.

As usual, our language is important. Again, in these typical lines, the better comment follows the wrong one.

"How stupid of you to lie. Dad will surely have a punishment."
"What was the reason for telling that lie?"

"You broke that toy! Well don't cry, we can get another tomorrow."
"Unfortunately, you can't play with that toy until it's repaired or you save the money to replace it."

"You found some money in the yard? Just put it on the counter."
"You could have just kept this money, but it was right that you brought it to me. Mike lost it so I know he'll be glad to have it back."

"How dumb to forget your spelling list at school. I guess you'll just fail the quiz."
"Forgetting to bring your spelling list home means that, instead of play, we'll have to go over to Dan's and copy the list."

"You know that we don't want you to use alcohol, so stop it."
"I'm glad you admitted that there was alcohol at the party. Let's talk more about drinking. Then I want you to set up the rules and what happens if you break them."

When children are toddlers, there is a fine line between fantasy and reality. It is here that a parent must determine the difference between unintentional untruths and intentional lies. When a child lies, look for the cause of the lie. Get rid of the cause and you get rid of the need to lie. Make these facts known to your child:

"I really appreciate your telling me the truth, as hard as it was to tell."
"If you hadn't told the truth, the punishment would have been much more stringent."
"I know that you can sometimes get away with telling me a lie, but *you* will always know that you did wrong."

"I want to trust your word and let you do certain things completely on your own."

Emphasize the good feeling that comes with honesty and a clean conscience. Don't play prosecuting attorney with your child. If you see chocolate crumbs leading up to your child's feet, don't ask him if he's eating chocolate cookies. You know it. If you suspect that a young child is lying, role-playing may be a solution. Ask a child to act out what has happened. Or, ask him to tell you once more, being very careful to tell all the details honestly. This second—or third—chance often brings the truth to the surface.

A child who steals or shoplifts reveals her motives by what she does with the loot. If she shows what she has stolen to no one, she wants it for its own sake. If she shows it to her friends, she is seeking their approval. If she shows it to you or another adult, she's asking for help. Be alert to these signals and take appropriate action.

The smart child should want to do the right thing just because *it is right,* not because of fear or because of what others may think. Don't make a child promise never to lie again; rather, encourage him to try very hard not to lie. Let kids know that some lies seem to go undiscovered, but that wrong is eventually punished.

Although honesty is taught at home and beyond, ethics are learned almost entirely at home. The schools have enough subjects to teach without having to give special emphasis to the question of ethics.

We send strange ethics messages to a child when we say, "Never tell a lie," and then say, "Act as if you're only eleven so we can get you into the movie for half price." Or when we make a generalization about ethical standards, such as, "All politicians are crooked," and yet our child notices that we vote just the same. (Are we voting for crooked people?) Or when we voice hopelessness about corruption in corporate business, yet the child is aware that the parent pads her expense account or brings home supplies from her office.

The high standard of ethics that is important to your child's well-being must start in the home. A child's ethics must be independent of what may be going on in his view of the world. That "everyone else does it" doesn't change wrong into right. You must be alert to the influences of a child's peers and the peers' families. You may have to say, "I know that Marty's family does it that way, but we do it this way." You must speak honestly and act ethically. And, above all, you must praise—and praise again—a child's honest and ethical behavior.

It is entirely up to you whether your religion is going to be an active and useful part of everyday life or a boring ritual that a child must suffer through until she is old enough to escape. Do you parade your religion only on Sundays and holidays? Or is it integral to every part of daily life? What religious traditions do you have? Do you explain them and encourage them wholeheartedly?

If your own religious training is inadequate, you should take the time to learn right along with your child. Again, your example is most important. If you tell a child to pray about a problem, but the child is aware that you never pray about challenges, you're relaying the message that prayer isn't worthwhile.

Selection of a church home is one of the best decisions parents can make when a baby is born. Learning about God and his care for his children, learning of the challenges and triumphs told in the Bible, and learning about the religious beliefs of others brings wisdom, stability, and tolerance to the smart child.

Lessons taught in the Bible are applicable to every aspect of life: schoolwork, sports, social relationships, sibling rivalry, physical disabilities and sickness, love and marriage, parenting, grief, war and peace.

An easy place to start is with a Bible reading at breakfast and a prayer before bed. The Commandments and the Beatitudes provide good guideposts for relationship problems that come up during the day. Your own family rules can be based on contemporary applications of the Commandments. Thus, "Thou shalt not steal" becomes "Thou shalt not shoplift." "Thou shalt not kill" becomes "Thou shalt not glorify the torture and killing shown on T.V."

Sexual morality is another topic that is best taught within the family. Nowadays the pendulum is swinging back from promiscuity and sexual freedom (which really isn't freedom at all) to more self-control and safe sex practices. Young people are finding that abstinence is a feasible premarriage option.

Spend some time at the library looking at books on teenage sexuality. Choose the ones that best tie in with your own ideas, and see that your child has the necessary facts. Keep the lines of communication open and your shock-threshold high. Don't back down from what you believe is best for your child just because it isn't popular. Youngsters need to know your feelings and expectations. These can be a strong support when a young person's sexual standards are tested.

Faithfulness in marriage is one of the most valuable lessons a child learns by observation at home. This relationship between parents, more than any other factor, creates the guidelines for the child's own dating and marriage. Children are quick to pick up on parental strife and are usually aware of infidelity, no matter how carefully a parent tries to hide it. The unrest that comes from an unstable marriage carries over into every aspect of family life. When a child sees that one parent cannot trust the other, it undermines his own trust in both parents. The example of a strong and loving marriage is a foundation on which a child can build his own successful adult life.

When there is a separation or divorce in the family, parents need to unselfishly explain to the kids not only the changes that will come about, but also some easy-to-understand reasons for the change. When parents think that youngsters are "too young to understand," the children often mistakenly think that they are the cause of their parents' unhappiness.

One research project has shown that children who were under six at the time of the breakup recover more quickly than older children. Preschoolers often exhibit regressive behavior, a subtle cry for attention, but respond to a parent's love. Grade-schoolers openly show their grief and anger, and need better communication with the parent at a time when the parent is often preoccupied with his own problems. Teens are usually the most damaged, with 68 percent exhibiting their confusion and hurt by engaging in some sort of illegal or destructive activity following their parents' divorce.

Parents should be aware of how much their own marriage influences a child. Marriage vows to love and honor should be mentally renewed each day with honesty and fresh commitment.

Reverence for country, family observances of patriotic holidays, conversations (not on just what is wrong with the country but also on what is right), participation in political and economic issues and a discussion of these with children—all these build both patriotism and political awareness. This kind of home education goes beyond saluting the flag and makes a child a more intelligent part of the community and world.

Regularly remind kids that doing right is not always rewarded, and that a clear conscience should be enough of a reward. And be sure to show that a person of integrity can still have fun.

On the subject of improved moral values, a young woman wrote this to me after the birth of her first baby:

I gave up smoking when I became pregnant and decided never to start again. My husband quit using four-letter words so the baby wouldn't mimic them. We started a savings account because we wanted her to have the funds for college. We cleaned up our house and made some improvements so the baby would have a nice place to play. We even planted a tree our child would later climb. We made a commitment that for her sake—and ours—we'd work hard at keeping our marriage loving and strong. We found that we stopped doing little borderline dishonest things because we didn't want her to pick them up. We looked for other couples to socialize with—ones who no longer smoke pot, get drunk, or gamble their savings away. And we thoroughly enjoy these new friends with better values. We always *knew* what to do, but the baby was our impetus to do it. We've found that we feel good about what we're doing, and best of all, our life is still a lot of fun.

5. *Responsibility, Poise, Leadership*

Teaching a child to be responsible is basically giving her freedom, loosing her (not losing her, but permitting her to carry the weight of certain things herself). A child who is constantly reminded and prodded doesn't learn to act on her own. When you have taught your child the right and ethical things to do, you can loose her more confidently.

This loosing goes on little by little as you allow her to make more choices for herself every year. A child needs to see the relationship between doing something—or failing to do it—and its effect (success or failure, harmony or confusion, completion of an assignment or work left undone).

Loosing in no way means you lose a child. Loosing means that he takes onto himself two things: the choices suitable to his age and the results of those choices. For example, each year your child becomes more responsible as he moves from picking up his clothes, to selecting what to wear, to mending his clothes, to laundering his clothes, to buying his clothes with your guidance, to selecting clothes on his own within the confines of a clothing budget. The result of those choices is the increased feeling of being in control, a nice feeling for kids to have.

But you must be willing to let a child suffer the consequences when he chooses wrong or fails to carry out his responsibilities. Only by tasting both success and failure can he choose the better way. Some parents, out of a mistaken sense of love, try to save their children from mistakes. This itself is a mistake. Certainly we would keep a child from making a dangerous mistake, but we must let him try his wings in most areas.

When a child understands the basics of being responsible, she is ready to be a leader of others. A leader is one in whom others have confidence because of her good ideas, her willingness to work, and her ability to get people to work and play together. Most parents want their children to be responsible and responsive leaders—responsive to the world around them. And we want them to have the poise to know how to handle themselves in public situations.

Poise and leadership in public start with opportunities for poise and leadership at home. When two young children are playing and it's time to put the train or game away, put one in charge and let the other be the helper. Switch the jobs the next day. This teaches both leadership and followership. A smart child needs to learn how to work amicably with others in the dominant position as well as in the nondominant one. Kids soon learn that they get more cheerful help if they aren't bossy.

Older children can work together in a similar way, as a team to clean up the kitchen or reorganize the garage. Again, put one in charge and one to help. Knowing that he will take part in both leadership and followership tasks within the family teaches a child the importance of being a kind and fair leader and a willing follower. In home, school, sport, and club activities, the wise parent, teacher, or coach provides opportunities for the so-called natural leader to be a follower as well.

When an event is over, whether it is a birthday party or a baseball game, talk with children about the event and how it went. Listen to their reactions; find out what in their estimation went well, what didn't, and why. This conversation after an event is vital, and you can learn much just by listening. Next consider together what might be done to make the event even better.

A poised child knows how to act when things are going smoothly and especially when they aren't. Poise is not just good manners. Far more important than knowing which fork to use is knowing how to act in an emergency, when under pressure, or when the issue is emotional. These important aspects of poise are learned from your example. Your reactions (calmness, hysteria, anger, forgiveness, confusion, thoughtfulness) will be the ones your child will be most apt to choose when in similar situations.

In addition to this vital aspect of poise, there is the social side of poise, which includes:

● *Table manners.* At mealtimes, practice good manners: elbows off the table, no talking with the mouth full, passing things around (not across) the table, which silver to use, how to order from a menu, making table conversation, requesting a courtesy serving, asking to be excused.

● *Introductions.* Even young children should introduce you to their friends. Practice the actual words. Insist that you be introduced to anyone a child brings into your home or your car.

● *Safety.* Practice fire safety, as well as what to do when the child is alone, lost, being followed, or when a stranger tries to touch him.

● *Compliments.* Practice how to accept a compliment and what to say when given a gift. Parents need to emphasize these social skills before a child has her first party.

● *Older-child social skills.* How to ask for a date and make conversation during a date, how to dance and what to do when a dance is over, how to act in a public place when others are misbehaving, opening doors, offering an arm or a hand, talking with older adults, how to refuse alcohol politely, how to dress appropriately for special occasions.

● *Conversational skills.* What to do when the conversation stops dead. (Remember the five topics?)

Anticipate a youngster's needs for poise or social skills. When a child is going to give a speech, have a party, stay overnight with friends, and so on, take a few moments to go over the correct behavior. You may have talked of it once, but it helps if you reinforce it again.

And don't forget the praise. A child will feel good about the responsible or poised behavior she has shown if you compliment her on successes. Parents use praise too sparingly, yet it is one household item that doesn't run out.

4. Self-government, Orderliness

If you were to stand over your child and give orders—"Get dressed," "Do your homework," "Thank Grandma for the gift," "Go to bed now"—your child would do those things, like a robot.

But we want a youngster to do the right things *on his own,* by his own choice. We want him to think about what he is doing and why he is doing it. We want him to be self-governing in areas appropriate to his age. This self-government stems from learning to make choices.

We let young children choose what to wear, which of two T.V. shows to see, what snack to have, or where to play. We permit older children to choose what club to join, what lessons to take, how to spend an allowance, what kind of party to have, when during the day to put away toys and crafts. And we encourage teens to choose what classes to take, when to do homework, how to spend a clothing budget, how to get weekend chores accomplished, what to buy as gifts, what extracurricular activities to join.

When we give kids the opportunity to make *many* choices completely on their own, they are more willing to make certain choices with our guidance.

Part of learning to be self-governing is learning to accept the consequences of a wrong choice. This will be discussed more fully in the next chapter, on discipline, but remember that rules—and punishments for breaking them—permit kids to be self-governing within the framework of the family.

When a rule is understood yet broken, permit no second chances. Mean what you say. Children are more comfortable when they know just how far they can go and what will happen if they go too far. Let children choose to do right or wrong and reap the reward or the punishment. Only in this way will they learn.

Thus, if a child is careless and breaks something, she helps repair it or pays for the repair or replacement. If a youngster oversleeps and misses the bus, let her walk to school or, if that isn't possible, charge $2 to drive her. If she wants to live in a messy bedroom, that's fine as long as she tidies it up the day before you clean. Otherwise, you tidy it up before cleaning, and she has to do another task (such as weed the lawn, clean several cupboards) to repay you for your time.

Regularly give children plenty of choices so they feel they are in charge of their lives. You never want a child to say or think: "I have no say around here." So give choices often. Here are typical choices for younger children:

"You may have a friend over to play on Friday or Saturday. Choose the day you prefer."
"You may buy this racing kit or this truck, but not both. Which one do you want most?"

"You may eat your breakfast since it is good food, or you may throw it on the floor or waste it and then be punished. It's up to you."

"You may stay up late tonight or tomorrow night."

"You may choose to write your thank-you note to Aunt Sheila now or after supper before playtime."

Of course, as a child gets older, you must allow even more important choices:

"You may come in on time, or come home late and have to stay home all next weekend."

"You may make three five-minute phone calls or one fifteen-minute one. Please use the timer."

"You may buy a used car now with the money you've saved, or save for another year and possibly buy a new one."

"You may borrow my sweater today and return it to me in good clean condition tonight, or you may borrow it and have it cleaned so I can wear it Friday."

"You may buy one $40 shirt or two $20 shirts."

"You may sleep all morning or get paid for cleaning the garage."

Sometimes it is hard for a parent to follow through with the announced conditions, but consistency is necessary if you really want to teach your child. You want your child to mean what she says. You, in turn, must mean what you say.

Teaching a child orderliness can save him time. Organization lets him cut through the routine and get on to the pleasant things of the day. Don't wait until a child is in school. Start teaching basic order and organization to toddlers, explain why a routine is important, and then sit back and enjoy a household that runs smoothly and happily—at least most of the time. Teach your child these basics:

- To get up when the alarm goes off
- To accomplish his morning tasks before play
- To be punctual
- To complete homework
- To remember what must be taken to school or Scouts
- To make a list of what must be done on an especially busy day
- To keep his clothes in order—clean and mended—with your help
- To put away toys in his room at least once a week
- To understand priorities—what must be done first, what can wait

- To keep important things in a special place: a box for jewelry, a bank or wallet for money, file folders for important papers or awards
- To throw away junk regularly, to recycle paper and cans, to give outgrown clothing, books, and toys to a charity
- To write down phone messages and put them on your desk
- To return telephone calls
- To borrow from others rarely and to return in good condition what has been borrowed
- To be aware of the family calendar of events, particularly when scheduling his own activities
- To accomplish assigned tasks with a minimum of reminding
- To make a note of something special or important and put it on the bulletin board
- To remember the motto: "Don't put it down, put it away!"

There are few obvious rewards in life for orderliness. Nobody's job resumé says "Keeps room neat." But a sense of order and priority does make for home happiness and business success. Organization makes one feel more sure of one's self, more in charge.

A child who feels in charge of her life and her environment has a feeling of satisfaction. She is not rushing to grow up too fast, she is enjoying life to the fullest right now.

3. Intelligence, Creativity, Inquisitiveness

Life is not a game show or a lottery—we shouldn't expect unmerited awards to fall in our laps. Teach children that knowledge and success usually come from study and work. Teach them how to work, why we work, and the value of work well done.

Never put down a child's intelligence. Don't ever label him (in your words or your thoughts) as slow. Children develop at varied rates. Labeling a child a slow learner can become a self-fulfilling prophecy that may take years to overcome. This doesn't mean that you ignore a child's educational problems. A wise parent is patient, but when there is a need the parent must get help sooner rather than later. The home attitude toward learning (discussed in chapter 15) is highly important.

One study conducted over an eight-year period showed that young children who are talked to, touched, and questioned, develop intelligence 40 percent faster than those who grow up in an atmosphere that lacks caring and stimulation. This should be sufficient encouragement to parents to communicate intelligently with their children.

Poor communication actually destroys rather than nurtures a child's intellect. Here are some typical put-down comments followed by better responses:

"It was dumb of you to flunk the test."
"The test must have been very hard."

"I'm busy, you'll have to figure it out yourself."
"I can help you in about fifteen minutes."

"I don't know; don't ask me."
"I don't know, but we can look it up together."

"You're too young to understand."
"Let's see if I can explain it another way."

"Don't argue with me about it."
"We disagree so let me hear your reasons."

"You can't have a theater in this house! It will make a mess."
"Let me find some old sheets you can use as a curtain."

"Clean up this junk!"
"The toys can be there until Saturday at 10 A.M."

"Let's see what's on T.V."
"What would we all like to do tonight?"

If you want wise, imaginative, creative children, these ideas are important:

● Teach a love of reading, starting with an infant in your lap. Encourage family members to bring articles from the newspaper to share at supper. Read a chapter of a book at supper. Give a child a magazine subscription. A love of reading is the single most important skill for a smart child.

● Talk with your child; ask questions. Take a child with you on errands and walks for one-on-one chats. Don't ask questions that require a mere yes or no answer. Challenge a child to think through problems and find solutions.

● Cut back on television viewing time. Provide alternative activities that are as engaging and far more educating.

● Carefully select the gifts you give. Choose gifts that foster creativity—drawing paper and paints, tools, books, chemistry sets—and provide simple instruction and enthusiasm to whet interest.

● Purchase a current encyclopedia and dictionary and encourage looking up things. Provide a quiet atmosphere for doing homework.

● Take children to the library, plays, museums, and music events as often as to movies and amusement parks.

● Encourage lessons in music, sports, drama, and more, but leave time for creative spur-of-the-moment play.

● Make learning fun. Set aside a time weekly when all the family works together on one creative project—building a tree house or solving the Sunday crossword puzzle.

● Keep getting smarter yourself. Take a class. Study and work *with* your children—read when they do, write or paint while they do homework, be a team for home repairs, let them visit your office and see your new computer. Let them know that you are still learning.

● Show that you value your child's work, the time she spends in school. Make grades important and help her work to improve them. Support school activities. Be aware of homework assignments. Be alert to signs of boredom or discouragement. A good education is a lifelong gift.

2. Love

How do we foster love and caring in our children? In two ways: by being loving and caring ourselves, and by giving them opportunities to show these important traits.

Through all the challenges of parenting, we *do* continue to love our children with a deep and unconditional affection, but sometimes our language doesn't reflect this. Have you ever said:

"Nobody loves a naughty boy."
"You have to earn my love."

"If you loved me, you wouldn't do that."
"What am I going to do with you!"

Such statements may seem minor to us, but said often enough they begin to erode a child's feeling of being loved. This is damaging because it is difficult for a child to be loving when she doesn't feel loved herself. How much better it is to let your child hear these words and for you to prove them:

"I love you no matter what."
"I'll always love you."
"I'm so happy you're my kid."
"I love you too much to let you do this."

Don't confuse love with overpermissiveness. Love has principle. Love has standards. Love doesn't make excuses. Love is forgiving. Love is more than saying the words. Love is shown in the way we treat our children. When children are little we hold, hug, and kiss them. And we walk hand-in-hand, hold them in our lap, and fireman-carry them. Expressions of love in words and acts should continue as kids get older. This touching, this affection, is natural when it starts with young children and continues as they grow older. And it must come from both mother and father.

A child knows we care for him when we ask about his activities or bandage his hurts, he feels special when we set aside what we're doing to give him help or praise his work, and he knows we love him when we guide him with both consistency and affection.

A child knows we care for others when we speak of them with affection, take cookies to new neighbors, read to a shut-in, run an errand for a senior citizen, give some of our free time to a community project. Try to include your children in these activities, all of them demonstrations of sharing love outside the home.

Love from a parent to a child starts in babyhood when a parent introduces words such as *love, thank you, I care, you are good, I'll always love you.*

It is easy to love a child when she is good and successful, but she needs your love even more when she fails or faces a challenge. Love never gives up.

You encourage love from your child when you verbally appreciate the loving and caring things she does. Look for such an opportunity every day. And when a child says "I love you," don't take this for granted. Respond happily so she knows that this love is important to you.

Help your child make surprises and do caring things for her other parent and other children. Encourage good deeds in the family. Start loving traditions: bedtime hugs, hello kisses, appreciative notes.

Sibling rivalry is a chief concern among parents (and rightly so if the disharmony is constant). However, be slow to use that phrase. Friendly competition, some teasing, and minor disagreements shouldn't be escalated in the parent's thinking into a major problem, and a parent can do much to ease these relationship difficulties.

Rivalry between siblings often starts with the arrival of a new baby, who takes away the parent-time formerly spent on the first child. A parent needs to reinforce her love for the firstborn, and she needs to point up the differences between the first child and the baby.

"You're my big boy, and you can do so many more things than the baby."
"I hope you will help the baby grow up into a nice person like you."
"Oh my, the baby is crying; would you comfort him for me?"
"Let's talk about how you're treating your little sister. Is this the way you'd like to be treated?"
"If you can't get along with a member of the family, it wouldn't be good for you to go out and play with anyone else."
"I know he's little, but is there any way to include him in your play?"

It is important for a parent to give the older child opportunities to play without the younger child. And the older child needs to know that certain of his toys and possessions are safe from destructive younger fingers.

The wise parent takes the older child on extra excursions and shows him that his age and maturity give him privileges that the younger child doesn't have.

Learning to share is one of the important lessons of early childhood. When there is only one child in the family, the parent must still see that the child knows how to share. For example, have just one muffin at snack time and let your child cut it in half for the two of you, offering you the first choice.

Inviting other children to your home for playtime is important for the single child. When there is a one-of-a-kind toy, a timer will help, giving each child the opportunity to play with the toy.

Toys that require cooperation also cut down on sibling and peer rivalry. Building sets, race car sets, a small playhouse—such toys teach young children to play together harmoniously. And of course, when you notice children happily playing together, don't forget to compliment them!

Occasionally a parent will have to prod children into doing loving things for the other parent (making a birthday card or selecting a gift). It was sad to hear of the young mother who never received a Mother's Day card, but the fault was as much her spouse's, because he didn't help the children to remember this important occasion.

To love and to be loved—what more can we ask for!

1. Self-esteem

Of all the gifts you give your child—your time, your patience, your love—the gift of self-worth is one of the most valuable. Self-esteem requires self-knowledge, an understanding of what each of us—parent and child—knows within his heart is true about himself. So we want regularly to remind a child who he is, how important he is to us, that there are some things only he will do in this world, and how precious and unique he is.

Children with low self-esteem often live in a home where they hear these depressing words:

"You never do anything right!" (Some days you really have to look to find something a child has done right, but you must do it!)
"Who do you think you are?" (The child thinks she is nothing if her parent doesn't know who she is.)
"I don't care what you think!" (The child assumes her ideas don't matter.)

A child with self-esteem is a candidate for success. He can accept some failures, he is ready to try again, and he is willing to work harder. He has felt success before, he knows that he is appreciated, he realizes that he has worth.

A child without self-esteem is a candidate for failure. He soon doesn't even try for success. If he's done things correctly, no one has noticed. And sadly, a child who doesn't feel he has value is apt to try suicide. "I'm not worth anything, so better to end the misery." Suicide is now the second cause of teenage death (drugs are first).

Attempted suicide is often the anguished cry for help, the cry to be noticed, appreciated, and loved. Suicide statistics cross all socioeconomic barriers. In fact, suicide is on the rise among children of affluent parents where love for career and status may have replaced love of family. These children feel a lack of intimacy as well as the pressures of competition with their parents' other time-consuming interests.

Never make light of a child's threats to commit suicide. Even if he is not sincere in that desire, he is saying that he feels his life isn't worth living. You must get professional help at once. Your minister or family doctor can recommend a specialist, or you can inquire about the social services in the town where you live. Many "yellow pages" directories list suicide prevention services.

A child gains in self-esteem when she hears these words:

"You tried, and that's good. You'll get it the next time."
"I'm glad you're my kid!"
"I know you can do it. Let's figure it out together."
"You were good today!" (We always find the time to tell a child when she's bad, but do we give the same time to compliment her on goodness?)

Research shows that children who have high self-esteem come from parents who believe that a child is basically good and has value. A child files away experiences according to two categories: things that are a success, things that are a failure. We need to give children opportunities to succeed so that successes will outweigh the occasional failures.

Of course, "winning" or being the best shouldn't be a prime emphasis. Doing a good job, working up to one's capacity, doing better than before, finishing the task, are all very acceptable results. One Olympic athlete said, "I always felt my parents' support—even when I lost." Can your child say and feel that you are always supportive of *her,* not necessarily of everything she does, but of *her?*

Some parents make the mistake of trying to protect a child from failure. They wake him in the morning so he won't be late to school, correct his homework, argue with the coach, do all his shopping, clean up after him, never criticize him or make strong suggestions. The real world can be a cruel awakening for such a child. Only by doing things himself can a child taste the sweetness of success.

Your best tool for developing self-esteem is giving children a life of opportunities, a life beyond school and television. And then, give praise. When a child catches on slowly or makes many mistakes, you have to really look for something you can honestly praise, yet honest praise bestows self-esteem. The child says to herself, "Hey, I'm not so bad!" Praise encourages a child to try again, to hold her head high, to speak up, to accept a challenge.

When there are failures, don't ignore them. Rather, help your child learn from them and then move on to better things. Degrading a child over a failure erodes his self-esteem and can actually be a form of child abuse. Degradation and unfounded criticism take away the security you work so hard to build.

You can take your child on a trip around the world, you can buy him a car and send him to the best schools, but the things he'll most remember about his childhood are when you displayed his clay piece in the living room, when you took him out for a hamburger after he struck out in the 9th, or when you said you learned a lot about gas-powered model airplanes from him. He knew he was precious. He had self-esteem!

Parenting Point

Although working parents have limited time, they must be alert to the occasions for teaching good traits—essentials for a smart and happy child. Don't ignore bad habits or encourage unethical behavior by looking the other way. Teach your child the difference between right and wrong, good and evil, love and hate. Because of your love, you can do it!

Chalkboard for Chapter Nineteen

Each day, look for these opportunities to build your child's feeling of self-esteem:

- Find something to praise.
- Give a child opportunities to do things on his own.
- Be supportive of his ideas.
- Encourage him to try new things (and to try again).
- Help him to conquer fear and live adventurously.
- Remind him of an earlier success when he fails.
- Uncover something special he can do well.
- Tell him you love him—each and every day.

Twenty

Discipline and the Happy Child

Because Brittany and Barry were such charming children, it was hard for their parents to discipline them. Liz and Steven loved them so much and wanted them to be happy all the time! Once, Liz made Barry sit in the corner when he was naughty, but he just giggled and then he did the same wrong thing again—and again. When the kids started nursery school and Liz went back to work, Steven helped Liz make a few family rules in hopes of having some peace and order when they came home tired. Brittany regularly broke those rules, but Steven was so soft-hearted he couldn't bring himself to punish her. Besides, he and Liz didn't have time for meaningful punishments other than shouting and a few quick spanks. As the kids got older and seemed to need more direction and correction, both Steven and Liz wished they'd found a good means of discipline when the kids were little.

Just how could they correct their kids so that they wouldn't keep repeating the same wrong behavior?

Hindsight regarding discipline doesn't always help kids behave better! Teaching obedience is possible when kids are older, but it is also more difficult. Most parents in our survey wished they'd set down more perimeters when their kids were young. With older youngsters discipline is often needed to correct aggressive and willful behaviors. Unfortunately, these behaviors become more ingrained as years go by; hence, the need to check them as early as possible.

Many working parents find it difficult to discipline their children at the end of a working day. Yet, discipline is the second most important parental role, right after nurturing. When a child breaks a rule, parents have an obligation to impose some form of discipline. Doing so gets the child's attention. It says, "See, we were telling you the truth." This consistency is one more way parents demonstrate their reliability to youngsters.

We've come a long way in disciplining children: from putting kids in the stocks and beating them with a leather shaving strop! Experience has shown that such physical methods—even spanking—simply don't work as well as ones that compel a child to *think* about the right thing to do.

The reason that spanking, slapping, and other forms of physical violence are often used is that they appear to have an immediate effect, and the "tool" for discipline, the hand, is readily available. But, beyond this immediate effect, they don't succeed in changing a child's behavior as well as other methods, which may take more time. Since a change in behavior is what we're after, why not take the action that brings results? Our aim isn't to show a child that we are powerful or mean. Our aim is to show him a better way to act.

Spanking teaches a child that a form of violence (spanking, hitting, slapping) is an appropriate and adult method for solving a problem. (This leads a child to adopt the same method when he has a disagreement with a playmate.) Spanking makes a child resent authority, and a resentful child is difficult to teach. It also identifies adults with hurting and pain, thereby cutting down on closeness between parent and child. Spanking doesn't permit the child to reason, since he is busy focusing on the discomfort of being spanked, rather than the wrong action. Research shows that when a child is spanked, he remembers the hurt and humiliation more than the wrong behavior. There is a better way to change behavior.

Discipline is defined as "training that produces self-control." Proper parental discipline leads to a child's self-discipline. Self-discipline contributes to self-esteem. Thus, we want a form of discipline that encourages a child to exercise her self-control.

You can't possibly be with your child every minute of the day for eighteen years, telling her the right things to do. So you want to raise a youngster who knows the right thing to do when you aren't on hand to remind.

Preventive Discipline

We usually think of discipline in the form of punishment as a *curative* method—something we do after a child has exhibited unacceptable behavior. But equally important is the form of discipline that is *preventive*—something we do to keep a child from making a mistake. To make this vital preventive discipline work, there are three essentials:

1. Your child must respect you and want to please you. This comes about because he knows you love him and will treat him fairly.

2. Your child must understand what you mean when you use basic words such as: *yes, no, maybe, stop, I want you to . . ., I don't like . . ., please do this.*

3. You must know the things that are important to your child (a certain toy, a special privilege, a particular activity).

It is imperative to start our obedience lessons with very young children. As one example, if we can't convince our three-year-old daughter that it's wrong to draw on the walls, how can we hope to convince her at thirteen that it's wrong to use drugs? We need to start with babies to teach right from wrong through obedience to sensible parental rules. These rules can help to prevent those mistakes that would cause us to punish and our child to be miserable.

Family Rules

The rules and traditions that prevail at your house are a strong force for right behavior. You need to have rules and your child needs to understand them. You cannot punish a child for breaking a rule if he doesn't know the rule exists. So, you need a means of informing your child of the rules.

Start when children are toddlers. Actually write down the important rules. Illustrate them with pictures cut from magazines. Put them in a looseleaf book. Read the book to the child each week. Discuss one rule each day.

When our children were young, our rule book was called "The Good and Happy Book." All rules were simply stated in two-line rhymes that were easy to remember: "When I get hungry and want a treat, / I ask permission before I eat." "When Mom or Dad calls my name, / I come as fast as a speedy jet plane." Although the poetry wouldn't have won any prizes, the rhymes were learned and followed.

As a child grows, update the rules; add new ones, and delete those that are no longer pertinent. Be sure to cover problem areas that are especially bothersome. Let older youngsters phrase the rules themselves.

Making such a rule book is a good rainy day activity. Of course, each family will have different rules and some rules won't be needed since the right behavior has already been established. But if in doubt, include the rule. It will save an argument later.

In many cases, you can let the punishment for breaking a rule be known. For example, when a youngster comes home after her curfew, she knows that she is campused one night for each fifteen minutes late. Or, if a child takes candy at a non-snack time, he gets to think about it as he sweeps all the porches and patios. Let older children determine some of the penalties. You will find that they often devise punishments that are more stringent than you would have suggested.

Include rules concerning privileges and put these in your book in advance of need. This helps a child anticipate the privileges and saves you from being pestered with requests that begin "When can I . . .?" Examples are:

At age five you may cross the street.
At age nine you may go to a movie alone.
At age twelve you may have your ears pierced.
At age fourteen you may go on a date.

Make your rules very specific. Consider these areas:

1. Answering and opening the front door
2. Answering the phone and taking messages
3. Answering the phone when alone at home
4. Going around the neighborhood, crossing streets
5. Getting into cars, dealing with strangers
6. Knowing when to come home from play
7. Time and place for eating snacks
8. Going to bed, repeated getting out of bed
9. Table manners
10. Car safety, fastening seat belts
11. Borrowing and returning things
12. Knocking before opening a closed door
13. Putting away toys and crafts, bringing toys in from outside play
14. Bathroom etiquette
15. What to do when something is broken or lost
16. Handling anger
17. What to do when delayed in returning home
18. Curfews and what happens when late
19. Fighting with siblings and peers
20. Sassy behavior toward adults
21. Profane or foul language
22. Completion of chores
23. Cleanliness, dress code, hairstyles
24. Use of drugs and alcohol
25. Teen car use and driving rules

When rules are written, there is no occasion for the old "I didn't know" line. If you make a rule book, keep it up-to-date and discuss it regularly; you are giving your youngster the security and comfort of knowing just how far she may go. And amazingly, kids like that!

Dialogue

If you talk *with* children—as opposed to talking *at* them—they can learn right action before making a mistake or breaking a rule. This family dialogue is a natural and pleasant way of behavior training for both parent and child.

Talk about good behavior more than the bad. Before a child goes to a birthday party, a wedding, or an overnight at a friend's home, talk about what will happen and what may happen. Don't just lay down a set of negative rules. Let the dialogue first come from him, then fill in the blanks.

One further step in dialogue is the family meeting, a forum for talking about correct behavior, and a good place to consider rules and, if needed, to air gripes. A once-a-week get-together can be informative (regarding holidays, excursions, trips, parties) and also corrective:

"How can I get everyone to breakfast on time?"
"Who took the keys and didn't put them back?"
"Let's change the weekend bedtime rules now that it's summer."

In a democratic meeting, kids will be able to bring up requests for rule changes and special privileges. And a strong disagreement between two children can be calmly arbitrated. Work to make such get-togethers pleasant. Make a pact that everyone will remain calm—no raised voices, no hurtful remarks. The setting should be pleasant too, perhaps by the fireplace with popcorn and apples to eat.

Curative Discipline

Sometimes rules and talk about them (preventive discipline) just doesn't work and it's necessary to use some form of punishment: curative discipline. The time, place, and method will vary, but a parent needs to think about punishment before the occasion occurs.

When to punish? As soon as possible, unless your anger is out of control or the offense is so serious you want to think about it or consult with your spouse. Sometimes a working parent is told of disobedience at school or hears of it from the baby-sitter, and so must deal with it after the fact. Even when you can't discipline immediately, do it as soon as possible.

Where to punish? Home is best. Punishment in public is more difficult and may compound the wrong behavior by adding humiliation. However, when away from home you can always talk about what will happen when you get home. If you're at the grocery store and your daughter keeps punching her brother, you can say: "I can't discipline you here, but believe me, if you don't stop that immediately, you are going to receive a really big punishment as soon as we get home." And when you say this and she continues the punching, you have to follow through on your threat. So when you get home she is deprived of going out to play with her best friend.

Who punishes? The parent or authority figure on the scene should do it. In the case of serious offenses, both parents may consult and then carry out the punishment together. But don't always deliver the unfair line, "Just you wait until your father comes home!"

If one parent seems to be more in charge of discipline during the week (usually the mom), then the other parent should become the authority figure for the weekend. No parent wants to be the ogre, the disciplinarian all the time! And show kids early that when they've been given a decision by one parent, they may not appeal to the other for a more favorable opinion.

At what age do you start to discipline? Training starts with babies when you use a pleasant voice and a smiling face for happy times (such as when a baby eats willingly) or a deep and stern voice with a somber face for unhappy times (such as when he throws his toys out of the playpen).

Many very young children can be disciplined by simply ignoring them. For example, you try to pick up a young child and she kicks and screams. Set her firmly down in a safe place on the floor, say nothing, turn away, and walk out of sight. Being deprived of an audience is often sufficient discipline and a child will learn from this that the behavior was wrong.

A simple "No!" can also be effective. Sometimes it is sufficient in itself. Sometimes it deserves further explanation. But in either case, a child should respond to the *no* before asking "why?"

Remember that you can't punish for every little wrong in the day. You have to ignore some small things. If a child is dropping his peas into his milk glass, you can laugh and say, "That's silly; please don't do that." Then make sure he eats the peas and drinks the milk.

When a child tries a power play, give him a choice: "Stop the kicking or there will be punishment." Stay calm and in control when the child is neither calm nor controlled. Don't be taken in by power plays. This is a behavior you must discuss with your child later, and then decide how he will be punished if he repeats the offense.

Mean What You Say

Many parents in our survey spoke about the importance of consistency. One said, "Because I'm not home all day, I haven't got the time for giving second chances. My kids know that I mean it and they don't expect to be told again!" Don't threaten to punish when you cannot carry it out. The moment you do, you open the door for kids to behave as they please without paying any heed to your words. For the safety of your child and her future success—as well as for harmony in the home—you want her to understand the meaning of words and the consequences of not listening to them.

If there is one piece of advice the survey parents wanted to pass on to other working parents, it was this: "Teach kids that you mean what you say!"

Humiliation

Punishment does not need to involve humiliation. You can correct a child without eroding his self-esteem. Humiliation is a not-so-subtle form of child abuse.

One parent whose four-year-old wet his pants made him spend the rest of the day in the wet pants. A mother whose child dumped milk off the high chair made him eat on the floor. This kind of response to wrong-doing is wrong in itself. Such accidents or provocations can be frustrating for a busy parent; however, humiliating a child, instead of helping him, only makes the matter worse. When you are in the pants-wetting and milk-dumping years, it seems that these tendencies will never end. But it is comforting to know that few children go off to college with these habits! So be patient. Put this problem aside and focus on another goal for a while. You will find that success in the new area often brings success in the problem area.

Isolation and the Thinking Bench

For children under ten, isolation is one of the most effective forms of punishment. It takes a child away from the mistake and lets him focus on what he has done. This is how it works:

Your son Daniel is playing in a little car and his friend Eric is on a trike. You see Daniel purposely bash into the trike, knock over trike and rider, take the trike, and ride away, teasing Eric, who is crying on the patio pavement. When you've ensured that Eric is all right, quickly pick up or lead Daniel away to a quiet place. This place should *not* be his room since that is his "castle" and should have pleasant connotations. So, take him to the laundry room, kitchen, or garage, and put him firmly down on the Thinking Bench.

The Thinking Bench is any low step-stool or bench that you will use regularly when children need quiet time to ponder their behavior.

First, establish why he is there by simply stating the unacceptable behavior: "You took Eric's trike, you knocked him over, you made fun of him." You can tell him this was wrong behavior, or let him tell you. In either case, the offense should be clearly understood.

Next, state that there must have been a better way to act: "I want you to think of another way you could have gotten to ride the trike. I'm setting this timer for three minutes; then I'll return. If you leave the Thinking Bench, you'll have to sit there for *six more minutes.*"

Then leave, staying nearby though, so you can return in three minutes. Next, say, "Since you wanted the trike, how could you have gotten to use it?" He may come up with some of the answers or you may have to prompt him (asking for the trike, taking turns, offering to trade, etc.).

Finally, make your closing statement: "You got excited and could have hurt your friend. Because of what you did, you missed a lot of playtime—how sad!" Then, let him go back to play with the understanding that he play harmoniously and also tell his friend he's sorry.

Now this procedure does take time, but only at first. It will take you less time in the long run since your child has seen the consequences of wrong behavior and won't want to go through that routine again and again.

Isolation and the Thinking Bench give a child the time to calm down and think. They let him realize that there are right and wrong ways to achieve things. And you will find that another time he may remember this lesson and save himself time and punishment.

Isolation on the Thinking Bench helps cure many of the mistakes of early childhood.

Cleaning Up the Mess

When a child has made a mega-mess, having to clean it all up can be sufficient punishment. (Remember though, playing with numerous toys is not something to be punished. Toys are part of creative fun.) Making a mess is spilling paint, taking out six decks of cards and throwing them on the floor, dumping out a drawer, emptying a box of nails in the garage, or throwing all the sand out of the sandbox. Such messes a child should clean up entirely *by himself,* with a few suggestions from the parent on hand. The parent may be able to do it better or faster, but the child mustn't be deprived of the lesson gained from the clean-up.

Show young children how to clean up spills and other messes, but don't be their servant. Let them realize that it takes time to clean up a mess and they must be responsible for their actions.

Having shelves, boxes, and bins helps a child keep her possessions neat and accessible. When the time comes to clean up the family room or her bedroom—daily or weekly—give some pointers on putting things away properly. Then let her do it on her own.

Even Steven

Sometimes there is absolutely no way a child can undo what he has done wrong. Perhaps he has cut a hole in his best shirt or taken up thirty minutes of your time by being late when you come to pick him up at the playground. When a child needlessly takes your time (that required for mending the shirt or waiting at the playground) he needs correction. In return for taking your time, he pays back your time by doing a special task. This makes it an Even Steven punishment, and there are many Even Steven punishments you will be able to think up.

A young child may deliver laundry or may dust. An older child may scrub a floor or weed the lawn. The Even Steven task should be one that the child does alone, in quiet; this provides him the opportunity to think about why he's incurred this penalty.

There's no way to get the wasted time back, but at least he can help you in order to make up for his mistake.

Deprivation

The most effective form of punishment is probably deprivation. It can be used for kids as young as three and on up through the teens. Because a child has disobeyed, she is deprived of something she likes: a possession or a privilege.

This method of punishment succeeds only if you know your child well enough to know what is important to her. Don't be like the dad who deprived his daughter of using the phone, forgetting that they were new in town and she had no friends to call. And don't do something dumb like the parent who deprived the entire family of going to a movie because one child refused to eat his peas! Deprive only the wrongdoer.

Parents who participated in our survey reported that deprivation worked well for kids of *all* ages. Younger ones can be deprived of a favorite toy for a week, or not be allowed to watch television for four days. Older ones can be deprived of riding their bikes or using the telephone for a week. Others can have social privileges, borrowing the car, or spending money rescinded. (Never deprive a child of his allowance; instead, refuse to let him spend it.) In each case, be very sure you are removing something very important to the youngster.

Deprivation teaches a child that the loss of self-control and the resulting wrong behavior mean the loss of privileges. The real world works much the same way: If we speed or steal, we lose our driver's license or our freedom. If we borrow money and don't return it, no one will lend to us again. If we slurp our juice and talk with a full mouth, we're unlikely to get many party invitations.

When using deprivation, it's important to follow through even though you may feel sorry for the child. Don't say, "If you don't improve your spelling grade you can't be on the soccer team" unless you intend to stick to your decision. Rarely make a concession in this area, but if you do, make it understood that this is a *very* special occasion and not likely to happen again.

Regarding time deadlines (to come home from play, to go to bed, to return from a date), set a time range of fifteen minutes. Say, "Your bedtime is 7:45, but I won't fuss until 8:00." Or, "I want you home by midnight but I won't start worrying and telephoning around until 12:15." When you've made a deadline, stick to it all the time.

Some deprivations can be known in advance: If your grade-schooler gets a C-minus, there will be no weekday T.V. until the next grading period and an improved grade. If your toddler disobeys a sitter, he will be put to bed before the sitter comes the next time. If your teen fails to be where she said she'd be, and doesn't phone with the change of place, she's campused for one night. If a teen gets a C-minus, his car keys and license are taken away.

Most youngsters prefer this system of knowing the rules and what happens when they break them. It works exceptionally well in those areas where definite limits are set: time (bedtimes and curfews), boundaries (you may go here but not there), and behavior (you may do this but not that). *Deprivation* is a big word, but start using it when your kids are young—it will improve their vocabulary and their behavior.

The Mini-lecture

The serious talk or mini-lecture is very effective for children under ten. You must be a good speaker and you must keep a straight face! The child should be seated and you should stand in front of him. Let's say you asked him to brush the baby's hair before the excursion, and instead he used hair spray and got it in the baby's face. Your lecture might go like this: "What you did could be dangerous and it's certainly not funny. I love you too much to let you do foolish things like this. You made me very worried and you made the baby very sad. Now we're so late in starting on our errands we can't stop for ice cream. Nothing good resulted from what you did. Let me read to you what it says on this hair spray can . . ."

Use the mini-lecture to impress a child who has done something dangerous or thoughtless: playing with matches, running into the street, playing with a gun kept at a playmate's house, rough-housing and hurting the cat. Make your lecture long—very long—and don't hesitate to repeat your message many different ways. Repetition makes the session tedious for the child, but it does make the message stick.

Letters and Notes

Children of all ages respond to a written correction. This works best if you type the message, or write legibly. Here's a letter a mother wrote when she'd asked a child to do his tasks and tidy his room in the morning, since Grandma was coming to visit:

"Dear Kent,
My morning was going well until I found what you had left for me. It was my only day off from work and I had just finished my own chores when I went into the kitchen and found I had to clear your dishes and put away the mayonnaise, lettuce, and juice. Then I tidied your bedroom. Finally, I realized the dog had no food! You know how I was looking forward to going shopping with Grandma, and then we were coming home to make cookies. Well, she arrived while I was still hurriedly doing *your* work. Your thoughtlessness—I could almost call it selfishness—put my whole day out of whack. In the future, I'd like you to start your day in a more orderly way and this will help me start mine on a happier note, too. I would like to have some ideas from you. Will you think about this problem of not doing your tasks in the

morning and come to me with suggestions before bedtime tonight? You know how much I love you—even when you make me upset.
Mom"

A child getting such a note is impressed. He thinks, "Hey, she took the time to write it down, so it must be important!" He reads it again and actually thinks about it. Yes, he will think of some ways to do better next time!

Along with disciplinary letters, don't forget to write complimentary ones! Tuck your appreciative notes under a child's pillow or in a lunch box. Sometimes a very brief note is exactly the lift a child needs during a busy day. And it takes so little time to write a love note. If you write such messages I bet you'll receive a few, too.

The Special Project

Occasionally a child's disobedience is of such magnitude that you must devise a unique punishment: the Special Project. You do this in the hope that he will *never* repeat the mistake. Usually, the Special Project discipline is reserved for occasions where a child has done something to endanger his own life or the lives of others. Dragracing, playing with guns, and trying drugs fall into this category. A father reported success using the Special Project punishment when his daughter had broken an important family rule. It happened this way.

The family rule was that the kids weren't permitted inside the swimming pool fence without an adult. He wasn't worried about his preteen daughter; he had made the rule for the safety of the two younger children. So you can imagine his surprise one evening when he returned home and a young son reported that his sister had broken the rule and shown the pool to a school friend. In fact, they had begun horsing around inside the fence and both had fallen into the water!

He knew he had to come down hard on his daughter, even though she was a "first offender," so that the other children would abide by the rule. So, the Special Project punishment was used. First, the daughter had to write a paper on responsibility and safety, including library research and interviews with neighbors. For one week she had to spend at least twenty minutes a day on the paper. The second week he enrolled her in an after-school CPR class for young people. After that, she read her paper to the family and gave a home CPR demonstration. She completed her punishment without too much grumbling.

When it was all over, one of the younger children said, "Wow, I'll never go in the pool without you, Dad. I don't want that kind of punishment to happen to me!" And the father smiled quietly and never had any further trouble.

If you need to use the Special Project punishment, you'll want to tailor it to the age of the offender and the seriousness of the offense. But it *does* work!

When Discipline Is Over

There may be occasions where apologies are needed. Teaching children to say "I'm sorry" makes everyone feel better. But when the offender has been punished, that's the end. Then a parent should give a hug and forget the incident, not bringing it up again at supper, to neighbors, or to grandparents.

Use these lines often:

"I'm hoping you won't make that mistake again."
"I love you too much to let you break the law. I want to trust you to do the right thing when I'm not watching over you."
"The punishment is over so let's go and do something that's fun!"
"I appreciate the good way you behaved this time."

Parenting Point

Consistent discipline is most important when there are others who help care for your child. Discuss your policies and rules with them and ask for their support. When you set standards at home and see that children follow your rules, you give them the know-how to do right at the day-care center or at school. Work together with your child to accomplish this! You can do it!

Chalkboard for Chapter Twenty

List the five areas in which your child needs the most discipline:

1.

2.

3.

4.

5.

Consider each one of these areas and see if there is an underlying reason for the misbehavior.

Next, talk about the five problems with your child. Tell her that you would like to correct these and would like her help. Decide together on fair punishments for these problems if she cannot control herself. Decide also on a small reward for a child who does not need any correction in these five areas for a week.

Twenty-One

Cross-Country Forum

Hundreds of working parents took part in the survey that provided many facts and figures for this book. At the end of the survey form, these parents had the opportunity to share practical ideas and pertinent thoughts that were meaningful to them.

Good ideas came from all parts of the United States and four foreign countries. They came from both moms and dads, older and younger parents, married and single parents—and some even from their kids.

The best of these helpful suggestions are shared here in the hope that some of them will be useful in your important parenting job. More than mere theory, these are ideas that have been successfully tested and used by other working parents.

THE COMPLAINER. Our son was grumpy about anything he was asked to do around the house. I put a jar on the kitchen counter with five dollars in coins in it. When he harped about something, I took out a nickel. At the end of the month, he got what was left. Believe me, he was cured in just a few months!

BABY'S TO-GO PACK. In a jumbo zip-top plastic storage bag I have a change of baby clothes, pacifier, wipes, wrapped crackers, and a toy. I keep this in the car so that it's handy for emergencies.

BULLIES. We went to a PTO meeting on the subject of bullying and found that parents of bullies use more put-downs, sarcasm, and criticism than affection when interacting with their children. This made us alert to how we treat our youngsters.

ALLOWANCES. Because we give our kids a regular allowance each month (instead of their just getting money from us piece-meal), our kids feel more in control of their money and actually save more. And if they run out of funds, we have jobs they can do to earn money.

FREEZER LIST. On the inside of the freezer door I keep a list of all the precooked frozen foods that can provide quick meals. This list is on a piece of chalkboard, so I can just wipe off an item when it's used. I make a quantity of soup for freezing and keep English muffins in the freezer too. That combination is a favorite emergency supper— and we have lots of emergencies!

BOX GAMES NIGHT. One night each month we play box games as a family. We mark the night on the calendar and all look forward to it.

ORGANIZE, ORGANIZE, ORGANIZE. Three jobs (my career, my family, and my home) take a lot of time and energy. To do it best I read everything I can on time management. I've picked up countless ideas that have freed up time I can have with my spouse and my children.

WASH AND WEAR. Now that our kids are old enough to read the use and care labels on clothes, they're alert to items that need ironing. If they insist on buying such clothing, it's understood that they'll iron these pieces themselves.

FULL DISHWASHER. Sometimes we come home and find a full dishwasher of dirty dishes. It's no problem since I keep some inexpensive paper plates on hand. My wife has also installed a paper cup dispenser in the kitchen, which saves a lot of glasses.

BIRTHDAY PARTY GIFTS. When we visit the toy store to buy a gift for a birthday party, we also buy a spare gift. Sure enough, quite soon it comes in handy and we save that last-minute shopping hassle.

QUILTS. When my wife suggested I take over the bed-making, I found a great solution. Now each bed has a large quilt or comforter that replaces the blankets and spread. The kids like this quick way to make the bed look good and so do I!

PRIME FORCE. I wanted to be the prime force in my youngster's growing up years—a hard task for a single parent. But one idea that works well is to make our "out" times coincide. If my daughter is going to a movie with friends, I make that my night for visiting or shopping.

CATALOG SHOPPING. I save time and gas by doing much of my shopping by mail. When sending a gift, I have the company wrap the gift, include a card, and mail it for me. And I've found that many catalogs have "800" phone numbers, and some even have a pick-up policy for returns!

REPOTTING. Once each year, usually during the kids' vacation, we move into a new house. Not really, but it seems like it! We can't afford to move, but we can afford to spend a weekend redoing our home. It's fun when everyone helps. We repaint dinged walls, rearrange the furniture, change pictures and posters, get rid of old books and clothing, put out different art objects, rejuvenate the plants, clean out the worst cupboards. By Sunday night, we feel as if we have a new home.

I DON'T WANT A DISHWASHER. I really look forward to the fifteen minutes after supper. Each evening I wash the dishes and a different child dries them. It's our special time to talk and I find the kids actually enjoy doing dishes.

THE ABSENT PARENT. When my wife died, I found it very difficult to talk with my son about her. But when I realized that he had feelings of fear and guilt, I started a dialogue and in the past year this has really helped to answer his questions. I have to be away on business, too, and I make sure he knows why I'm gone and exactly when I'll return. I phone him daily on these trips. I guess what I'm saying is that we need to communicate on the hard topics as well as on the easy ones.

THE BEST PET. Working parents want their children to have an interesting pet, yet one that can be left alone much of the day. We suggest guinea pigs! They love to be cuddled, the plastic cages are easy to clean, they live about eight years, and their progeny can be shared with other kids.

CRYING BABY? I know there are lots of clever devices you can buy, but my home-made system works well. When the baby starts to fuss, I put my loud-ticking kitchen timer near the crib and set it for fifteen minutes. This gives baby time to settle down and time for me to collect myself. And usually the baby is asleep in less than ten minutes so I remove it before it rings!

SAFE BIKE SEATS. One of our best investments was a child bicycle seat. Although our youngest is still too little to go hiking, he loves to go bike riding and it's wonderful exercise for the rest of us. In fact, when I come home from work, we often go for a ten-minute ride before I tackle supper.

WHAT'S MEMORABLE? Several times a year we ask our kids what are the most memorable and enjoyable things we've done as a family. We're often surprised with their answers! And we get ideas on what to repeat and what to drop.

STEP-MOTHERING. Some of the lines I used often when I first became a stepmother were these: "Yes, I know I'm not your mother, but I am your parent. As your parent I have certain obligations to fulfill in seeing you grow up correctly. And I have certain rights that you must respect, just as I respect your rights." It wasn't always easy, but we became a real family.

CAN'T READ YET? When reading a book to a young child, involve him in the reading by having him watch the pictures and point to each of the objects you're reading about. This improves comprehension and lengthens his attention span.

HEALTH AND STRESS. I find that as a working parent I need to be selfish about my own well-being. Once I got sick from overwork and that made home life a mess! Now I make sure that I eat a balanced diet, talk out problems that could cause stress, and get some daily exercise. I do the latter by parking my car in the parking lot at the farthest point from the office. I leave my lunch in the car. That way I get four brisk walks every day.

NEVER TOO EARLY. I was so sure our kids would never get involved in drugs, but nonetheless, when the kids were in grade school, I attended the program on drugs presented by our parent-teacher organization. It gave us pointers on what to be alert to. Then our family read together the book *It's OK to Say No to Drugs* (Alan Garner, St. Martin's, 1987). I think this book made the difference in keeping our kids out of drugs.

BAGS FOR ORGANIZATION. The reclosable zip-top plastic bags have saved us a lot of work. Our child uses them for crayons, puzzle pieces, small toys, hair bows, and small game pieces. She also has one bag she calls her mystery bag where she keeps unidentified items she finds on the floor! It saved us a lot of work when we realized we'd lost a key. It was safely in the bag!

PET ABUSE. We found that our daughter was taking out her frustrations on our cat. Counseling helped her handle this aggressive behavior before it turned into more-violent acts.

FATHERS AND DAUGHTERS. It was easy for my husband to find an activity he enjoyed with our son. But, what about with our daughter? When I was asked to be an assistant leader for her Camp Fire group, the late hours of my job prevented it. But my husband volunteered to try it once; he's been doing it now for six months and really enjoys it! I guess I just underestimated his abilities.

DIVORCE. When my husband and I split up, I found the public library the biggest help. I'd like to suggest these four books:

Two Homes to Live In; A Child's-Eye View of Divorce (Barbara Shook Hazen, Human Science Press, 1978)

A Look at Divorce (Margaret S. Pursell, Lerner Publications, 1976)
Two Places to Sleep (Joan Schuchman, Carolrhoda Books, 1979)
The Boys and Girls Book About Divorce (Richard Gardner, Aronson, 1983)

THE FIVE C's. We have a sign on our refrigerator to remind us of the concepts that make our family work. The five C's are: Cooperation, Communication, Compliments, Commitment, Compassion.

SINGLE PARENTING. My daughter feels important if I involve her in some of the decisions that I'd normally make with a spouse. We set goals together, plan the monthly calendar, and decide the most important things to do around the house.

SIBLING RIVALRY. At the shower for our second baby, a thoughtful guest brought two gifts for our first child. Our daughter was thrilled with the one marked "grown-up toy." This made us realize the importance of showing her all the more grown-up things she could do and could later teach to the new baby. The other gift was the book *Betsy's Baby Brother* (Gunilla Wolde, Random House, 1982) and we all learned from it.

SAVE SOME IDEAS FOR LATER. With our large family, I found that some activities have to be reserved for certain age groups. As an example, first-graders should not have sleep-overs. That's an enjoyable privilege for later. Don't let your kids grow up too fast.

THE FEELING OF COMMUNITY. Because we both work and our children attend schools outside the immediate neighborhood, I feel that our children lack that feeling of community we had when growing up. We've now started a neighborhood potluck supper once a month. We parents also went together and bought some outdoor play equipment that all the children can use. We put up signs on our street indicating that children are playing. This is helping to generate a local community feeling.

THE GLAD GAME. When our child is cranky, we play the glad game. We alternate telling something we're glad about at that moment. For example, I may say, "I'm glad we're together." My daughter may then say, "I'm glad I have new sneakers." We try to see how many "glads" we can get before we decide to happily do something else.

MY FRIENDS, YOUR FRIENDS. Being a single parent, I date different people. At supper, I ask my son about his friends. Then it's natural for me to tell about my friends at work and also those I'll go out with. Then he isn't surprised when I have a date, and he feels more comfortable meeting my friends.

NEW KID IN THE NEIGHBORHOOD. We move often because of our jobs. We take slides of each house we live in and also of the kids in that neighborhood. Then, when we move to a new place, we let our kids invite the new neighborhood children over for ice cream and a little slide show. It breaks the ice and helps our kids make friends.

I WAS HESITANT about teaching my child about sex, yet I felt that it was best taught in our home. Two books helped: *What's Happening to My Body*—there's one for boys and one for girls (Lynda Madaras, Newmarket Press, 1984, 1983). I read the book first, then gave it to our son, and later we had a good talk about it. It opened the door for further conversation, and I felt much more competent on the subject.

OUTDOOR SHOWER. We hooked up a simple shower spray outdoors in a private corner. On warm summer evenings when children have played hard, they enjoy the outdoor shower. It takes care of the business of cleanliness and makes it seem like more outdoor play. After the shower they slip into clean clothes or pj's.

NO SITTER? Sometimes my husband and I need "time for us" on the weekend. So we have a "date" even if we don't have a sitter. After the kids are in bed, we change into nicer clothes, I serve a light supper by candlelight, then we look at a rented video. Before bed we go out on the patio and talk in the dark under the stars. Not bad for two old married folks!

BABY HELPS CLEAN. I have a baby backpack with hip strap that allows me to work around the house yet be with my baby. I also put extra baby food in an ice cube tray and pop out a cube as needed. Since I don't sing well, I have a cassette of lullabies our baby loves to hear at bedtime.

TALK IN THE DARK. At bedtime my kid likes me to turn out all the lights and sit on his bed. Somehow he's more apt to share problems and confidences in the dark. We've had some great bedtime talks this way.

SAY NO. When someone outside the family asks me to do something extra, I give it this test: Will this activity really mean something to the community, to me, or to my family? Will it provide me with new opportunities to be with my husband or child? Is it something that someone else can do better? Is it something that I can do better another time? I often say "no," but having thought it through, I don't feel guilty.

BEFORE-SUPPER SNACKING. It's always a rush to make dinner for the starving kids. I have found that a good pre-supper snack is frozen peas, beans, corn, or diced carrots! They're tasty, don't spoil supper, and I know that my kids are eating their vegetables!

TIME ALONE. Each member of our family is encouraged to have time alone each day to think, relax, regroup. Often this is the time just before going to bed. Some of our best ideas come from these quiet moments.

WRITTEN NOT ORAL. When you want to be sure a child remembers to do something, write it down for him (or better yet, have him write it). I use yellow 3×5 cards that are easy to spot.

TWIN STROLLER. If you have two children under the age of three, invest in a twin stroller. It will make walking trips more enjoyable.

MANY TREES. When we go shopping for our Christmas tree we always ask if there are any small trees—ones that may be misshapen or unsalable. We let each child choose one as an "ugly duckling" tree for his own room. After helping trim the family tree, they love making the little tree beautiful with their own decorations.

PLAY DOUGH. Here's my great recipe: 1 cup flour, 1/2 cup salt, 1 cup water, 2 teaspoons cream of tartar, 1 tablespoon vegetable oil, and a few drops of food coloring. Mix all ingredients together in a pan over medium heat, stirring constantly until a ball begins to form. Remove from the heat and cool. Store in an air-tight container in the refrigerator until modeling time.

JOIN A SERIES. Our family joins an inexpensive community concert series. Although we don't all go to all concerts, we feel that our children are learning to appreciate good music in an informal atmosphere. And the season tickets are reasonably priced. When we can't go, we give them to the kids' school teachers who really appreciate going.

BIRTHDAY CARDS. I keep a supply of birthday cards at my desk and sit down once a month and write them, putting the date to mail where the stamp will eventually go. This saves time and apologies for tardy cards.

EXPLANATIONS. When I was young and asked questions about drugs or sex, my parents just said, "It's wrong!" and that was the end of it. For our own children, we try to have a discussion and give them some reasons and some facts. We've heard that they share the facts with friends.

BE A CHILD. We tell ourselves regularly that our children *are* children. We remind them that they have our permission to act like children, not like adults. They know that acting as a child doesn't mean being tardy or naughty but being happy and good.

CROSSWORD PUZZLES. Starting when a child can read, provide simple crossword puzzles. As children get older, encourage their work on harder ones. These puzzles are wonderful vocabulary-builders.

TARDY BOOKS. When we borrow library books, I note on the family calendar the day that books are due back at the library. We haven't been fined in years!

FOUR RULES. Here's my short but important advice: Be organized. Prioritize. Don't try to be a perfectionist. Enjoy being a parent.

Thanks for sharing!

Twenty-Two

Step by Step Together

Claire loves her family. Although her career is demanding, she spends much of her off-the-job time with her children. And in her own leisure she reads books on parenting. How she wants to do it right! There seems to be so much to do, but she makes it her goal to organize the everyday home tasks into a time-saving routine. That way she saves up time for more creative and adventuresome activities with her family. She's decided that for these years when the kids are at home, the family will be her priority. Her husband, Jeff, agrees with her, and though she loves him dearly, she realizes that it's going to be her leadership that will make family life special. Can she do it?

From the first moment you hold your baby in your arms to the day you hug him and send him off on his own, you have the wonderful job of parenting. And it *is* wonderful. Yes, there are days it doesn't seem so wonderful: Things go wrong, there isn't enough time, mistakes are made. But those less-than-wonderful events hold lessons somewhere within them—lessons showing the need for more patience or organization or listening or care.

Only if we ignore these subtle messages do we have real failures and regrets. When we do pay attention and think how to do better the next time, we turn a bad situation into progress and success. No one said it was going to be easy!

As you work at parenting you grow, and that's what life is about: becoming a better, more useful, more loving person. When you explain to your child that you are learning right along with her, that you're both going in the same direction, you elicit from her more helpfulness in the growing-up process.

There is so much you want to share with your child. The thought of eighteen years of parenting seems endless at the beginning and so short as it nears the end. But, little by little, you can achieve your aim and be that working parent with a happy child.

Back to Basics

Teaching your child how to live in this changing world is really teaching some very basic ways of acting and thinking. Robert L. Fulghum, in his book *All I Really Need to Know I Learned in Kindergarten* (Villard Books, 1989), says it well:

Most of what I really need to know about how to live, and what to do, and how to be, I learned in kindergarten. Wisdom was not at the top of the graduate school mountain, but there in the sandbox at nursery school.

These are the things I learned: Share everything. Play fair. Don't hit people. Put things back where you found them. Clean up your own mess. Don't take things that aren't yours. Say you're sorry when you hurt somebody . . . Learn some and think some and draw and paint and sing and dance and play and work every day some.

When you go out into the world, watch for traffic, hold hands, and stick together. Be aware of wonder . . .

Think of what a better world it would be if we all—the whole world—had cookies and milk about three o'clock every afternoon and then lay down with our blankets for a nap. Or, if we had a basic policy in our nation and other nations to always put things back where we found them and clean up our own messes. And it is true, no matter how old you are, when you go out into the world, it is best to hold hands and stick together.

Holding hands and sticking together—that's really what you're doing as you teach your youngster to draw, paint, sing, dance, play, and work.

A New Generation of Parenting

During 1988 and 1989, more than 500 interviews were made in writing and in person with working parents. These parents came from the United States, Canada, Mexico, England, France, and Australia.

The parents represented various races and socioeconomic levels. The survey included single fathers and mothers, remarried couples, parents who had to travel for business, foster parents, adoptive parents, parents who worked part-time as well as parents who worked full-time, moms who worked by choice and moms who worked because of necessity.

Each participant answered thirty-seven questions and had the opportunity to share additional ideas.

New statistics as well as new ideas came from the survey, and many of the results are covered in this book.

These parents in our survey had some definite ideas on parenting and how it would differ from what they experienced as children. An *overwhelming* number—more than 80 percent of those answering the question—said that they'd be more communicative with their children. Almost as many said they would be more open in expressing love and affection.

Love. Isn't that why we want to do our best for our children? We love them so much. We want them to be happy and good and wise. And we remember to love "no matter what." Our unqualified love is our greatest gift to our child.

The Good Family

Don't try to do it all alone. A good family has many helping hands. Friends, relatives, support groups, books, and classes will give you fresh inspiration for every one of the eighteen years together. Be humble enough to know when you need help, and reach out for it.

Work to make *family* a lasting concept in your child's life. This will help your child to include those beyond the family in the larger family of all humankind.

And what makes a good family? Not just sleeping under the same roof!

The good family cares about one another.

The good family shares the work of making the home a pleasant place.

The good family spends time getting to know and enjoy one another.

The good family values honesty within itself and in the outside world.

The good family respects the privacy and possessions of one another.

The good family worships together.

The good family appreciates one another and often says so.

The good family can laugh at itself.

The good family doesn't ignore problems; it works hard to resolve them.

The good family expresses love in words and actions.

The good family reaches out beyond itself and shares its bounty.

The good family is forever.

Holding Hands

You will hold your child's hand through many of the challenges of growing up. You'd like to be there for *all* the important times when a little hand-holding is needed, but a working parent may miss some of these times and that's the way it must be. So, you teach your youngster the importance of the family, and that means you'll always stick together even when you live far apart. Hand-holding takes many forms and continues all through life. When you love your child, hand-holding never ends.

When your child is a tiny baby, you let his whole hand curl around your little finger.

When he is learning to walk, you hold his hand as he takes the first unsteady steps.

When he is first learning to cross the street, he trustingly takes your hand.

When you gather around the breakfast table, you all hold hands for a quiet moment.

When the family goes for a hike, you hold hands in the steep places.

When he leaves for camp, he gives you a brave handshake in front of the other guys.

When he doesn't feel well, your hands lovingly nurse him back to good health and you sit by his bed, holding his hand.

When he has car repairs or a tough school assignment, you give him a helping hand.

When you fall behind with the chores around the house, he gives you a helping hand.

When he goes on his first date, you press an extra bit of cash into his hand.

When he gets his first after-school job, your hands applaud his achievement.

When he graduates, you give his hand a loving squeeze, and then you give each other a "High Five."

When he leaves home, your hands touch briefly in a proud good-bye.

Then come hands across the miles. You mentally hold his hand through the trials and triumphs of learning to be on his own.

And throughout all time, your hand of love will reach out and support your child.

And now it is up to you. Take the hand of your child. Go forward together as a family. You can do it!

Parenting Point

Don't put it off. The sooner you start to make a good family at your house, the sooner you'll enjoy the benefits of good times, good ideas, good feelings. Working parents, take a firm grip on family life. Step by step you can do it!

Chalkboard for Chapter Twenty-Two

Using a marking pen, print these words on a sheet of paper and put them somewhere you'll see them often—refrigerator, bedroom mirror, desk. Look at them, think about them.

Working Parent
Happy Child
Loving Family
I Can Do It
Step by Step
Starting Now

Index

Absenteeism from work, 72
Activities
  afternoon, 37, 85
  evening, 117-28
  fathers and daughters, 300
  for parents, 243-46
  for Saturday mornings, 144-48
  parental involvement, 197
  when child is home alone, 89
Activities, extracurricular, 190-202
  age to start, 195
  costs and commitment, 191-92
  group, 194
  how many?, 193
  popular choices, 192
Affection. *See* Love
AIR: acknowledgment, interest, relaxation, 95-96
Alarm clocks, 45
Allowances. *See* Money
Aloneness, 197, 303
Art
  at home, 209
  at school, 209
  books, 209
Art museum visit, 206-10
Astronomy, 228
Attitude
  child's positive, 260
  on the job, 75
Auto
  care, 238
  time savers, 252
  See also Commuting

Babysitters. *See* Sitters

Bathing
  before bed, 131
  outdoor shower, 302
Bed making
  morning, 47
  quilts, 290
Bedtime, 129-41
  getting out of bed, 136-38
  importance of routine, 130-35
  reasons against the family bed, 138
  setting bedtimes, 139
Bicycling safety seats, 279
Birthday
  cards, 304
  gifts, 298
Books. *See* Reading
Botany, 228
Breakfast, 54-61
  affection, 60
  confidence building, 59
  eating, 49
  education, 58
  essential conversation, 57
  importance of, 56
  preparation, 48
  togetherness, 56
Budgets
  clothing, 133, 222
  family, 221
Bulletin board, 249
Bullies, 297
Business and industry, understanding of, 221

Calendar for family events, 248

311

Car. *See* Auto
Car pools, 63
Career. *See* Work
Character traits. *See* Traits, eight
    great
Cheerfulness, 257-60
Child-care. *See* Day-care
Choices, giving children, 267-68,
    270-71
Chores. *See* Tasks
Church. *See* Religion
Clothes
    budget for child, 133, 222
    fads, 132
    selection for next day, 132
Clutter, getting rid of, 254
Communication, 261-62
    importance of, 24
    in writing, 262
    tape recording in car, 66
    to nurture intelligence, 273
Commuting
    activities, 64-67
    alone, 65
    with child, 85
    with others, 64
Complaining child, 296
Computers
    at home, 231-32
    for use with homework assign-
        ments, 232
    in schools, 232
Confidence. *See* Self-esteem
Consistency in discipline, 271, 282,
    287
Conversation and discussions, 261-62
    about discipline, 285
    at breakfast, 57
    at social events, 262
    at supper, 109
    hidden messages, 262
    in car, 63
    in the dark, 302
    putting off, 96
Cooking together, 253
Creativity, 273-75
    and gifts, 274
Crying baby, 299
Cultural events for weekends, 153

Dance. *See* Music, ballet
Day-care, 169-76, 178-80, 184-88
    at the work place, 175
    premature education, 174
    problems, 187
    selection of, 171
    vs. home-care, 186
Deep-breathing time, 67
Deprivation of privileges, 290
Desk supplies, 247-49
Dinner. *See* Supper
Discipline, 281-95
    consistency in, 282
    curative, 286-94
    dialogue, 285
    humiliation, 288
    isolation, 288
    power plays, 287
    preventive, 283
    rules, 283-85
    spanking, 282
Discipline, forms of, 289-93
    cleaning up the mess, 289
    deprivation, 290
    even Steven, 290
    isolation, 288
    special projects, 293
    the mini-lecture, 291
    time out, 288
    written notes, 292
Discussions. *See* Conversation
Dishonesty, 263-67
Disobedience. *See* Discipline
Divorce, 266
Drama. *See* Theater
Drug use, 300

Eating
    snack before supper, 97, 303
    too slowly, 55
    See also Breakfast, Food, Snacks,
        Supper, Touch-base time #1,
        Touch-base time #4
Eating out, 114
Economy, understanding of, 221
Education
    at breakfast, 58
    at supper, 209
    contract, 189

premature, 174
See also School
Efficiency
at home, 240-55
at the office, 72-78
See also Home management
Enrichment at home, 203-39
Entertaining at home, 244, 254
Errands on weekends, 147
Ethics, 263-64
Evening activities, 117-28
importance of, 118-20
with gradeschoolers, 122
with teenagers, 124
with young children, 120
Exchange students, 226
Excursions
indoor, 153
outdoor, 152
with twin stroller, 303
Extracurricular activities. *See* Activities, extracurricular

Failures, coping with, 277-79
Family, attributes for success, 307
Family bed, 138
Family rules, 270, 283-85
Family time events, 151
Fears
at bedtime, 135
of separation, 24, 58
File folders, 247-49
Files, bring-up, 248
Flexibility in daily routine, 259
Food, list of foreign words, 235-36
Food, menus, 65
Food preparation
breakfast, 48
dinner, 100
lunch, 49
Foreign food terms, list of, 235-36
Friends. *See* Playmates
Fun in family life, 20, 142-56, 203-39, 305-10

Games and puzzles, 121-23, 297, 304
Gardening skills, 237

Geography, 225-27
maps and globes, 225
Gifted child, 184-86
Gifts
birthday, 298
creative, 274
scientific equipment, 229
Going shelf, 49, 133
Grades. *See* School
Grandparenting, proxy, 39
Grocery lists, 65
Group activities, 194
Grumpiness, 301
Guilt, 26, 70, 75

Happiness, 259
Headquarters, home. *See* Home management, headquarters
Health
of child, 35, 72
of parent, 72, 300
skills for personal care, 238
Help, professional, 34
Helps. *See* Tasks
Hints from working parents, 296-304
History, 222-25
History, important dates in, 223-24
Home management
children's contribution, 242-43
morning desk check, 49
parents' contribution, 242-43
repotting, 298
toy organization, 300
Home management, headquarters, 247-49
bring-up file, 248
bulletin board, 249
calendar, 248
desk projects, 252
lists, 249
scrapbook, 249
Home repairs. *See* Repairs
Home-care vs. day-care, 186
Homecoming, 95
Homework, 90, 98, 180-84. *See also* School
Honesty, 263-67

Housecleaning
  morning pick-up, 48
  on weekends, 146
  skills, 237
  spring, 253
  with baby, 302
Humiliation, 288
Humor, sense of, 257-59

Illness. *See* Health
Incentives for accomplishing tasks, 251
Indoor excursions for weekends, 153
Inquisitiveness, 273-75
Intelligence, 273-75. *See also* School
Isolation as discipline, 288

Job. *See* Work
Joy, 259

Kitchen
  efficiency, 253-54
  hints, 297-98
  skills, 237, 297

Language skills, 233-37
  common faults, 233-35
  foreign food terms, 235-36
  parental example, 233
  second language, 235
Latchkey children, 87-91
Laundry, 253, 297
Leadership, 267-69
Lessons
  practicing, 196
  variety of, 192
Library books. *See* Reading
Literature. *See* Reading
Love, 274-77
  at bedtime, 134
  at breakfast, 60
  for family, 275
  for others, 275-76
  permissiveness, 275
  sibling rivalry, 276
Lying, 263

Management of home. *See* Home management

Manners
  at the table, 111, 269
  introductions, 269
Marine biology, 228
Marriage
  and divorce, 266
  communication with spouse, 253
  date at home, 302
  division of work, 242-43
  faithfulness, 266
  importance of social life, 243-46
  keeping it together, 241
Me-time, 45
Menu-making, 65
Money
  allowances, 222, 297
  clothing budget, 222
  family budget, 221
  savings account, 222
Morality, 265
Morning, 43-55
  dressing, 47
  purpose of activities, 44
  schedule, 46-52
Movies. *See* Theater
Music, 217-21
  at home, 218
  at supper, 110
  ballet, 221
  choral, 219
  classical in car, 66
  joining a concert series, 303
  lessons, 192
  list of composers, 219
  musical comedy, 220
  opera, 220
  popular, 220
  practicing, 196
  symphonic, 218-19
  terms, 219

Nap time. *See* sleep
Neighborhood
  new family, 302
  sense of community, 301

Obedience. *See* Discipline
Office. *See* Work
Optimism, 260

Orderliness, 269-72
Organizational abilities, 271-72
Outdoor events for weekends, 152
Outreach beyond family, 246
Over-programmed children, 198

PACT: place, asking, checking, talking, 180-83
Parent-teacher associations, 35
Parental enrichment partner (PEP), 29
Parenting
    attributes of good family, 307
    basics, 15-27, 306
    generational differences, 307
    hints, 296-304
    holding hands, 308
    home management, 242-43
    single, 40, 298, 301
    successes and failures, 305
    See also Support for working parents and Table of Contents
Patriotism, 266-67
Pediatricians, 34
Pen pals, 226
PEP, 29
Permissiveness, 275
Pestering
    at bedtime, 136
    of parent after work, 96
Pets, 299, 300
PGPs, 39
Phone calls. *See* Touch-base time #2, 81-83
Play dough recipe, 303
Playmates
    at your house, 199
    ideas for play, 200
Poise, 267-69
Politics, 222-25
    participation in school, 225
Positive attitude, 260
Power plays, 287
Praise, 265, 269, 278-79, 293
Profanity, 234
Professional help, 34
PTA, 35
Punishment. *See* Discipline

Quality time, 18
Quiet time, 98
Quiz
    for kids, 17
    for parents, 16

Reading
    after school, 90
    at supper, 110
    before bed, 133
    encouragement, 210-14, 273, 299
    finding time for, 253
    recommended lists for children, 211-12
    recommended lists for high schoolers, 212-14
    Saturday morning, 145
    while commuting, 66
Religion
    and ethics, 229-31
    attendance at services, 154, 265
    Bible characters, 230
    importance of choosing a religion, 230
    list of leaders, 231
    list of terms, 230
    practicality, 265
    prayer at home, 265
Reminders of 3 × 5 cards, 303
Renaissance Child, The, 204
Repairs with child's help, 146, 253
Repotting, 298
Responsibility, 267-69
Restaurant, meals, 114
Rewards for homework, 183. *See also* School
Roots and wings, 19
Rules for family living, 270, 283-85

Safety of child home alone, 88
Saturday morning activities, 144-48
School, 169-89
    educational contract, 189
    expectations of grade school, 176
    expectations of high school, 177
    homework, 180-84
    homework checking by parent, 182
    homework questions to ask, 181
    PACT for homework, 180-83

School *(continued)*
  paying for grades, 183
  preparing for college, 186
  progress of child, 178-79
  support of gifted child, 184-86
  visits and questions to ask, 178-79
Science and the environment, 227-29
Scrapbook, 249
Self-esteem, 277-79
  esteem, confidence building at breakfast, 59
  humiliation, 288
Self-government, 269-72
Separation
  child's fear, 24, 58
  parent's concern, 71
Sex education, 302-4
Sexual morality, 265
Shopping
  by catalog, 298
  list, 254
  on weekends, 147
Sibling rivalry, 276, 301
Sickness. *See* Health
Single parenting
  absent parent, 298
  decisions, 301
  social life, 298
  support team, 40
Sitters, 32, 39
  trading partner, 40
Sleep
  for parents on weekends, 144
  hours needed, 141
  preschool nap time, 172
  See also Bedtime
Sleepy children, 51
Snacks
  after school, 86
  before bed, 133
  before supper, 97, 303
Social events
  for kids, 149
  for single parent, 298
  importance for parents, 148, 243-45
Social service agencies, 35
Social skills, 269

Spanking, 282. *See also* Discipline
Sports, events and team practices, 147
Spouse, helpfulness, 52, 242-43
Stamp collecting, 226
Step-parenting, 299
Success, encouragement of child's, 277-79
Suicide, 277-78
Supper, 103-16
  activities, 108
  advance planning, 100
  alternative places for, 107
  book reading, 110
  clean-up, 113
  conversation, 109
  hour before, 93-102
  importance of, 104
  music, 110
  preparation, 100
  table manners, 111
Support for working parents, 28-42
  enrichment groups, 37
  for single parents, 40
  friends and relatives, 38-39
  group leaders, 37
  groups, 35
  religious workers, 36
  teachers, 36
  trading partner, 40

Table manners, 111, 269
Tasks, 249-52
  for after school, 90, 100
  for grade-schoolers, 251
  for high schoolers, 251
  for weekends, 145, 147
  for younger children, 250
  incentives, 251
  morning, 48
Teachers, importance of, 36
Telephoning, Touch-base time #2, 81-83
Television, 157-68
  alternative activities, 164
  and book reading deal, 165
  and sex, 161
  and violence, 160
  benefits of, 159

family viewing, 126, 163
gaining control of, 162-65
parental responsibility, 166
Saturday mornings, 145
statistics, 160-62
video games, 165
viewing rules, 164
Theater, 214-17
in the home, 217
list of actors, 216
list of playwrights, 215
play-reading, 215
quality movie-viewing, 217
school productions, 214
terms to know, 216
Thinking bench, the, 288
Time abuse at work, 74
Time, importance of unstructured, 193
Time management, 25, 240-55
Time-out, 288
Togetherness
in religious activities, 154
rating, 126
weekdays, 22-27
weekends, 142-56
Touch-base times, 23-26
#1, 54-61
#2, 80-92
#3, 93-102
#4, 103-16
#5, 117-28
#6, 129-41
Toy organization, 300
Trading partner, 40
Traits, eight great, 256-80
#1, Self-esteem, 277-79
#2, Love, 274-77
#3, Intelligence, creativity, inquisitiveness, 272-74
#4, Self-government, orderliness, 269-72
#5, Responsibility, poise, leadership, 267-69
#6, Honesty, ethics, religious faith, patriotism, 263-67
#7, Ability to communicate, 261-62
#8, Cheerfulness, 257-60
Travel, 225-27
family trips, 226-27
school trips, 226
travelogues, 226
T.V. couch potato test, 167

Unstructured time, 193

Video games, 165
Vocabulary, basic for young children, 172
Volunteer work, 303

Weekends, 142-56
cultural events, 153
importance of family activities, 143
indoor excursions, 153
major work projects, 151
"must do" and "might do" activities, 143-54
outdoor events, 152
social events, 148-50
sports events, 147
Work, 69-79
absenteeism, 72
appearance, 77
as an escape, 76
attitude, 75
criticism from others, 70
fatigue, 76
gossip, 73
guilt, 70
motive for, 75
part-time, 176
performance, 70
professionalism, 77
time abuse, 74
unpaid leave, 176
Work projects for weekends, 151